Memories Are Beyond Forgetting
No Matter How Bitter They Are

Reminiscence

(third edition)

J.R. ARRANGUEZ JR.

Ordering Information:

Prime Seven Media
518 Landmann St.
Tomah City, WI 54660

Printed in the United States of America

In memory of our beloved parents:

Jose M. Arranguez Sr. (1905-1976)
Federica Rosell Arranguez (1907-1990)

Their parental love and their guidance,
the moral and financial support they extended made
us, their children, achieve our dignity to live.

Reminiscence is a historical/multicultural fiction based on a true story and inspired by actual events. This book is dedicated to all Filipinos working abroad; to the children all over the world who are growing up without a father, and to the Filipina nurse I happened to meet more than a decade ago on whose life story the herein plot is based. As I promised, her real identity is being kept confidential.

I address this book to my family:

my spouse, Edna; my daughter, Gypsy Rose,

&

my sons, Jiffy Jon and Rez Robby,

and to my son-in-law, Eric Shimizu.

In one way or another,

my family helped me realize this book.

Special mention goes to my first grandchild.

Ryleigh Akemi Arranguez Shimizu

was born on June 12, 2020.

Preface

I used to watch my mother gazing at the eastern skies where, she believed, Vietnam lay beyond. When I was a child, in so many times my mother told me that my father was there, living there in Vietnam, but she said he would be returning home someday. My mother waited for a long time for that someday to come. And so, did I.

When my country sent more volunteers to the Vietnam War in October 1968 in response to America's request, my father was one of them. He left my mother an address where to write him; he left home with a promise that he would be back as soon as he had the chance; he left when my life was about to creep inside my mother's womb.

My mother wrote to him about her pregnancy but never got a reply. She speculated that he had no time to write back because he was in the country at war, yet she kept on writing him and only stopped when my grandfather, a veteran of the Second World War, told her that incoming letters may be banned in the US camps in Vietnam per military policy.

One early morning in June of 1969, my mother received the news that my father was among those who died in an ambush while doing reconnaissance patrol in Vietnam's Quang Nam province, a bailiwick of rebel forces. Severely devastated, she passed out after reading the obituary. She woke up in the hospital and found out she had given me birth by inducement.

A week later, Mama got a letter without a return address. Surprisingly, it came from my father, detailing that ambush in Quang Nam. That enlivened back my mother's senses and rekindled her hopes that my father was alive and would be returning home someday. In November of that year, Ferdinand Edralin Marcos was reelected as Philippine President.

The first major event Marcos did in his second term was withdrawing the entire Philippine forces from Vietnam. The last group of returnees came home in February 1970, but my father wasn't with them. Yet my mother did not lose hopes for his return. She kept on waiting for him even long after the Vietnam War was over, but my father never came home.

Years passed. The absence of my father in my life did not matter anymore when I came of age and started dreaming of coming to America and living there with my mother for good. There were times I thought I might step into my father's life someday, but my American dream was more compelling. In my country, some people thought of America as a paradise.

My dream to live in America came into fruition; I had reached the land of paradise only to find out that its grandeur won't be enough to fill the hollow within me for leaving my mother alone at home in the meantime that my American citizenship was not yet realized. Depressions kept recurring in those years and the more I turned despondent over my fate.

Old folks said I brought bad luck to my parents because of my name. I may have reached my dream but the thought that I brought bad luck to my parents was still bothering me. Why should it be my name? I thought of seeking an answer from a soldier of God. One day at the sanctuary of St. Mary Magdalene in the town of Apex in North Carolina, I met him.

In the Sanctity of a Name

Names are primarily for identification,
may denote something but has
nothing to do with fate.

Father James O'Brien looked back when I entered through the front door of the church. It was past three in the afternoon when I came in. The priest must have finished praying; he was about to stand up from kneeling when I was closing back the door. He sat on the bench behind him and watched me approaching. The cascading black hair that gave my face an oval outline, the shape of my eyes, and the tiny mole above the left corner of my mouth could have made him remember me so well.

It was also a Wednesday, at the same time in the afternoon inside the same church the first time I met Father James, a good-looking priest perhaps in his early fifties with a clean-shaven face, and of medium built. He was walking down the aisle in white habit on his way to the main door when he saw me approaching. He stopped when

I got nearer. I introduced myself. My Spanish-sounding surname and my Asian looks might have told him I was a Filipino. He had mentioned of having stayed in the Philippines for a couple of years when there was the heavy influx of Vietnamese refugees after the fall of Saigon.

"I'm not here for confession, Father," I said with utmost courteousness when he told me to wait for him in the confessional. "I'm here to solicit your opinion."

The priest looked deeper into my eyes; a faint smile beamed in his face when he asked, "Opinion . . . on what?"

"Let me ask you first, Father James, does a name effectuate a person's fate?"

The priest settled himself on a pew and gestured me to take the next bench. Impulsively, I thought I shouldn't have come to him, but the faint smile that dangled on his lips when I asked him the question gave me assurance I had come to the right person.

"Names have nothing to do with fate," the priest opined after I had seated myself. He was looking outside through the glass-paneled window while I waited for him to say more of his wisdom. He looked back at me after a moment – stared again into my eyes as if to measure the level of my understanding of the complexities in life.

"If it is so, Father James, why . . ."

"Name-choosing is incidental," the priest cut in abruptly. "Or it may be by fascination like a flower's name for a daughter and a historical or biblical name for a son." He paused for a few seconds then continued with a chuckle. "My Da who loved biblical names named me after the Apostle James. I may not like the sound of it but think of the trouble I'd been through writing my name if it was Nebuchadnezzar."

The priest's impassive countenance struck a humorous impact that sent me laughing loud enough to stir the serenity inside the church.

"Pardon my irreverence, Father James. I forgot we are in the house of God."

"Laughing is good . . . good for your health . . ."

"It cures anxiety," I implied. "Anyway, your name sounds suave and saintly."

"It is most common. How many James had been U.S. Presidents? I am counting to six. And not all named James are virtuous. You must have heard of the outlaw named Jesse James. Wild Bill Hickok was also James. In college, I thought of making my name be well-revered after my death. Is 'Saint James of Dublin' a good moniker?"

I freed a little laughter to his jest.

"Is it the Dublin of Ireland?"

"Yes, it is."

"So, you're Irish!"

"Aye, I am . . . born and raised in Mullingar. I only became a resident of Dublin when I was in college. I took up law thinking I would fit well as a secret agent like my namesake James Bond 007."

I suppressed myself from laughing.

"So, names are contributing factors . . ."

"Actually, they aren't the factors at all," the priest butted in. "It's the environment and family upbringing."

"Genetics and education are also considered, am I right, Father?"

"And do not forget the will of God. It is by God's will that I turned into a priest."

"Seriously, Father James, what do you think of my name?"

The priest stared at me again and somewhat looking worried, he asked, "Why, my child? Is something wrong with it?"

"Some folks in our town said that it was because of my name that my family suffers bad luck. I may not have believed it, yet that worried me for it might be true. I took advantage of it by not giving up easily on anything. I succeeded on some things, but I also suffered losses."

"Faith makes things happen if you believe what people say, but if you don't, why worry about it? It is a mere superstition."

"But it won't have passed through generations if . . ."

"Names have nothing to do with fate. Life's a game; winning and losing are parts of it. If you have your ups, you might have your downs as well."

There was a brief silence between us. I was giving his words a thought when I heard some movements. It was the church caretaker turning off some lights. Except for the three of us, everybody was gone. I looked around and my attention was caught by the multi-colored figures on a window panel. I was figuring out the biblical event depicted there when the priest interrupted my thoughts.

"What did you say your name is?"

"I wasn't named after a saint, Father," I replied without looking at him.

"You don't need to be named after a saint to be benevolent."

I gave the priest a query look then leaned back in deep thoughts.

By confiding to the priest my worries, would it set me free from anxiety? It might not. Would it reduce my misery to a lesser degree? It might not. Why then did I come to him? What really did I want?

Some seconds had passed when I heard the priest asking again for my name.

II

The Fate of my Father

My father died in a foreign land
without a dying wish, without a mound,
and without a headstone to remember him by.

I would have been named after my father, but Grandma said the name Romula sounded too masculine for a baby girl. Consonant to my birth month, she named me Jin and added Ceres after the Roman mythological goddess with the C changed to X to signify the tenth of June I was born.

"Your Grandpa gave you his name as your father was no longer around," said my mother one day on the thought that I might have been wondering why I had my grandfather's surname. I was five then - had no idea what was going on with my life. I was already in school when I learned that Grandpa drove my mother out of his house on learning of the affair she had with a military man. That pained my mother so much that she promised herself never to live anymore in Villa Zaragoza. Upon learning her daughter was conceiving,

Grandma told my mother to return to the villa, but Mama already had pride. She opted to stay in the house where my father left her with me growing inside her womb.

My father left home at the onset of chilly days in 1968. My mother thought he was joining the revival of the *Pulahans*, a band of the pre-war revolutionaries which dissipated at the start of the Second World War. It reactivated as *Hukbo ng Bayan Laban sa Hapon (HUKBALAHAP)* when the war was about to end, disbanded when war was completely over and intensified again in the late 'forties when the government allowed foreign ownership of the country's land and natural resources. So, in the early fifties when the Koreans were at war with each other, my country also had a little civil war to fight out.

A Second World War hero named Ramon Magsaysay, then Secretary of National Defense, persuaded the rebels to lay down their arms. The man could have been the country's first President reelected had he not met his sudden death. That was when his presidential plane Mount Pinatubo crashed in Cebu's Mount Manungal on March 17, 1957.

After Magsaysay, two more people took turns in the handling of the country's Presidential affairs. During their reigns insurrections were slowly reactivating due to continuous corruption in the government. Then came the term of Ferdinand Edralin Marcos, the first Philippine President reelected even if his term went awry with rampant corruptions that caused the rebirth of the *HUKBALAHAP* as the New Communist Party of the Philippines, better known as the New People's Army or NPA. In the last two quarters of 1968, the chaotic atmosphere between the military and the NPA rose to a higher level.

My father wasn't joining this outlawed organization, but the civic group dispersed to Vietnam in October 1968 per America's request. To Grandma, Filipinos in Vietnam were but cannon fodders with a fifty-fifty chance to come home alive. She was aware how uncertain fate is for a soldier in war. When Grandpa was called for active duty during the Second World War, the fear of whether he'd be coming back alive was gripping my grandmother constantly. My father joined the PhilCAG in his desire to study Law with the remuneration that America promised to volunteers. Grandpa signed his concurrence as the town mayor but did not inform my mother about it. Then my father left; he left against my mother's will; he left without knowing he was siring a child.

In America, protest demonstrations against the sending of troops to Vietnam were gathering momentum. Due to this situation, Democrat's L. B. Johnson, who assumed the presidency after the death of JFK, didn't run for a term in 1968. Richard M. Nixon was elected president with his political campaign "to end the Vietnam War." Nixon failed to end the war, however repatriated American soldiers from Vietnam upon assuming his post.

In my country, meanwhile, discontentment in the government was mounting that the NCPP had grown stronger when it celebrated its Founder's Day on December 26, 1968.

A month before I was due, Mama was notified of my father's death. Per obituary, he was with three Green Berets and two Vietnamese soldiers patrolling in the hinterlands of Quang

Nam Province when ambushed sometime in May 1969. The thunderstorms occurring that night prevented rescue attempts; subsequent searches were futile. After months of continuous search and no remains were found, all of them were presumed dead.

My mother passed out after reading the obituary. She woke up in the community hospital and found she had given me birth by inducement.

Father John, the town's parish priest, said it was better if my father was blown up dead than captured alive by the commies who were known to torture their prisoners. He would've been brutally executed and thrown into the Mekong River where tortured bodies of American soldiers were retrieved. He was dead whatsoever, but Mama did not receive indemnity from America; the Philippine government denied receiving such grant.

My father perished like he never had existed at all. He died in a foreign land without a dying wish. There neither was a headstone nor a mound to remember him by. His unburied remains, withered through the years, were then windblown to nowhere.

A name may have nothing to do with one's fate, but even then, there are those who have the flair of concocting a name with events – weaving it intricately so that it sounded believable. I heard some folks say I was culpable for my father's fate because my name suggested curse. Contrarily, it was the death of my father that caused me to be born a month ahead I was due. Therefore, asserting that my name caused my father's death was an illogical concocting of nonsense – neither with rhyme nor reason.

And so, my father died not knowing he sired a daughter. It was unfortunate for my mother who kept hoping for his return and was unfair to me - born like a true bastard.

But then, about a week after my birth, came a letter. It was from my father! That brought back my mother's hope that my father was coming home someday.

I was taken out from my mother's womb on a rainless summer when the temperature was on its peak; when the muddy ponds, where carabaos skulked to get rid of the incessant heat, were baked into pools of mud cakes; when seeds sown in farmlands may have popped off beneath the dried soil, when a great famine was coming. The Lord must be at the helm of punishing humankind for defying His will that only on Earth man should govern.

It was the era when two of the world's greatest nations were locked in a race for outer space supremacy. If Russia launched its *Sputnik* in October 1957, America had its Explorer I in January 1958. In April 1961, Russia sent its Yuri Gagarin to orbit the earth and so did America in February 1962 with its John Glenn Jr.

The race went on, but it was America who first landed on the moon.

On July 20, 1969, a Sunday, while the world was watching Neil Armstrong taking *'a giant leap for mankind'*, I was baptized.

If 1969 was a glorious year for the Americans, it was a victorious year for the Filipinos. Before America conquered the moon, Gloria Diaz of the Philippines conquered the year's Miss Universe title. And while these nations were in celebration, people in South Vietnam were either living in distress and desperation or dying of holocaust and hunger.

When Marcos withdrew the Philippine forces from Vietnam, insurgency in my country was intensifying. He found a perfect alibi to place the country under military rule.

On September 21, 1972, Marcos declared Martial Law over the entire archipelago through Proclamation 1081 as drafted by the so-called 'Rolex 12'. It was rumored that Mr. Marcos gifted each of the 12 Martial Law architects with a Rolex wristwatch and awarded them all prime jobs in the new government for helping organize the military takeover.

In America that year, Nixon was reelected. Through his efforts, the Paris Peace Accords between the warring Vietnams was signed on January 27, 1973, but that was not carried out for both parties disagreed on some points. The 'Vietnamization' - leaving South Vietnam on its own went into effect, however, the supply of war aids continued.

With the outburst of the Watergate Scandal in August 1974, Nixon resigned; Gerald Ford took over his post and drastically cut off America's substantial aid to South Vietnam. Due to lack of ammunition, Saigon fell into the hands of the commies on April 30, 1975.

Meanwhile, my mother was still waiting for my father's return. I grew up watching her wait for his coming. There were times I saw her cry; that worried me much for I only had her to count on, the only one I had in the world.

Mama kept telling me I was the only one she had to live for. She inculcated in me values and virtues to guide me in life. From her, I got the answers to things that baffled me. Even if she ignored some of my nonsensical inquisitions, I learned her wisdom. By the weed that crept through a crack in a concrete wall or pavement, Mama pictured to me how precious life is that even the most disabled beings in the world strive hard to live.

Only God can take back the life He gives, but when hatred dominates humankind, people learned to take away lives so easily that some even take their own. Some even dare to snatch an innocent's life from its mother's womb.

"All of the living may end up dying," my mother said at one time. "You'd bear the pangs of pain of being left behind more bitter than when your time to leave had come."

I did not mind what my mother had told me as I did not bother to know why the moon waxes and why stars pop up only at night; why do we dream and what are they for? I was not worried whether daylight was coming back or what the day would bring for me. If I had air to breathe, had food to eat and water to drink; if there was a home for my mother and me - a place to play and sleep and dream - everything was fine.

Life is but a journey that starts at birth and ends with death. I cringed at what my mother said – that all the living things God created in this universe end up dying. I begged the Lord never to take my mother away from me. She was my guiding light. In my desperate moments, she was there to cheer me up. From her I learned what values are; I learned the Bible; I learned how precious a human life is. From her I learned my country's history and the important global events that happened in and before my time and I came to know stories of my ancestors which I was always eager to hear from my mother even repeatedly.

III

The Family Zaragoza

It was not because she was the lone heiress of the Torreses.
Margarita was as beautiful as the night of full moon.
That made her attractive to the choosy Aragon.

Politics in my country had become like a family business. Some political figures must bestow their elected posts to their inheritors as if those were family inheritances. Clan members, even without the knowledge, ran for public office banking on their wealth and the name politics established.

My grandfather, Aragon Zaragoza, was a scion of a well-respected political clan from the capital city of Cebu. He worked as personal secretary to the provincial governor while studying Law at the Gullas Law School that's known today as the University of the Visayas College of Law situated off historic Colon, the street known to be the country's oldest.

Uptown was the Colegio de la Immaculada Concepcion, a convent school of academic excellence and discipline, from where Margarita Federica Torres earned her Home Economics degree in 1937 at the age of twenty. Right after graduation, she got a teaching job in her hometown's central school too alluring for one so young and fresh from college.

Meanwhile in Europe, the Nazis had started the mass murdering of the Jews in Hitler's desire to conquer the entire continent; they won Italy to their side.

In the Pacific, Japan was Hitler's major ally.

That year, peace still reigned in my country, but apprehensions beset its people after Japan's vicious attack in Nanking, China, in July of 1937. If America got involved with this conflict, so were its territories and that included my country, the Philippines.

By this time, Sacandaya was preparing for its annual fiesta to be held by the end of August. That year's celebration was highlighted with the coronation of a fiesta queen amidst ballroom dancing. Margarita Federica Torres, a ravishing beauty at 21 of Spanish-Filipino descent, was the Executive Committee's unanimous choice as the town's first beauty pageant winner. The Governor recommended his private secretary to be Margarita's royal escort which Feliciano Torres, Margarita's maternal grandfather, hadn't refused.

Margarita instantly fascinated the choosy Aragon, considered the most elusive among the Zaragoza men for staying a bachelor at 24. Since then, they gathered envies among Sacandaya youngsters but earned rapturous admirations from the town's society circle: God created Margarita for Aragon as Eve was for Adam.

At the last sunset of 1939, when people were preparing for the coming of the New Year, Aragon's parents came to ask the Torreses for the hand of Margarita. No less than the Provincial Governor came to speak for the Zaragozas citing the potential of his personal secretary as an ideal husband. It was a Filipino custom of marriage proposal called *pamanhikan* in our national language; it is *pamalaye in* Cebuano, our local dialect. Persuasions entailed long deliberation. By twilight, the proposal was accepted. The wedding day was set and planned. A celebration followed. Per tradition, the groom was to shoulder the expenses. The bride's parents asked the Zaragozas a house for the newlyweds as dowry but the Torres patriarch, who planned to return to Spain for good, offered his palatial abode as a wedding gift to his only granddaughter. Prominent elders gave the would-be couple advice on the "dos and don'ts" before and after the wedding. Superstitious beliefs sound preposterous but in many instances were proven true.

The magnificent wedding ceremony of Aragon and Margarita was held on a Sunday in March of 1940. An elegant wedding dress for Margarita by Pining's Elegance, Cebu's most sophisticated dressmaker in that era, made my grandma an envy of every bride-to-be.

The newly married couple honeymooned around the country by boat reaching the island of Mindanao, then known as the 'Land of Promise' when opposing principles between Christians and Muslims were not yet advocated and the notorious bands of the *Ilagas* and *Barracudas* were yet unheard.

When schools opened in June, Aragon pursued his studies in the city. Margarita went back to teaching elementary Home Economics in Sacandaya Central School. By the summer of 1940, before he could return to Spain, Feliciano Torres fell ill and succumbed.

Early morning on December 7, 1941, Japan invaded the United States with a massive sudden attack on America's Pacific Fleet at the Pearl Harbor in Hawaii's Oahu Island.

The following Monday morn, a drone of Japanese air squadrons attacked Manila, the capital city of the Philippines. Pandemonium broke out in the city of Cebu. People feared it was Japan's next target being the country's second biggest city. Establishments and schools were closed. Students from the other provinces panicked for a ride back home.

Aragon missed all the trips to the North. He wired Margarita that he would be with her by any means. By that time, all means of transportation and communication were deliberately cut off. By then, Aragon Zaragoza, an ROTC officer in his Pre-Law years, received a call for active duty in the military and he had to report immediately.

The enemies infiltrated the province of Cebu in the summer of 1942.

One day, a group of Japanese soldiers invaded Sacandaya. Houses were burnt, and young men suspected of being guerillas were huddled up on the streets and were massacred.

Villa Zaragoza, known then as Casa de Torres, did not escape from the eyes of the invaders. Margarita and her parents were watching the burning of the town when three Japanese soldiers broke into the house. Margarita's father gunned down two of them, but the third one got him dead. Margarita grabbed her father's rifle and felled the raging soldier before he could swish his blade on her. Watching her pregnant daughter in the brink of death, Margarita's mother suffered a stroke and succumbed.

After wrapping the dead bodies of Margarita's parents with linens, the whole household fled and found refuge in an abandoned small house deep in the woods far from the villa. In the dead of the night under a limpid moonlight, the helpers buried the corpses nearby while Margarita was birthing her first child. Amid grief and fear, when the world was about to reach its peak of dread and anger, Aunt Merriam was born.

On April 9th of 1942, about 75,000 Filipino and American guerrillas surrendered to the Japanese Imperial Army after General Douglas MacArthur, the Supreme Commander of Allied Forces in the southwest Pacific, left for Australia upon President Roosevelt's order. The surrendered soldiers were made to walk about a hundred kilometers from Bataan to a camp in Tarlac province barely with food and water. It was henceforth known as the infamous 'Bataan Death March' as tens of thousands of the guerillas died along the way.

Aragon Zaragoza was one of those who survived the march, but after a year in the camp, he was accused of keeping a day-to-day diary that was prohibited. He was impounded in a bamboo cage, subjected to frequent interrogations, mentally and physically tortured, and fed with only a small quantity of boiled rice; his strength drained.

On October 20, 1944, MacArthur returned and liberated my country.

President Franklin Delano Roosevelt of America died on April 12, 1945, and Harry S. Truman assumed presidency. By this time, Germany surrendered. On May 8th that year, the Allied Forces celebrated the Victory Europe Day.

War was going on in the Pacific. With President Truman's command for Japan to give up being ignored, America dropped an atomic bomb called 'Little Boy' in Hiroshima on August 6 that year, followed it up after three days in Nagasaki with another atomic bomb named 'Fat Man', which forced Japan to surrender on the second of September 1945.

The Second World War was over.

Aragon returned to Sacandaya harboring an immense hatred against the Japanese whose hostilities during the war bore him a gruesome pain. He had witnessed the atrocities of the Japanese soldiers towards his comrades during the Bataan Death March; he, himself, suffered the same. To him, the most horrendous was how a Japanese soldier impaled the body of a little girl for giving water to an American prisoner. Aragon saw the girl writhe in pain, blood squirting from her back that made Aragon Zaragoza wept unabashedly. He calmed down only when another Japanese soldier doused his face with ditchwater.

Those untold war miseries tormented my grandfather in his sleep even long after the war was over. Unless he could exact a full payment from any Japanese-bloodied, to Aragon Zaragoza, the war hadn't yet ended.

In March 1946, my grandparents renewed their marriage vows. The couple wore the same outfit they had six years ago. This time, the bride's wedding gown had turned tighter; Margarita was five months heavy with her second child. Cebu's local dailies dubbed it "the wedding anniversary of the century." Bigwigs from rival political parties, the *Nacionalista* and the *Liberal,* stood as primary sponsors;

both wanted to have the groom be its prime municipal candidate in the coming local elections. They saw in him the epitome of a political kingpin for the medals of heroism he garnered during the war. In that occasion, Margarita informed her friends that Casa de Torres should be known henceforth as Villa Zaragoza in honor of the town's returning hero.

In accordance with the act that the U.S. Congress passed in 1934, America granted my country independence on July 4, 1946. My mother was born that day, christened Patria Independencia shortened to Patricia. My country celebrated its independence on this date thereon until it was moved to June 12th, the date when Filipinos declared their independence from Spain in 1898. Thereafter, the fourth of July had become the American Friendship Day in the Philippine calendar.

My grandfather, Aragon Zaragoza, passed the Bar in 1949, joined the *Nacionalista* Party and ran for mayorship in 1953, a position he held for twenty solid years. In my country that era, the incumbent could run for the same position as many times as he wanted. To Sacandaya housewives, the big force behind Aragon's political success was his spouse. Margarita was not only rich and beautiful to be humble and dignified; she had the milk of human kindness that was not common then among the illustrious.

A paragon of human virtues, Margarita Federica Torres Zaragoza was always the choice to chair many organizations; had been adjudged "Mother of the Year" both in the municipal and provincial levels. Grandpa was voted twice as one of the ten "Most Outstanding

Citizens" in the province. Seldom would a weekend pass by without one of them attending as a primary sponsor in a baptismal or wedding ceremony. Twice in a row during my grandfather's tenure, Sacandaya was chosen as the country's most beautiful town, and it was elevated to Class A from level D.

My mother's profession was considered of lower caliber. Grandma said that teaching is a very dignified job, but whereas my grandmother married a scion of a well-to-do family from the city, a would-be lawyer who became a great political figure in our town, my mother engaged herself with an army sergeant, a son of nobody who came from nowhere. My mother's father showed his vehement protest of the relationships for it was a grievous disgrace to the family, but my mother, who was known in town as a dutiful daughter, followed her will. With what she did, the family Zaragoza suffered a great embarrassment. My grandfather threw her away from the villa for insubordination and for a while, disowned her. Finding no one to turn to, sans the benefit of marriage, my mother lived with my father, the soldier drafted in town whose ancestors were not even heard of in Sacandaya.

From Flora, Grandma had known that my mother was in the family way. Feeling her daughter's pain living alone with me getting heavier in her womb, she asked her daughter to return to the villa, but Mama had learned to wear pride.

Aunt Thelma was secretly seeing my mother. From her, Mama learned that grandpa had a mild stroke; that Uncle Ralph was into priesthood; that Uncle Benito flunked out in his medical studies in University of Santo Tomas in Manila and had transferred to Cebu's

Southwestern University; that the family was preparing for a big event - the marriage of Aunt Merriam to a lawyer from the city – a celebration that didn't need my mother's presence.

One day, my grandfather personally handed to my mother the notice that my father died in an ambush in a place called Quang Nam in South Vietnam. She passed out after reading the obituary and gained consciousness in a community hospital where I was forcibly taken out from her womb. About a week after that, she received from the post office a typewritten letter that detailed the ambush that happened in Quang Nam. To her surprise, it came from my father, but it bore no return address. That was the only letter she got from him. Nevertheless, it made her believe my father was alive and so, she kept on waiting for his return and I had learned to wait for the coming of a father I never had seen. It was like waiting for the end of forever.

My Countrymen

We were not known then as Filipinos.
I wondered how my ancestors were referred to
before Mother Spain called our country Las Islas Filipinas.

The occurring drought coupled with the rampant corruption in the government made people suffer extreme hardships. The insurrections that fizzled out during Magsaysay's term resurfaced in the early part of 1968 during the Marcos presidency and got stronger after his reelection in November 1969.

In September 1972, before his second term was over, Marcos declared Martial Law using the resurgence of insurgencies his alibi. Together with his spouse, he governed the country with Presidential Decrees, which the media dubbed 'conjugal dictatorship'. They purged adversaries from their respective jobs and gave their allies high-ranking positions in the new government. They suspended the Philippine constitution, closed Congress, and sequestered big private firms, shut down TV and radio stations and publications identified as anti-government. Journalists could not write anything that transgressed to the government guidelines. The writ of habeas Corpus was suspended. Opposition leaders were jailed without warrants. Those forewarned sought asylum in other countries. Benigno S. Aquino Jr., the President's most critical foe, was arrested allegedly for murder and rebellion, convicted after a biased trial, and was imprisoned with solitary confinement. Grandma said it was the Japanese torturing Filipinos in the Second World War; during Martial Law, Filipinos were persecuting their own compatriots. The so-called "Manila's Finest Police Officers of the Year" was hypocritical; some of those cops were abusive according to the rival political party: they ransacked houses and arrested residents on suspicion they were drug users or pushers or forced them to admit they were insurgents. Under duress, some admitted the accusations only to give the cops a reason to keep them incarcerated.

"Ang Bagong Lipunan" which in English means "The New Society", a marching hymn that tells false praises on the new government was enforced in all government institutions like it was another National Anthem. That could have been the beginning of a possible monarchial government with the country's ongoing President as its prime ruler.

When I was not yet in school and Mama was at work, I spent my day at the villa until Mama had come to pick me up. Staying at my grandparents' house with nobody to play with or talk to was boring. Seldom would Flora talk to me; Santiago never did; he was always busy attending to Grandma's plants and Grandpa's fowls.

I could not move freely inside the house. I had to be extra careful in moving around because I might break an antique jar which, as

Flora said, could be more precious than me. So, all I did there was to sit and watch cartoons on TV or listen to Flora's tall tales. Whenever Grandma was around, she let me read the books of fairy tales that I always carried with me. She enjoyed listening to me read those books in English and coaching me if I could not pronounce some words correctly.

My mother started teaching me how to read when I was five. She did it at night before my time to sleep or she would be telling me bedtime stories or Flora's kind of tales. Then she would lull me to sleep with her rendition of *"Matud Nila",* a post-war classic composition of Ben Zubiri, whom Grandpa got acquainted with during the Fall of Bataan. Mama said it was my father's favorite. It had become a favorite Cebuano song in many generations, but my mother would sing it as if she was in agony, sounding like the howling of a dog that sees a ghost passing by; worse than how those farm boys would belt out their kind of songs while pasturing cows in the meadows. How I wanted to stop my mother's singing but that would be impolite of me especially since she was a schoolteacher. I would have to pretend to have fallen asleep to stop my mother from howling.

In my country, it had been the duty of schoolteachers to teach their pupils to love and respect their parents and be polite to elders. Children are taught to use a prefix in addressing older people. So, it was 'Manang Flora' whenever I called her. For older men, it is *'Manong'* like how I addressed Santiago. Relatives are addressed accordingly. We learned this from the Chinese who were trading goods with my ancestors long before the Spaniards claimed to have discovered my country and named it Las Islas Filipinas. The Chinese traders were the first foreigners to have known my ancestors. They introduced values and beliefs which are now part of Filipino culture referred to as *'sinofications'*.

We were not known then as Filipinos; it puzzled me how my ancestors were referred to before the Spaniards gave us identity. My country was said to be in a single landmass and disintegrated into more than seven thousand islands and islets during the great flood. In my own belief and Flora's, it was not only Noah's Ark that was saved from the Deluge as it was not only Adam and Eve who were the first people in the world. Every race had its own first couple, but God had the Garden of Eden His 'pilot project'. Or how could humanity populate the world with different races if humanity descended from one couple alone? And so, there are whites as there are blacks, and yellows, and reds, and browns.

Filipinos are brown, said my first-grade teacher, but did not say why God made us brown. We're not descendants of Adam and Eve for we have different facial and bodily features. Flora must be right in saying that God brought forth our ancestors from a giant bamboo tree He planted in the heart of our country when it was a single landmass. Out of a node came a brown man God called *Malakas*, which means 'strong' and a brown woman He called *Maganda*, meaning 'beautiful'. Over the years, people of assorted colors came.

According to our History, Chinese traders influenced my forefathers with their culture and beliefs. In the 1520s, Spanish explorers brought Christianity and traditions to my country and named it *'Las Islas Filipinas'*. We were known as Filipinos since then.

In 1898, Spain ceded my country to America for $20 million. Then came American settlers who introduced the Commonwealth form of government. They educated my ancestors with British English and renamed the islands 'The Republic of the Philippines'.

In the 1940's the Japanese invaded and occupied my country for about three years. America rescued my countrymen from the Japanese atrocities and granted my country complete independence. Interrelations occurred that made Filipinos a mixture of different races but still identified as browns and even then, *'sinofications'* had been part of our culture. A close-knit family was and still is highly advocated. Divorce is not recognized by law and regardless of age, children can stay with the family unless they get married and only then are they given the freedom to live apart.

I did not like attending parties in the villa because most likely, I'd be meeting Grandma's relatives and had to show them my utmost respect by kneeling before the elder ones and pressing the back of one's hand on my forehead one after the other. It's a conveying of blessing that had become a tradition out of the culture in Filipino Christian society. My mother then would show her wide grin in return for their compliments: *Oh, Patricia's daughter is not only pretty but very polite. Where did she get it but from her mother!* My failure to do it was offensive and they would say: *Patricia, aren't you teaching your daughter good manners?* Then Mama would make me contrite at the prayer room while she'd be delivering her litany of censure messing up my prayer that I had to say it all over again. She'd stop only if her mouth had dried up of mincing words and end her sermon by saying this: *Don't ever, ever make me mad again,* to which I'd silently respond: *Amen.*

At night when the moon was bright, older people went out dawdling while children played on the streets. Gone were the roaring of motor vehicles but the laughter of the kids and the voices of young lads singing serenades.

At the blare of the curfew siren, everybody must be home for no one was allowed to walk around on the streets. What remained roaming were stray cats and dogs and the men in uniform patrolling around town. The rest of the night went to deep slumber while the breeze gently blew from the mountaintop down to the valley, swooped over town and swayed into the sea. Silence fell over Sacandaya as the town listened to the chirping of the crickets and cicadas, and the tweeting of the sparrows chanting the night away.

Curfew was over at four the following morning. The town was alive again. Farmers poured down to the market to meet buyers of their farm produce, while fish vendors swarmed to shores to retail around town what fishers caught from deep sea fishing.

In my country as of today, parents have the right to discipline their youngsters. On moonless nights, the kids must be home before Angelus, or they get scolded. Outrageous punishments are somehow not tolerated by the government. The Social Welfare Administration is there to oversee the safety and protection of children.

The heaviest punishment I got from my mother was when she caught me lying. It was what people call 'white lie' and I thought that would have saved me from my mother's anger but unfortunately a white lie for my mother was still a lie. And so, she punished me by rubbing my mouth with *siling labuyo*, a tiny red pepper native to the Philippines that was spicier than the *jalapeno*. I felt my lips swell so much I cried harder and harder after Flora told me that my lips would remain thick forever.

"Do you know how precious you are to me, Jinee?"

"Yes, I do, Mama."

"Then stop crying. Don't be mad at Mama for God doesn't like kids who harbor ills against their parents. What I did was for your own good - to let you know that lying is bad. You would know this when you have a daughter of your own."

"I'm not mad at you, Mama. I cried because I felt bad offending you."

Although my mother never said sorry to me, in her sighs I felt her rues for inflicting me pain and that soothed the embitterment in me. When I asked if I were a burden to her, she said I wasn't heavy to bear for God gave me the same kind of a heart she had. She loved to boost my ego with what I got from her, always from her. I wondered what I got from my father.

My Mother's Woes

Through the years, I had seen how unhappy my mother was.
I promised myself that someday I'd make her
the happiest mother in the world.

My mother said I got my father's eyes. I was skeptical about it because in the picture of my father, the only one that Mama kept, he was wearing shades like the sunglasses that General MacArthur got. My father came from the province of Leyte, born on the day America dropped an atomic bomb in Japan's Hiroshima, baptized on the day the United Nations Organization was established and was named after Carlos P. Romulo, the Filipino statesman who co-founded the UNO.

"What about his family? Mama, I don't even know any relative of his."

"Seldom did he mention to me his parents, had no siblings, and never talked about any other relative save the First Lady whom he claimed his mother's first cousin."

Mama learned about my father's parents by fragments. Piecing these fragments, she concluded my father was illegitimate. His mother, a schoolteacher, was dismissed from teaching for immorality. My father's father, a former Japanese soldier of the Second World War, who deserted his comrades, was murdered before my father was born.

"Wasn't there anything good about my father? He was a bastard, right?"

"That doesn't mean he was despicable."

"What is that?"

"People are born to parents not of their choice. Like you, your father lost his father before he was born but while your father's father was a traitor to his countrymen, yours was a patriot."

"Why?"

"He was fighting for Democracy in another country."

"Why?"

"Also, he was after of the remuneration that America promised to pay soldier volunteers, so he can further his studies in college."

Mama said that my father aimed to be a lawyer, but the death of his mother dissuaded him from pursuing his ambitions. He then joined the military.

"All his dreams are gone if he really had died in Vietnam. But your father is still alive and will be returning home one day," Mama said in the same way Miss Via said that Christ was coming back to the world which never had happened.

My mother was teaching History in Saint Martin de Porres High School, a private institution run by Catholic nuns when she got involved with my father. Aunt Merriam heard about this from her mahjongg playmates and informed her parents. Grandpa was against my mother's involvement with the military man. Enraged, he threw her out of his house.

"It was late in the night. I was all alone in the dark but even with the opacity of the night, I feared no evil because the Lord was walking with me; He was my light and salvation," Mama said with her eyes fixed at the window that framed Villa Zaragoza at a distance. She saw herself shoved outside by her own father one midnight. There was no other one that my mother could turn to but my father, who, at that time was assigned to monitor the illegal dynamite fishing that some fishers of Sacandaya were practicing. She had no choice but to stay with him. Eventually, they got married by a civil authority.

During a long break from school, Mama shut off herself from friends and relatives by skulking inside my father's station. Flora, who couldn't keep secrets, found where my mother was staying, and Mama's family must have known where she was hiding.

Talks about my mother's elopement dissipated like the dark clouds after a heavy rain. She submitted her resignation from her job to save the reputation of the institution where she was teaching, but the school's Mother Superior said there was nothing wrong living with a man if they were legally married. The nun encouraged them, however, to get married in church which they put aside momentarily on financial reasons.

Unbeknown to my mother, my father had enlisted himself as a volunteer of the Philippine Civic Action Group bound for Vietnam. He was after of the monetary consideration that America would remunerate to a PhilCAG volunteer. That would help him obtain his passion to become a lawyer and be a man of distinction. If my father really had died, those dreams of his had died with him.

"To be left behind is more painful than leaving," Mama told me this one day. "Be ready of it for this would be happening usually in one's life."

My mother had been in that situation. She cried hard the night she left her family and harder the morning my father left her. She couldn't stop washing down her pains with tears. To her, crying is as beautiful as laughing.

On some nights, with the aid of a little lamp, Mama would read on the porch the letter from my father. Or she would bide her time there brooding on a recliner from where she could see the ancestral house that had been her home while growing up.

My mother had a happy childhood, I had a miserable one. She grew up with a happy family complete with parents, brothers, and sisters that I could have wished for, and lived in a manor house I could only dream of.

I couldn't help wondering how it was to live in a manor. I grew up in a single- bedroom house made of palm shingles for a roof, thin bamboo sashes interweaved for a wall, polished bamboo slats for a floor, and with a ladder of sturdy bamboo trunks. Small as it was yet it had sheltered me from heat and rain and saved me from lightning and thunder. This had been my parents' home and had been mine as far as I could remember.

Villa Zaragoza should have been a home for me. It was of me that Grandma persuaded my mother to come back to her family, but deeply hurt when Grandpa banished her notwithstanding her pleas for mercy, Mama reasoned out she already had a family of her own and my father was coming back as he promised. She stayed where my father left her and kept hoping for his return even if the length of time in waiting measures the degree of pain she would suffer in case of frustration.

There's nobility in waiting and the realization is its prize, my mother told me. She believed my father was still alive, but I didn't care anymore whether he'd be returning to us, his family. I didn't feel intrinsically my father's absence; he didn't care about me, anyway, but I had my mother's pain as I watched her watch the passing of forever.

The Town Fiesta

Introduced from Spain centuries ago,
this celebration was handed down through
generations and had been a notable Filipino tradition.

Through the years, I witnessed how sadness drained off the better of my mother and it was a burden for me to bear. Only once did I see her laugh heartily and it was a long, long time ago when Sacandaya celebrated its annual town fiesta in 1974.

A fiesta is a notable celebration in my country, comparable to Thanksgiving Day but not a nationwide festivity. Introduced from Mother Spain, fiestas are held on different dates - on the feast day of the saint the town venerates. Unless it falls on a Sunday for an ecclesiastical law that prohibits the holding of a fiesta on this day, the celebration is either held the day preceding or moved to the following Monday.

Sacandaya's patron saint is Saint Rose of Lima, an American of Peruvian descent whose feast day falls on the 30th of August; the biggest annual event that townsfolk look forward to. Fiestas are held for two days. Visitors start coming in on the morning of the opening day Sacandaya folks called 'The Vesper'; the following day, the culmination, is known as 'The Fall'.

Preparation for the fiesta usually would start a month ahead. Streetlights were posted and streams of buntings would be hanging crisscrossed over the streets; arches were erected at the main entrances as welcome indications for visitors. Stalls of itinerant merchants were popping up like mushrooms on the sides of the town's main streets displaying their wares. Traffic had to be rerouted because these thoroughfares would be crowded with shoppers.

Fiestas were highlighted with the selection of a beauty pageant winner in the evening of the vesper. In 1937, when pageantries were of beauty and brains, Grandma was chosen as the town's first beauty pageant winner. In the late 'forties the process changed. Pageant candidates were to raise funds to defray expenses the municipal government incurred for the celebration. The highest fund-raiser won the title. It had been the practice since then.

That fiesta of 1974 had my grandmother as the *Hermana Mayor*. She headed the executive committee and accommodated in her abode not only the guests of honor but also barrio officials with their retinues and people who introduced themselves as relatives or political associates – faces that I saw only on this occasion. In other words, my grandmother was the benevolent benefactor of gatecrashers. I was five then and Mama had to tug me to the villa; she had to be there to help prepare food for the guests – invited and uninvited.

Some visitors came not to pay homage to the town's patron saint but to witness the grand coronation of Miss Sacandaya and to dance until the early morning hours of the next day. Some came for the food the townspeople lavishly prepared. Sacandaya was known for its pomposity in holding fiestas and residents were noted for their hospitality.

The vesper that year opened with the municipal band marching around town at early dawn to signal the start of revelry while the Zaragozas were rushing breakfast for the congressman's entourage was expected to arrive early that morning. There was a special meal of anise-flavored *torta* which tasted exceedingly good with a cup of flavorful coffee. Also, there was everyone's delicacy called *suman*. It's made of glutinous rice which blends perfectly to one's taste with a ripe sweet mango from Cebu City's Guadalupe. This tastes better with a cup of freshly brewed chocolate from the Brazilian cacao beans that Grandpa grew in the backyard.

Lunch was a variety of specially prepared food complemented with a *lechon,* a young pig fermented with spring onions and lemon grasses and roasted golden brown and crispy over a bonfire of wood charcoal. Cebu's *lechon* was, and still is, a delicacy known worldwide for its exotic deliciousness. Grandpa personally prepared the Congressman's favorite *kinilaw,* a local delicacy of raw tuna or salmon fish fillet. It comes very appetizing between sips of imported wine that politicians and sugar cane magnates preferred over the locally brewed San Miguel beer. Traditional desserts and savories ordered from Inday Loring's were laid at another table with the famous *royal bibingka* of Manang Pesit Gomez which was more palatable than the special rice cakes from the city of Mandaue. It was my Uncle Ralph's favorite dessert.

Uncle Ralph, who was studying for priesthood in the city, arrived that morning with three other seminarians in a red car owned by one of them. They joined breakfast with Aunt Thelma's guests who came by bus earlier. The girls' eyes twinkled when the boys huddled with them. They talked of nonsense, laughed and munched delicious looking seafoods that Flora prepared and to any delightful things one had said, somebody responded it with *'I drink to that'*, seconded with *'let's toast'* until the boys got drunk and carefree that it seemed they didn't care anymore of going back to the seminary.

Mama and Flora, while preparing a cassava cake, were listening to their street lingo which I thought was taboo, but which heartily amused Flora. The guests from the city were lucky my grandmother was attending a meeting at the municipal hall that morning. They would have had the lecture of their lifetime.

After lunch, Aunt Thelma led them to the beach. Uncle Ralph wasn't coming so my aunt brought me along. One of the male guests had a car but everybody preferred to walk across the town to the shore.

On our return to the villa, the boys still had their wet trunks on, and the girls were in their skimpy bikinis except for Aunt Thelma who was in a shirt and shorts. I was walking behind them, and I couldn't help laughing at the wiggle-waggle of their butts.

We were stranded at the corner of the main streets where people huddled as they watched the parade pass by. The elders leered at Aunt Thelma's friends; kids ogled at the sight of almost naked bodies. They got the attention of the fiesta dignitaries who were in the car that was trailing behind the float that carried the queen of the fiesta that year. The guests from the city stole the whole grandeur.

In the evening, the guests witnessed the proclamation and coronation of the queen by the Provincial Governor assisted by the congressman's wife. It was held in Sacandaya's open auditorium, the public place where big town events were usually held. There was the grand ballroom dancing that night which lasted until the wee hours for curfew wasn't imposed in places celebrating fiestas.

That was when Sacandaya natives who had been residing abroad chanced to hobnob with old acquaintances. The gentlemen were more distinguished. To any of them, the 'reigning queen' of the fiesta would offer a stem of fresh American rose and the pleasure to have 'a special dance' with her. In return, he would give a monetary donation to the fiesta executive committee which was publicly announced; the bigger the donation, the louder the applause and those gentlemen competed on who would get the loudest - a grandiose display of ego and pride.

That was a night of vanities: the men in their hand-embroidered 'barongs', and the women in evening gowns, matched with glittering earrings, necklaces and bracelets, shoes and purses – the vogue of the seventies, competing for the most bejeweled lady of the night. Nobody in town, and that included the Zaragoza women, had ever outdone the congressman's wife. Mrs. Sarmiento had beaten them all three years in a row – always breaking her own record as the most decorated person of the evening – spectacular from head to toe! Her earrings were dangling with clusters of fake diamonds matching the choker that was really choking her robust neck, and the bracelets that looked too tight for her fat wrists. Her gown, a yellowish satin, had in the skirt patches of green rhinestones embroidered in the form of mango leaves that matched her gold high-heeled shoes complemented with a green-sequined purse. With all that glitter in her body, she reminded everyone of the sparkles in the Christmas trees the rich people in our town were competing with at Christmastime. A walking Christmas tree, kids said of her and laughed.

Mrs. Sarmiento was wearing a scarf of yellow laces clipped with a gold tiara over her head which made her looked like she was to dance the Spanish flamenco. Grandma had asked her to dance, not the flamenco, but the *curacha,* a folk dance that originated from the Spanish time which only old folks loved to perform. It tells the old practice of Filipino courtship between a man and a woman. Specifying it as the *Curacha Boholana* to honor her home Province of Bohol, Mrs. Sarmiento and her Congressman husband were ever prideful in offering this to the fiesta queen. Unlike any other dances, the *curacha* steps couldn't be executed with any other music but the *curacha* itself.

As the emcee mentioned her name, Mrs. Sarmiento grandiosely swayed to the center of the dance floor where she held the audience's eagerness to watch her do what she had been known for. In her right hand was a black fan of Spanish lace opened into a semicircle covering the lower portion of her face.

The orchestra started playing. Mrs. Sarmiento turned around to the beat of the music, trying hard to be graceful in moving her left fingers, flicking them like she was flipping castanets. Congressman

Sarmiento, who was as robust as his spouse, dramatically stepped up and danced his way toward where his wife was positioning herself. In rhythmical motion, she fled at his approach, her big butt wiggling. He chased her and they whirled all over the dance floor chasing like chickens on mating with the lively beat of the music until she fell into his arms in time when the music ended.

A thunderous applause followed; the couple vowed in acknowledgement. Mrs. Sarmiento giggled and waved her hands in appreciation of the yells and whistles. All the while she tried to make her eyes sparkle by batting her false eyelashes in quick succession and as she was catching her breath, her nostrils were constantly flaring. She stole the whole show from the fiesta queen. With those glittering ornaments she wore, it wasn't hard to tell where the congressman's wife was seated even if complete darkness covered the whole town that evening for a quarter of an hour due to a power outage.

VII

The Guests from the City

Friends are like the clothes you wear.
Those that wouldn't give good impressions.
must be discarded; only the good ones remain.

A Holy Mass for the town's patron saint was celebrated early the next morning - the feast day of Saint Rose of Lima. As had been the practice, the town's first family did the offertory. Aunt Thelma's friends heard the Holy Mass while the would-be priests were still in bed suffering from hangover. The church was crowded mostly by the poor residents of the municipality while the rich who crowded the ballroom the previous night until the wee hours were still in deep slumber. Father John was right to say in his homily: *'blessed are the poor for theirs is the Kingdom of Heaven'.*

Back to the villa that morning after church, Aunt Thelma's friends, while on the breakfast table, were talking in whispers about who was the 'hottest' among the seminarians, not knowing that Grandma, who was baking her favorite chiffon cake was silently listening to them. When the boys came out for a cup of black coffee, the girls showed them their cutest smiles. I saw embarrassments in the boys' faces. Shyly, they said "Hi". The girls reacted with their faint giggles, but Grandma heard them. Their reactions obviously displeased my grandmother. The boys, who were wearing almost nothing but their short shorts, immediately slipped back into their room.

Flora, who was watching them while preparing food for lunch, discerned what Grandma thought. When their eyes met, she burst out laughing and quickly suppressed it. I could tell Flora did it on purpose: to make my grandmother more upset. Shaking her head again with her mouth contorting, Grandma called out Aunt Thelma from her room.

"I thought you were going to the beach," Grandma told her daughter as soon as she came out. Apparently, Grandma wanted to get rid of her daughter's friends from sight.

"In the afternoon, Mama," Aunt Thelma replied. "They only want to see the sunset we have here. I told them it looks more spectacular than the one over Manila Bay."

I went with them to the shore and again without the kill-joy Uncle Ralph. When we returned, the guests walked in pairs, holding hands.

After supper, the visitors returned to the city packed in a red car. Back then, cars in my country were built without seat belts. With the guests from the city gone, Grandma reprimanded her children not to bring again those kinds of friends to Sacandaya.

"They were attention seekers. What's the right term, Flora?" The housekeeper was playing deaf, so Grandma raised her voice: "Flora, what did you say they were?"

"What was that *Senyora?*" Flora asked as if just aroused from a deep sleep.

Grandma spoke haltingly to emphasize every word. "What's the apt term for people who walk naked on the streets?" Flora couldn't answer so Grandma gave a hint to jog her memory. "You whispered it to me earlier after they'd left; what did you say they were?"

"Exhibitionists . . .?" Flora responded but hesitatingly.

"*Maria Santisima!*" Grandma exclaimed and made on her the sign of the cross the way she would at the strike of a thunderbolt.

"Miss Flora, you smeared my friends' reputation," Aunt Thelma reproached.

"Appropriate!" Grandma butted in. "Shame on them who had the nerve to exhibit their bodies in wet skimpy bikinis on the streets. They should have covered themselves with towels because the parade was passing by. Did you see the boys, Flora? Do you think they were brawny with their scanty trunks?

Flora nudged Mama: "What do you think, Patricia?"

Mama gave her a quick glance: "I wasn't there. I did not watch the parade."

Flora whispered: "Well, they came home like that: bold and bulbous."

Mama whispered back: "I didn't see them when they came. . ."

"Patricia didn't see the guys in bikini briefs, *Senyora*," Flora told Grandma.

"I was asking you!" Grandma yelled.

"Well . . . well . . . I d-didn't s-see their fronts, *Senyora*," Flora stuttered. My mother, who was composing herself in deference to grandma, laughed aloud.

"Miss Flora," Uncle Ralph said. "A poet once said that a thing of beauty is a joy forever, don't you think so?"

"Okay, but what's the connection to your friends' nudity?" Flora asked and swayed her hips at the face of Uncle Ralph. Everybody burst out laughing. That amused me, too.

"Well, watching a naked body is a joy, don't you think so?"

"Mr. Don't-you-think-so, it depends on the body. Is it a joy to everybody seeing me naked?" Flora answered chin up, posing like a teapot. Everybody laughed out loud again. It was the first time I saw Mama stooping down to the floor while pressing her belly out of laughing, but Grandma was wearing the same stern face.

"There would've been a thunderbolt if you did," Grandma's face scowled.

"But they would find joy watching me naked. Right, Thelma?"

"What we mean here are beautiful naked bodies," Aunt Thelma scoffed. "People surely enjoyed seeing my friends in their sexy swimming suits, right?"

"Were those swimming suits? I thought those were hankies covering their private parts," Flora commented, and my mother couldn't stop laughing so hard again.

"If those guys were guilty of it, what's your verdict?" Uncle Ralph asked in a prating manner which Flora ignored. She was reminding Mama of '*Maria Flordeluna*', their favorite radio soap opera to be staged at the plaza that evening.

"About the verdict, Rafael, ask your mother about it," Flora said and left.

"Spare me from that foolishness, Rafael," Grandma told her son with sternness in her face concealing her amusement over Flora's stint. "I was embarrassed . . . greatly embarrassed, when the Congressman and his wife asked me if those youngsters who were watching the parade in scanty suits were our visitors. Mrs. Sarmiento is from Bohol and most Boholanos are brought up with propriety, but here were your friends – baring themselves to the scrutiny of the public on a fiesta at the most glaring time of the day and on the street where the parade was passing by."

"Mama, they didn't mean to catch the people's attention."

"Yes, they did. They were displaying their bodies because they thought they had nice, beautiful bodies . . . huh! How brazen! Scandalous! Embarrassing! God couldn't have spared them from lightning. You were with them, Thelma, and you must have witnessed how people reacted. Do you think people loved what your friends were wearing? Thanks, you didn't have a bikini to wear, *ay Dios Mio!*"

Laughing, Uncle Ralph said, "Mama, Thelma's guests were city bred; they didn't come from the boondocks."

"*No solo las mujeres, Rafael, pero Tambien tus amigos . . .*"

"It's the same thing, Mama; my friends were city boys . . ."

"And to think that those friends of yours were aiming to become priests . . . to be celibates . . . *Que barbaridad!*" Grandma said in the language of her ancestors. "Not because all those friends are raised in the city, they're excused from the culture we have here. I expected them to behave naively here because they were strangers, but to my dismay, they looked so indecent, very indecent! How daring!"

"As if you don't know, Mama . . . it's no longer the twenties or thirties; it's the seventies and you know the evolution of vogues and cultures," Uncle Ralph reasoned out.

"Whatever! People here are not used to seeing lascivious attire displayed publicly. Your friends didn't care about morality as if they were movie celebrities. Did you see how they behaved? *Dios mio!* Miss Via, a proponent of morality, saw what they did."

"Those are city-bred, Mama. We cannot just change their behavior automatically."

"It is said that when you're in Rome, be a Roman. You should've advised them, Rafael of the culture we have in our town."

"My friends are all grown-up men responsible enough of what they are doing. If the girls weren't flirting..."

"What did you say? You misunderstood my friends' cordiality. Remember that those girls are students of Colegio de la Immaculada Concepcion, our mother's alma mater."

"Well, not everybody who comes from that school has Mama's good bearings. Your friends are descendants of Eve who tempted Adam to partake in the Fruit of Sin. My dear sister, you forgot that my friends are seminarians."

"That doesn't make them saints!"

"Stop blaming each other!" Grandma interfered. "Don't side with your *amigos*, Rafael. Those *hombres* took advantage of the girls' flirtatiousness. Are those the kind who goes for a vow of celibacy? Huh! You would never know if they're aiming for priesthood or for fatherhood. Maybe . . . no, I'm not just suspecting, you also behave like them whenever you're away from us. Do you? No, you could not answer that, Rafael, because it's true. *Santa Maria Purisima!*"

"*Mama mia . . .*"

"Listen! *Temo que al final no te vas a dedicar a ser sacerdote*, but a father in a family like those friends of yours. You better dissociate from them."

"Did you hear that? *Dissociate!*" Aunt Thelma told Uncle Ralph sarcastically.

"The same goes to you, Thelma."

"Mama . . . not as easy as that, Mama," Aunt Thelma's reaction was coated with vehemence. Uncle Ralph laughed out loud. Grandma shushed him.

"Friends come and go like the clothes you wear. Dresses that will not give you a good impression are discarded. Only the good ones remain. Your friends were flirting and fake. A woman wearing a heavy makeup is not wearing her true self. Your friends are fake and therefore not the right people to go with!"

"Ma, don't be irrational."

"Unpleasant habits are contagious," Grandma continued without giving Aunt Thelma a chance to interrupt. "Patricia, did you see one of the girls smoking?"

"What's wrong with smoking?" Aunt Thelma impulsively scoffed.

"The defense council is asking: What's wrong with smoking?" Grandma said mimicking Aunt Thelma's voice. "Flora, don't you have the answer for that?"

"Well, there is really nothing wrong with smoking if you can blow out smoke rings gracefully well. If you cannot do it, then you'd look like a cheap prostitute."

"Flora, that's not what I told you!"

Again, Uncle Ralph laughed out loud. Again, Grandma shushed him.

"And it causes lung cancer; right, *senyora*?"

"Exactly right! People think that a woman who smokes is either a socialite or a social climber or a prostitute. That girl did not look like a socialite, not at all, so what is she . . . a social climber or a prostitute?"

"I have the answer . . . she's a crossbred," Uncle Ralph said and freed out another sarcastic laughter that irritated his mother. Once more, Grandma told him to shut up.

"Okay, Mama. That is your opinion, but I can keep my friends and keep myself unaffected," Aunt Thelma disputed. "I know how to manage myself."

"Friends are influential and bad manners are viral so whatever your friends are, people think that you are not far different. You do not have to tell the town folks what you are but who your friends are," Grandma said and went to her room leaving her children blaming each other and laughing over their mother's antiquated outlook.

The town fiesta culminated with the staging of 'Maria Flordeluna' in the plaza that children and older women, who were following the soap opera over the radio on weekdays, did not want to miss. Flora brought a chair to sit on at the stage forefront; she also brought a towel to wipe her tears. She had been following this radio series every day while preparing lunch and how she cried listening to it. That night when Flora watched the radio actors performing in person the drama on stage, she cried a river, wailing so hard and loud unmindful of the people around who were helping her cry.

The fiesta was over. It left Flora with red swollen eyes for watching a schmaltzy stage drama the previous night; it left the town folks deep in debts for having pompous banquets; it left the town littered with pieces of trash as if a hurricane had just passed by. Schools cancelled classes the following day. Teachers and pupils had to help clean up the streets while municipal employees dismantled the arches and removed the bunting hanging over the main thoroughfares.

The Frolics were gone and so were the guests from the city. That day, after Uncle Ralph and Aunt Thelma had left for the city, Mama and I walked back to our house. From there, I could see Villa Zaragoza nestling alone in the hills, looking desolate once again.

VIII

A Psychic Came to Town

I saw nothing in the psychic's crystal ball.
Mama said 'twas because I was not a seer.
I did not have the mystique of a psychic.

Fiestas are special occasions to Christian Filipinos. That town fiesta in 1974 was the most crowded so far and the liveliest because of the presence of the circus and freak shows. More fiesta vendors came displaying their wares on the sides of main thoroughfares, so more people were crowding the streets; however, they made the occasion more jovial.

Among the vendors who came to town that year was Solvera. Her wares were her skills in future-reading and finding lost things.

Like a wild mushroom that pops up after a night of lightning, the seer's tent popped up in the plaza a week before the fiesta. She had a tarnished crystal ball and two packs of old reading cards - browned and enfeebled of overuse - on a black square table made of rigid plastic set between two folding chairs of the same materials and color. The self- proclaimed psychic claimed to have predicted the death of President Magsaysay, the rising to power of an Ilocano senator, the triumph of Gloria Diaz as Miss Universe of 1969, the escalation of insurgencies in late sixties and the declaration of Martial Law in September of 1972. Never did she touch events of global magnitude for she may not have known it. When asked if she had predicted the day man would land on the moon, she retorted: "What man? What moon?"

Solvera had her showers at the town's only inn where traveling salespeople and tourists sojourned. For fifty cents every shower, she can avail free use of restrooms. The inn housed the only baker in town where the seer happened to meet Flora one morning before the fiesta. Since then, many came to know about her. Flora suggested to Mama to solicit the seer's help on my father's whereabouts. Mama gave this a thought.

Solvera opened her business after Angelus. With hair brushed up with a bandana to show a pair of long fancy earrings, spic-and-span, she was ready to face her clients. Some people said the seer was good only on finding lost things not in foretelling, yet many believed in her especially those foretold of winning the lottery or going abroad or marry a foreigner. She ended up every session filling the client's heart with contentment and the earnestness to come back for another session. She closed business at the blaring of the curfew at 9:45 in the evening. By 10:00, the town become silent per municipal order.

The soothsayer never revealed her real age; I guess she was as old as Miss Via was. She said she never had tried any facial make up but a light puff of talcum powder. "Cosmetics cause skin sagging; it makes you look older than your age. "Simplicity is beauty," she would say.

When Flora complimented that her complexion looked as lovely as that of Susan Roces's, the most popular Philippine movie star that era, Solvera divulged her 'secret': She was using Chin-Chin, a face powder in solid form that she got from a Chinese merchant in the city. She was retailing the powder cake no bigger than a baby's palm at two pesos each. Flora tried using it but stopped after a month because her face remained as rough as ever.

When the fiesta was over, the psychic moved her business to a small place within the Chinese district. Her clients grew in numbers especially on Tuesdays and Fridays when her crystal ball was clear, and her card-reading was not blurry. On lost things, she would use the crystal ball and would charge twenty pesos for a thirty-minute session which ordinary people in town could hardly afford. For predictions, she had two different sets of cards to choose from. Clients who were adherent to card-reading said that tarot cards showed more accuracy. She charged five pesos for ordinary cards and doubled it if tarots were preferred, which at that time was already equivalent to a laborer's daily wage.

Anyway, there were clients who did not mind Solvera's high service fees. They had her assurance of authenticity posted at the entrance above her door in big bold letters:

****

SATISFACTION GUARANTEED

****

Chinese entrepreneurs paid more for the seer's services when the prediction augured well for their businesses. Their openhandedness made those Chinese her favorite clients - served them with hot green tea during the session complimenting it with '*good for your health*' to which the Chinese client would instantly respond: '*very*'.

When Solvera was preparing to move to her new place, Chow Pong Kang, the middle- aged Chinese merchant whose '*R*' sounded like '*L*' came to her looking for his young wife, who eloped with a young guy from the city after the fiesta.

"Your wife's not here, Mr. Chow," Solvera, while packing up her things, told the Chinese man who was standing by the entrance of her tent. "Why don't you try the 'lost and found' unit at the municipal hall?"

Mr. Chow didn't hear what the psychic said, he stepped inside the tent.

"Ask glass ball, okay?"

"Don't have time... moving out," Solvera replied instantly without looking at him.

The Chinese was insistent. From his pocket, he pulled a ten-peso bill.

"Pay you ten pesos, okay?"

"It's thirty and when it's emergency, fifty. Okay?" Solvera bluntly told Pong Kang, pronouncing the letter "F" crisply as a new fifty-peso bill would sound.

"Nevel mind. Wife only good ten pesos," Chow Pong Kang said dryly and was about to step out of the tent, but turned around in a second and gleefully asked, "Hey, how about cald leading? Yeah, find me new wife, huh?"

"For ordinary cards, it's five pesos; it's ten if I use the tarot."

"Talot." The Chinese responded in a heartbeat, nodding his head several times with a wide smile that exposed his uneven disarranged set of teeth.

The psychic squinted at him; the wider Pong Kang smiled, turning his eyes to slits.

"Did you say 'tarot'?" Solvera asked.

"Yeah, find me a new wife. Good wife."

"That is fifteen. I charge ten pesos for the tarot cards, and five for the **good**."

"Okay. Find me good, beautiful wife."

"That is twenty pesos already. Add another five for the **beautiful**."

"Okay, twenty pesos. Good wife also beautiful and young."

"That's already twenty-five. Another five for the **young**,"

Chow Pong Kang said nothing more. Silence means yes for Solvera. She took out her tarot cards. When she turned around Pong Kang was gone.

The psychic may be tricky but so religious she never missed church obligations. In the era when Holy Masses were said in Latin and women covered their heads with bandanas, she covered her head with black veil that draped down to her buttocks. With a loose white poplin dress hemmed at her ankles, people from the boondocks often mistook her for a nun addressing her *sister Solvera*. Inside the church, she would carry her wooden clogs and with head bowed as her gesture of humility, she would walk barefoot to the most front pew where she could have a closer look at Father John. People teased her that she had a terrible crush on the American priest to which she would retort: "So? Is it a sin? The Bible did not say so."

A religious procession in our town would not be complete without Solvera at the frontline. In her left hand dangled a huge cherry-colored wooden rosary and in her right, a giant white candle which she personally ordered from a candle factory in the city. She would hold this like how the Statue of Liberty is holding her torch. Impish young boys took turns tickling her armpit, laughed and ran, until she tucked down her elbow. She recited aloud her prayers and in a tremulous voice, sang the *Salve Regina* so melancholically that it sounded like the wailing of the dead. The soothsayer tried hard to deliver the lyrics articulately as if to let people know she could pronounce Latin excellently well.

One night after she had moved to her new site, we came to her place. Mama brought Flora with us. Knowing my mother as the mayor's daughter, the psychic gave her special attention; the first session was free.

"Don't tell me why you're here. Let my tarot cards find it."

Solvera shuffled the cards. Mama reshuffled them per her instruction. From the top of the pack, the seer drew three cards and said: "You lost your husband," on the first, "about five years ago," on the second, "in a faraway place across a great sea," on the third. Then she looked back at my mother as she carelessly dropped the pack on the table.

The impact on the psychic's accuracy astounded Mama and Flora. After glancing at each other, both hastily asked: "Can you tell if he's still alive?"

"Our crystal ball knows it," Solvera smiled appreciatively. A great excitement flashed in Mama's eyes. "However, this isn't a good night to read the crystal ball. Come back next Friday at eight in the evening. Don't worry about the fee. I'm giving a fifty percent discount to any member of the Zaragoza household."

It turned out that like the PAGASA, the seer couldn't predict the weather accurately. On the night Solvera wanted Mama to come back, the weather wasn't good and at times like that, she said the crystal ball was not in the mood to cooperate. However, she assured my mother that my father was alive in Vietnam but couldn't tell the place in particular because of the bad weather. Nevertheless, that fueled Mama's hope for my father's return.

The psychic rescheduled my mother to the first Friday of November which was yet two weeks away, but Mama was so antsy of my father's whereabouts that she could not wait for that day, so the seer told her to come back on the first night of November which was three nights away. The seer assured my mother that even if it were not a Friday, she still could rely on her crystal ball. Only on All Saints' Day and on Holy Friday that the seer could predict with ninety-nine percent accuracy even if it is not a first Friday.

IX

The Eve of All Souls Day

A something was behind me breathing out
chilly air smelt of incense and burning candles
that brought a dreadful sensation down to my spine.

In the Christian calendar, the first of November is marked All Saints' Day; the following day is the All-Souls' Day. Filipinos believe that spirits of the dead wander in the evening of All Saints' Day to visit the living and sniff the food relatives prepared for them.

That first night of November, when town folks were in their respective homes preparing food for the spirits or were in the cemetery lighting candles and offering flowers and prayers for the dead as had been the practice in a Filipino Christian community, my mother and I were finding our way in the dark in Mama's continuing search for my father's whereabouts. Flora could have come with my mother, but she was so busy assisting my grandmother preparing food for the spirits, and so I went with my mother even if I didn't like going outside that night; I couldn't let Mama trek in the dark alone. Our absence in Villa Zaragoza on that eve of All Souls' Day was conspicuous. Without doubt, Mama was the butt of their jokes again.

"Believing in a seer is a sin," Grandma had warned my mother about consulting a seer, but that didn't deter Mama's faith in the psychic.

It was a bleak night. Nothing flickered in the skies but the soundless lightning at the western hemisphere flashing intermittently like a matchstick that suddenly flared and instantly died down.

We reached the house of the seer and up in the roofless porch, we settled ourselves in a bamboo bench while waiting for the seer to open her door. Except for the chirps of the crickets and cicadas, the night was quiet and windless, but the breeze was chilly. Suddenly, two dogs from the back of Solvera's house simultaneously freed a long deep howling followed by barking in same resonance. Somebody admonished them. Seconds after, they whined again then growled. I imagined how their bodies wriggled, tails tucked between their legs as they yelped and writhed as though in pain. Flora said that when dogs behave crazily, something nonhuman is around. Fear bashed my heart, vibrated in my head, quivered down all over my skin, and crawled deep in my flesh, streamed into my veins and wriggled to the core of my bones.

I was pondering on my fear when the church bells rang so loud it jolted me and made me grip my mother's arm. The tolling of the bells at eight in the evening sounded eerie and doleful as this was followed with death knells like when someone in town just died. Fear shuddered my nerves again when I heard the dogs ululate again, more aggressive and agonizing this time and it made the night eerier. Again, somebody admonished them.

Not long after the death knells were sounded, the air was turning smelly of burning incense and candles. Flora had said that if these things are smelt, ghosts must be nearby. I swear I heard footfalls coming up, faintly audible, but made the sagging bamboo floor creak. Something or someone blew chilly air on my nape that sent a more dreadful sensation down to my spine. This time, I really wanted to cry out of fear.

I skulked airtight closer to my mother. Quivering in fear, I was about to place her arm over my shoulder when the door opened. A ghost appeared! I almost shrieked but Mama quickly covered my mouth with her fingers. It was the seer dressed in solid white with her face thickly covered with chin-chin. I was on the verge of crying.

An eerie silence was shrouding when we stepped inside the room that served as the psychic's session hall. The faint light from a half-melted candle that was fitted to a glass holder on the top of the small black table made the atmosphere creepier. My heart was beating faster this time; my hands were shaking as I tried to reach for my mother who had settled on a chair that was on one side of the square table facing the seer. I stood behind.

In a few seconds, the psychic started her ritual. There was horror in her eyes when she gave me a glimpse and with a dry shallow smile, whispered that she had unseen visitors around which were harmless unless provoked. I must avoid looking at her eyes for the more intense I watched them, the more fear they cast on me that shuddered the innermost fiber of my being. She was out to scare me; I was again on the brink of crying.

I wanted to avoid seeing Solvera's talcum-whitened face but couldn't help glancing at her occasionally over Mama's shoulder. Her head was covered with a black veil. With the faint light of the candle, the seer looked like how I imagined a ghost fresh from its grave. She glowered at me as she placed a finger across her lips. I kept myself mum, but I looked at her eyes closely and I noticed they were reddish like those of a stale dead fish. She was staring at the crystal ball when she told us to close our eyes. Mama did; I did not.

After a moment of silence, Solvera started to moan, softly at first while settling into a trance. Then her moaning gradually turned louder and her breathing harder sending shivers through my skin, and I was also breathing harder to get rid of the fear lurking inside me. My heart thumped faster when the dogs howled again blending inharmoniously with Solvera's agonizing wail. She had summoned all the wandering souls on the streets for I heard again the creaking of the bamboo floor.

The ghosts were gathering now around us. I was about to faint in fear right where I stood. I held my mother's arm tightly and closed my eyes to avoid seeing strange things that might happen there those moments.

Unperturbed, Solvera slipped deeper into her trance. Her mournful murmur, becoming more tremulous and chillier, sounded like it came from deep beneath the ground. She was murmuring a language that was incomprehensible. Twice, the seer blurted my father's name. 'Romulo' was the only word that was clear to me.

Slowly but constantly, my fear was ebbing away. The clairvoyant, the psychic, the soothsayer - whatever she was - surely did not know I was now observing her moves. She continued muttering in a singsong manner words that sounded like of a dead language – Latin – but it gave me a feeling that she just made it up to impress her client, my mother this time. I bet Solvera herself did not understand what she was mumbling.

The medium stopped chanting. She rolled her eyeballs as if listening to some movements coming and shifted her eyes from right to left in many times while my mother was staring at her for about a minute without blinking, looking curious of what Solvera was about to say of my father's whereabouts. She stretched out her neck, inhaled deeply and exhaled wearily as if giving up her search.

"I heard no answer," muttered the medium in a loud whisper.

"Does it mean he isn't dead?" Mama whispered back in a hesitating manner.

"When I conjured his spirit, he would have answered," said the psychic.

"Then it's possible that he's alive . . ."

"Yes, it is," the seer replied immediately following a sigh of surrendering. "It's possible that your husband's alive. Let's try again."

Solvera closed her eyes once more. Mama did the same.

I moved to the side where I could have an unobstructed view of both faces. When Mama opened her eyes, the seer was gazing into the crystal ball, throwing glances at my mother as she told her what the ball was showing. Mama's eyes were nailed at the psychic's face. She was inhaling deeply, holding it every time the seer was about to say something, and slowly exhaling her breath as Solvera shifted her gaze back to the ball.

Watching my mother watching the seer was quite amusing. I almost freed out a loud laugh to get rid of my dread. The seer's facial expression made me suspect she was faking, an inkling that helped relieve me of fear. I wondered how my mother, a well-respective schoolteacher in our town, could believe what the psychic was telling her.

I sneaked to the seer's back the moment she closed her eyes again. Peeping into the ball over the seer's shoulder, I saw nothing, but the faint blurry reflection of her face illuminated by the light from the burning candle. The ball wasn't even crystal clear - had a cloud of stain, its bottom a bit mossy. My suspicion grew - the psychic made up all those quaint stories. I couldn't care less anymore about her unseen visitors.

Unhesitatingly I told my mother outright that the psychic was playing tricks. Solvera heard it loud and clear and so she stopped her unintelligible murmur, opened her eyes, and cast them sharply at me as if wanting to engulf me in a single stroke. Again, that struck me with fear. Impulsively, I shied my eyes away from the psychic's gaze, crouched behind my mother and tugged her arm countless times hurrying her to leave.

With the session unfinished, Solvera told my mother to come back on the first Friday of November without me or she would lose my father's trace. I had stepped out onto the porch when I heard the seer telling my mother that the mole in my face where tears run through brought us bad luck. That was illogical. The seer was up to get even with me.

Mama was not bothered about the mole in my face, but the GMRC that the psychic said I needed. Without being told, I knelt before the small altar we had at home to show my remorse and suppress Mama's anger. While I did my contrition, she was behind me delivering her usual moralizing discourse that messed up my prayer I could not finish 'The Lord's Prayer' solemnly well and had to say it all over again.

"It was so impolite for a teacher's daughter to insult an old woman. Do you understand what a GMRC is? That's *good manners and right conduct*. Being a schoolteacher, I don't need anybody to tell me how to impose discipline on my own daughter. What you did embarrassed me! You embarrassed me!"

My mother discoursed with fire in her eyes until she cried again. I had to apologize for what I did to calm her down even if I thought what I did was right.

"But, Mama, don't you ever think that the seer is a fraud? She was concocting things for I didn't see anything in her crystal ball."

"It was because you were not the seer! You didn't have the mystique!"

Seldom Mama scolded me; if ever she did, I deserved it. I wasn't the seer; didn't have the mystique and it was useless to argue with my mother over that matter because she always thought she was right that in closing her admonition she'd tell me, *"Never ever make me mad again"*, and as always, I ended it with the sign of the cross on me and with a bowed head, whispered to myself: *"Amen."*

The Psychic's Clients

Except for one, they were all women.
No wonder women are referred to as the weaker sex,
the ones who are easily influenced; the ones who are easily fooled.

My mother was captivated with the psychic's eccentricity which to her was a 'mystique'. Her faith in Solvera was as strong as her hope to find my father alive even after the passing of many years.

I wasn't supposed to come with my mother the next time she went to see the psychic, but Flora was busy that night and Mama was afraid to trek in the dark alone. At the seer's house, Mama told me to stay at the porch. *Fine!* Anyway, I didn't want to see again that old woman's weird face. She looked scary when she did her under-a-trance act speaking in somewhat infantile manner, which she said, the voice of the Child Jesus. That would've provoked me into laughing were it not for my mother's indicative touch on my lips. The truth is the psychic sounded like the squeak of a mouse pinned down with a board. She was faking it yet got the nerve to use names of saints to make her clientele believe she was for real. I could hear Miss Via exclaim her animosity: *"It's blasphemous!"*

There were quite a few clients on the porch waiting for their turns. Except for one, they were all women and most of those were on their second or third visit. It proved once more that women can easily be gypped than men - more vulnerable to seduction. The half hour that Solvera allotted per session wasn't enough so that clients should come again for another session which means another five or ten bucks in exchange for false hopes and consolations. Anyway, they seemed satisfied of whatever the fake seer could sham on them, and Mama wasn't any different. The addiction to Solvera's mystique was turning viral among women in our town.

While waiting for their turn, some clients talked about the clairvoyant's accuracy in telling their past, looking quite amusing with their eyes popping, nostrils flaring, and jaws dropping in raptures. They giggled in appreciation of the soothsayer's predictions like good fortune coming in terms of going abroad or of marriage to big Americans - mentioning something obscure - about the private parts of those tall and big men, black or white. Saying the words with gestures, they broke out with boisterous laughter, pushing each other, their butts sliding off the bench until they dropped to the floor.

I didn't get what they guffawed about, but I laughed seeing them fall. Tears came out of their eyes suppressing their laughter. A thick fluid suddenly spurted out of one's nose. She sniffed it back. Slavers dripped from both corners of her mouth. She wiped dry the spittle in her chin with the hem of her skirt unconsciously exposing her red underwear to everybody's amusement as she spluttered her words in describing the private parts of big American men. An old lady looked at me and in a high-raised voice admonished them from talking scandalous things because "a kid is listening", but those girls couldn't stop talking about it and laughing out hard and only after they heard the psychic hiss that their voices toned down to whispers.

Mama came out from the session hall and those gullible women fired questions that led her to announce that my father would be coming home on a boat one stormy day when the wind was strong, and the sea was as restless as a mad dog gone wild. Believing it without hesitation, the ladies applauded and chorused: *We're happy for you, Patricia!*

I was the only one not happy about it - skeptical of Solvera's ability to foresee. She made my mother's problem worse by casting false hopes. Even with my father's failure to come back after many years, Mama's faith in his promise to return home one day was still strong and was strengthened more by the psychic's prediction that he was *'coming on a boat one stormy day'*. I wondered about it: *From where? How?* The answers lay ahead, which my mother endlessly waited for but which I doubted to happen.

Mama patiently waited for a strong wind to come and see a restless sea. Many stormy days had passed by and in a few times, I heard her say that she saw my father coming - running on the street amid heavy rain. Those were all hallucinations.

Meanwhile, Solvera's popularity was waning. Her predictions faltered. Nobody in town won the lottery. Town folks laughed about what happened to the women whom the fake fortune-teller foretold to marry an American.

There was this girl named Marissa who, indeed, married an American guy. Armed with a 'broken bamboo' English, she went to America with a fiancée visa. In less than a year, she returned not as passenger but a baggage in a crate, her body was beaten black and blue. Rumors had it that there were Americans who married Asian women, insured them, and murdered them for money.

The story about Marissa's fate landed in the pages of city dailies but that didn't prevent other women to seek for an American husband as it was the easy way to get out of poverty. They believed there were Americans who could proudly boast of happy marriage with an Asian woman, especially a Filipina.

Another girl Solvera predicted would marry her American boyfriend ended up a single parent. Nona's American pen pal was sincere in marrying her that he sent her big money for their wedding. So, excited about her fiancé's coming, Nona thought of surprising him with a new look. She had her nose lifted and slimmed at the sides; her slit eyes were turned a little bit bigger. Her skin was fully bleached; her bust turned humongous. If not for her voice, people would never recognize her as the same person they have known.

The American came but doubted that the girl who introduced herself as Nona was the girl he was to marry. She had her face looked different from the picture she'd sent him previously. The American guy cancelled the marriage and immediately left the town.

Nona was the talk of the town for days. Greatly embarrassed, she left Sacandaya after a week. Stories had it that she was working as a masseuse in Manila's Ermita and later, a hospitality girl in a nightclub where big businessmen and the 'honorable and decent' politicians were frequenting. Then she had gone abroad – to Japan – and not long after that she became a *japayuki,* a street lingo that describes a Filipina working as a club entertainer in Japan, selling her flesh on the side for real big bucks.

Nona came back to our town with a son sired by a Japanese businessman who married and divorced her after a year. With the child support and her monthly alimony, she ventured in money-lending business and in due time became a nouveau riche, envied by girls her age for young men in town were vying to marry her wealth. But the fanatic ladies of the Catholic Women's League rebuffed her donations for charity as she was rumored to have traded her flesh to Japanese clientele, imported young Filipino girls for a huge fee to different prostitution dens in Kyoto and had been a notorious mama-san in a teahouse along the avenue where men plied for a geisha's warmth.

There was Benilda, whom the psychic predicted would marry a wealthy American widower. That didn't happen; the girl's good-for-nothing childhood boyfriend persuaded her to elope with him in his fear that the seer's prediction might be coming true.

Solvera learned that Benilda's father, the town's Chief of Police, was looking for her to inquire into his daughter's whereabouts. Sensing she was in trouble, Solvera vanished as instantly as she had come to town before the police chief could contact her.

The fake psychic had stashed a good sum of money from the townspeople. One of those was my mother. Mama's sibs talked and laughed about her faith on the seer. Although that embarrassed me, I must stand by her.

With the seer gone from Sacandaya, talks floated that the psychic had been a vagabond for the kind of livelihood she had and, on some occasions, ran for her life. She alleged herself to be a seer, but she never had seen what livelihood was good for her that she wouldn't be running for her life anymore.

Christmas was in the offing. In my country, people start welcoming Christmas at the advent of colder days – probably in the month of September. As soon as they hear Christmas carols played over the radios, residents start hanging lanterns by the window in their houses. The affluent ones were competing to see whose Christmas tree was the best. We may never ever have a Christmas tree in our house, but at least, we were able to hang a star lantern on our porch.

As had always been every year, schools were closed when the celebration of *Misa de Gallo* started. It was for nine consecutive days starting on the 16th of December as early as when the Morning Star appeared in the Eastern sky.

Going with my mother to the church every early morning during those days was kind of exciting because we'd be having a breakfast of hot chocolate and *suman,* or other delicacies vendors displayed at the church's yard. This time of the year in my country may be cold, but not chilly at all.

Celebrating *Noche Buena* at the villa had been a family tradition. After a hearty dinner, we'd gather around a giant Christmas tree in the family room to open our presents. I'd have something from my grandparents and from Uncle Ralph and Aunt Thelma, even had something from Flora, but neither from Aunt Merriam nor from Uncle Benito.

A week before Christmas day had come, Mama mailed several cards to her friends and co-teachers. I sent only one and that was to Santa Claus asking him to grant me two Christmas wishes: One was for Solvera to find a permanent place to have a different and better means of living and the other was for the return of my father. It had been more than six years since he left home.

A couple of months passed, and the psychic was no longer heard of in our town. The poor woman must've found a place to stay and a better way of earning money as I had wished for her. As for my other wish, no streak of hope was coming. It was as dim as the end of the Vietnam War.

XI

Sundays in Sacandaya

This is the day the Good Lord made holy.
Let us rejoice and be glad about it.
(PSALM 118:24)

In those times I was still a child, and even years before I was born, a Sunday had been a get-together day for the Zaragozas which required the presence of everybody. Mama said my father never had the chance to hobnob with any member of the Zaragoza family. Not only my grandfather, but Aunt Merriam and Uncle Benito also despised my father vehemently.

Mother and I had to be at the villa after church to help prepare a sumptuous breakfast. We should stay there throughout the day and into the night until the curfew blared.

While the women were preparing lunch, the men were checking out which of my grandfather's gamecocks were going to the derby that day. In our town, cockfighting would start after lunch. Except for Uncle Ralph, all the other men and that included Santiago would be going to the cockpit to watch and bet for my father's roosters. Uncle Ralph would be playing scrabble with Grandma and Mama and Aunt Thelma. My cousins would be running around the yard playing "hide and seek". I would rather reread my books of fairy tales which I always carried with me than play with those cheaters.

Aunt Merriam would come at lunchtime and leave right away after lunch for a mahjongg session somewhere downtown; she lingered there and would only come back to her parents' house if she ran out of money to gamble. Unlike cockfighting, playing mahjongg will last until the early morning hours if the gamblers have money to bet or if they got tired and bored in scrambling and rearranging the tiles, decide to adjourn. In most times, Aunt Merriam would come home a loser but had plenty of gossips to tell. In this gambling game, players exchange a variety of talks while playing. My grandmother would know the latest talk in town from Aunt Merriam if not from Flora.

A mahjongg aficionado would say that the game has lots of excitement worth the time spent for with its ups and downs - the winner doesn't always win; the loser doesn't always lose but a mahjongg player must master the tricks of the trade to be considered a skillful player. Not only does a lucky streak help; the player must be careful of the tiles he or she should throw for all the players to see and be watchful of the tiles that any player has thrown to the center of the table. The player needs to have tricks and strategies in executing the game skillfully well.

Cockfighting on Sundays was and still is the favorite pastime of most men in our town. It would stop when the visibility of the gamecocks was no longer clear. Grandpa would bring home lots of money and the rooster he won over which Flora would stew for supper. Locally called *bihag*, its soup tasted very palatable if simmered with mashed ginger, slashes of green papaya and *kamunggay* leaves, flavored with stalks of lemon grasses. A stewed *bihag* would taste wonderfully great but I never saw my grandfather partake a piece of it for he treated fighting cocks like they were his pets.

After dinner, the grandchildren would gather in the living room to listen again Grandma's 'fairy tales' or to listen Grandpa retelling his heroic war adventures. The adults would be watching a live show on the TV if not playing scrabble.

A quarter before curfew, everybody in town started dispersing. Nobody could roam the streets after ten in the evening except stray dogs and cats and uniformed men on patrol.

One Sunday morning, I heard Uncle Benito say: *Here comes Solvera's heifer milking cow tugging her calf.* I saw Aunt Merriam force out sardonic laughter although it wasn't funny at all. They did it on purpose because they had been treating my mother as a laughingstock. In many times, it puzzled me why these two siblings of my mother found it enjoyable to hurt her. Mama didn't mind those despicable gestures of arrogance for it was a day of gathering and bickering among family members and should be avoided.

Pretending not to have heard the bad comments of her siblings, Mama greeted them gleefully, but they ignored her and left that instant; I saw the blush in my mother's face even if she tried to hide it from me.

A Sunday at the villa could've been a wonderful day for me if not for my cousins' indifference. Madel would lead the two sons of Uncle

Benito in making fun of me. They referred me as *"anak sa buho sa kawayan"* which literally meant I was conceived not in my mother's womb but inside the bamboo tubes like how the first Filipino couple originated per Flora's tale. My cousins' chanting of it was irritating, but I must ignore them for the louder they chanted if I got upset.

I didn't understand why my cousins found it funny calling me as such. I thought they were associating it with the house I and my mother dwelt in which was fully made of bamboo unlike theirs that were made of hollow blocks and bricks. Aunt Merriam found it amusing. I suspected she coached Madel to do it. Like mother, like daughter.

"Don't mind them," Mama had told me. "Your cousins are just jealous of you because you are your grandma's favorite grandchild."

I wondered how it would be if my father were there to defend me. Mama couldn't even defend herself. Clear as thunder, she heard Uncle Benito bad-mouthing her, but she had it in one ear and out through the other to save herself from trouble. Whenever we were at my grandparents' house, Mama would always prefer to spend her time at the kitchen to help Flora do her chores rather than share thoughts with her siblings because most of the time, the topic would be about her and my father's tragic end in Vietnam.

My mother didn't believe my father was dead on the strength of the letter she got from him. She'd been keeping it so well and had reread it a thousand times already that she must have memorized every single word that was written there. Besides, the psychic gave her assurance that my father was alive and well even if I doubted of it because the Vietnam War had already ended and all Filipino soldiers had come back home; they came home, but not my father.

XII

The Boat People

Seeing them, I could imagine how miserable
my father's life had been in the country
where the boat people came from.

The Vietnam War was perhaps the longest ever to happen in all Asia. It was France's war in the fifties and had become America's in the mid-sixties. My country got involved when America asked its nation-allies for soldier- volunteers. My father was with the second batch dispatched in the last quarter of 1968.

On the first working day of May in 1975, Grandpa held the monthly meeting of municipal officials at the villa. I was there the whole time listening what those people were discussing – it was about the end of the Vietnam War. Everybody in the council wondered how the great America lost the war to a small country called North Vietnam.

"President Ford ordered the evacuation of Saigon," Grandpa told the council. "Some people fled by the sea. It's possible that one of these days they would reach our littorals." I told my mother what I learned that morning. She already knew about it and was earnestly hoping my father would finally come home. Since then, every night before going to bed, she urged me to pray with her for the return of my father.

One early Saturday morning, I heard a woman's voice calling my mother from across the street. I sensed my mother hurriedly open a window.

"What's going on?" I heard my mother ask.

"There's a boat of people from Vietnam washed ashore," the woman shouted back. "Cheer up, Patricia. Your prodigal husband finally had come home."

Mama shrieked out. She roused me up and, in a hurry, took a quick glance at the mirror, brushed her hair with one careless stroke, took her jacket, and wrapped a beach towel around her hips. Then she dashed out like a hen squawking after laying an egg. Hurriedly, I pulled out a sweater and ran fast to catch up with my mother.

The southwest monsoon had swept in; the air was cold, and the sky was damp, but town folks were rushing pell-mell down to the shore to see how the people from a war-torn country looked like.

There were already innumerable onlookers when we reached the seashore. Mama left me at the top of the seawall where stood a few bystanders before she went down to the shore where the drifters huddled. The wind had gotten rough it made the sea restless like a mad dog gone wild – exactly how Solvera, who I thought was a fake seer, predicted. Furious waves were slamming the boat the refugees used which was carelessly left on the shore. At the boat's escutcheon was a word that had ciphers over some letters and that made me conclude the boat people were really from a foreign land. They looked famished and seemed smelly of fish and sea with their sun-tanned faces, soiled dresses, and wind- ruffled hair; white patches of dried salty water were visible in their skin. Looking at their faces, I wondered why they looked like they were Filipinos.

Mama came back after a while looking downhearted enough to tell me my father wasn't among those washed ashore. Tears flooded my eyes and no matter how many times I tried to dry out my swelling tears, they fell.

The refugees were led to the municipal hall for breakfast. Among them was this miserable-looking girl, barefooted and limping caused by a huge wound in her left thigh. There wasn't joy in her face even when she was offered a bowl of hot sweet rice porridge that was cooked with tender chicken and flavored with garlic and ginger exceedingly good to guzzle on a stormy day. It seemed she forced herself to consume it which could be unpalatable to her after that great ordeal across the vast South China Sea.

After breakfast, the refugees were led to my grandparents' *camarin* for temporary shelter. I went there at lunchtime and saw the Vietnamese girl dogging behind Grandma, limping like her sick little puppy. A white cotton bandage swathed her wounded thigh. I brought my old pair of shoes for her to use and the dress that Grandma gifted me the other Christmas which I already had outgrown. It was solid white with red and yellow roses embroidered around the hem. Her eyes sparkled with joy at the sight of it; a faint smile beamed in her face when she opened her arms to me. I presumed it was her gesture of gratitude for the things I gave her.

The little girl's name was Diep. I guess she was a little bit younger than I was and hadn't been to school. I was six, a year shy of first grade but I was admitted as a first grader because of my grandparents' influence. Anyway, Diep and I communicated with each other with hand and facial gestures. I spent some hours with her while teaching her the English alphabet which she was excited about that she memorized it in half-a-day.

Mama talked to the oldest-looking refugee who walked with us to our house. Tam Nguyen was a businessman from the Empire City of Hue. When the communist invaded the city, he and his wife fled to My Lai to be with their only son who lived in the village with his family. It shocked the old couple to learn that the whole village was brutishly massacred in cold blood by the American soldiers in the summer of '68 on suspicion that it was populated with NVA sympathizers; no one was spared.

In deep grief, the couple proceeded to Da Nang and stayed there for another few years. Sometime in the spring of 1975, they sought refuge in the capital city of Saigon, but then they heard that the communists from the North were coming and so, the city must be evacuated as quickly as possible.

Tam Nguyen and his wife reached the vicinity of the American Embassy in Saigon by daybreak when the evacuation coded as "Operation Swift Wind" started. In the rampage, his wife was separated from him, dragged away with the stream of people wanting to get inside the compound. He heard her calling him until her voice faded in the variant sound of voices and movements pervading in the air.

In frantic search for his wife, the old man squeezed himself in, jamming onto the gate of the embassy until he touched the iron bars where he held himself, unmindful of the American soldier who struck the knuckles of his hands with a rifle butt, slicing his skin. He felt excruciating pain but ignored it in his effort to catch a glimpse of his wife among the huddled masses all squeezing a way to get inside the embassy and to reach the staircase that led to the rooftop of the building where a helicopter was standing by.

Morning got clearer.

Tam Nguyen saw his wife at the rooftop of the building. She appeared to be searching for him among the people hovering along the fence. He called her, but his voice was drowned amidst the cries of people, pushing and banging against the chain-link gate while the American marines were jabbing them with rifle butts. He waved at her but with too many hands waving out, she failed to recognize him. He saw his wife pulled into the whirring chopper. The aircraft left and another came but Tam Nguyen was still locked outside the gate of the American embassy. He couldn't get in because he didn't have papers to show that someone would be supporting him in America; his wife had it.

By eight that morning the North Vietnamese Army had penetrated the borders. The last US chopper had left. Those left behind fled by the sea for fear of retributions in the new government. Tam Nguyen met other refugees who asked him to add fifty thousand piasters for a ferry boat that would take them to the evacuation ship in Vung Tau.

On their way to the beach, they passed by a little girl at the side of the road crying over a bleeding wound in her thigh. Her parents had left her accidentally. Tam Nguyen decided to tag her along. Twelve of them were originally planning to get into the evacuation ship. With the little girl, they numbered thirteen, an unlucky number according to the old folks in our town. And so, bad luck was stalking on them.

The old man stopped talking when we reached our house. Inside, Mama gestured to him to a chair. Staring at his face, I thought the Vietnamese man could very well be mistaken for a Filipino if not of his accent. He spoke ragged English and sometimes in pidgin with so much hand gestures and facial expressions even if Mama wasn't looking at him. He was always smiling making his eyes look like slits. His smile turned wider when Mama handed him a cup of freshly brewed native coffee which he quaffed right away as if it was cold plain water. Mama poured him another cup.

Fully energized, the old man kept nodding his bald head and saying *chao*. Mama asked him if he was familiar with the place called Da Nang and the old man readily answered in the affirmative. He said he often went to that city in the early seventies on business where he met a man who talked about the Philippines literally well. Mama told him about my father and showed him his picture which had his eyes covered with dark glasses. Tam Nguyen readily said *yah-yah*. Mama's grin stretched wide.

"You know him? His name is Romulo; remember that name Romulo Romualdez?" Mama gleefully said and she must be expecting the Vietnamese man would say *yah-yah*, but the old man said that the person he met in Da Nang, who spoke the Vietnamese language with thick foreign accent had a Japanese name and a family of his own. Therefore, it wasn't the person Mama had been searching for, I thought.

Drooping, Mama grabbed the rocker and slouched in there. The glow of hope in her face turned to despair. An abrupt silence fell between them.

We walked back to the farmhouse with lesser agility. Nobody was talking anymore. The smiles of Tam Nguyen were lost on the way.

XIII

The Search for a Sanctuary

"Give me your poor, your tired, your huddled
masses yearning to breathe free."
Emma Lazarus, a poet

At the camarin, I heard the same
old man retelling how his group escaped Saigon the day the city
fell. This time he had my grandparents for his audience. I heard my
grandmother sob while listening to his story.

Per his account, at the time the NVAs were storming Saigon,
refugees were crowding the shores of Vung Tau along South China
Sea racing for chances to board the rescue ship that would take them
to America. It was anchored about five kilometers offshore. Tam
Nguyen's group was a minute away when the rescue boat started
to depart leaving about a hundred fully loaded ferry boats drifting
offshore.

With paraphernalia for a long journey, the group decided to cross
the vast sea following the wind's direction. They were drifted to

Thailand, sought refuge but the Thai government was only kind enough to ration them with food and water but drove them back to the sea. Thinking of the danger to sail across the pitch-dark ocean, there was no other option for them but to spend the night in the shores of Thailand. Tam Nguyen slept late that night wondering what the next day would bring on.

Towards midnight a band of armed robbers assaulted the refugees, took away their valuables and raped the two teen-age girls who were with them. After the incident, Tam Nguyen decided to brave the night for a journey across the black sea before another band of bad Thais could come and do them more harm. Everybody in the group agreed.

Except for a single two-battery flashlight, which beam could hardly be detected on a foggy night, the refugees didn't have enough incandescent light to flare if ever a big ship was cruising across their way. They went on.

God must have cast His eyes on them when they fell asleep while traversing. They woke up to witness the shaping up of the sky but saw no wisp of cloud drifting above as no land horizon was in sight. All over was blue and boundless as if the world was made of nothing but oceans. Like seaweed they drifted. Nobody was paddling; all were dead tired even if the sea was as calm as it had been the night before.

Downwind they went.

After a few days of drifting, with all food gone, they must eat any edible things floating on the surface. With nothing to drink, they could only pray hard for heavy rain and open their mouths wide to catch raindrops as much as they could. Two elderly women gave up living one after the other. One man expressed the idea of eating some parts of the dead bodies to satisfy hunger, but Tam Nguyen vehemently opposed it. "We must respect the dead," he said. The remains of the dead were dumped into the sea.

In another morning.

A streak of horizon came into view, then a grey patch, a shoreline. Their senses enlivened. They paddled with their hands, their hearts strengthened with faith when suddenly a strong wind blew them back to the deep and further. Dark clouds were hovering over. Tam Nguyen feared a tropical storm was coming. They could only hope to reach the shore before the storm could swish down its fury on them.

The old Vietnamese man was in tears when he mentioned about his relatives and friends who were left behind. He made my grandmother cry when he talked about his son who had his family live in My Lai, the village the American soldiers massacred. Tam Nguyen believed his son and his family were among the casualties.

Tuesday morning, Grandpa commissioned a bus to transport the boat people to the refugee camps in Bataan, the place Grandpa had been to during the war. They would be hauled there to wait for the big ships that would take them to America.

There was Diep looking fresh like a newly bloomed white chrysanthemum on a bright summer day in the dress that I gave her. The pair of old shoes I gave fitted her well.

"*Buoi sang*," Diep said upon seeing me. "*Toi se di. Gap anh tai My.*"

"So long. See you in America," Tam Nguyen translated the phrase for me.

The bus started revving, we said our goodbyes.

"I always pray for you," I told Diep and hugged her. Although she may not have understood what I said, she smiled; her eyes squinting against the morning sunbeams.

Through the years, I often thought of Diep. History blew her off from her homeland, brought to our town by circumstance and was bound to reach a world where she could run freely and play with no bullets and bombs to scare her away. I realized then that I was not, after all, the most unfortunate child in the world. Compared to the children in South Vietnam who woke up to the world amid a war, I was luckier.

"Why do people fight, Mama?"

"A man's heart is filled with wrath; his head is full of pride," Mama answered but I could hardly understand what she said other than knowing that pride and wrath are two of the seven deadly sins; Miss Via said so.

My mother oftentimes told her pupils that the Vietnam War started during the fifties with France supporting South Vietnam against the communists from the North. It had become America's war in the mid-sixties, but notwithstanding of her being a History Class teacher, my mother didn't know why it had become America's war. Through all those years, countless Vietnamese children were orphaned, abandoned or deprived of longer life until Saigon fell into the hands of the communists and that ended the Vietnam War. Tens of thousands of Vietnamese fled out of their troubled country in search for a better place to live in as the poet Emma Lazarus says, "Where they could breathe free".

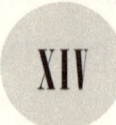

XIV

The Stormy Season

The Philippines is in the path of storm.
About 15 to 20 of them ravage
my country every year.

Even with the boat people long gone, Mama still hoped for my father's return. One stormy morning I woke up to see her bustling to open a window. In a rasping voice, she said that my father finally returned. I got up so excited with the thought that my father was on the street running across the storm. I thought I could see him finally; could touch his face, but to my dismay, I saw nobody but the heavy rain at the mercy of a blustering gale. Mama closed back the window and told me to go back to sleep; it was but her dream.

I feared what had become of my mother. I'd known her to be smart, but she was embezzled by a so-so soothsayer. If she listened to me on what I found out about the fake fortune teller, she wouldn't have become the laughingstock of her siblings. Or my mother might be just over excited at knowing where my father was if he were alive as the seer declared. Anybody in her place would feel the same way.

Many stormy days passed by, but no boat of refugees was ever washed ashore again. Nothing had been heard of Solvera, yet Aunt Merriam and Uncle Benito were still laughing about my mother's faith in the psychic. Behind her back, Aunt Merriam was calling her "Brenda", a coined name attributed to a woman suffering from brain damage and Uncle Benito called her "Aspie". I learned later in my adolescence that Aspie is the name applied to a person afflicted with Asperger Syndrome. My mother was called as such because she had a terrible inferiority complex; had difficulty in socializing even with her own family.

How have it been if we were staying at my father's side?

My father was a descendant of a big political clan from the province of Leyte. But except for my mother, no one among the Zaragozas believed it for no relatives of his came to ask for my mother's marriage. With his family unknown, my father was referred to by Mama's relatives as 'the Alien' and my mother's involvement with 'the alien' cast her out of Villa Zaragoza.

Per Flora's account, my father was with the 342nd Division of the Philippine Constabulary based in the next town. Some of its soldiers were either from the President's home province or were from the First Lady's and were known to be abusive. They earned the ire of the townspeople with their wanton display of arrogance. With rifles slung at their backs and machineguns mounted at the top of their vehicles, even the town's policemen cowered when they were around.

Mama said that my father was a dignified soldier loaded with humility and far different from his comrades. He was 22 when dispatched in 1967 to monitor illegal fishing activities on the town's remote coastlines. When the Provincial Governor was invited to crown the fiesta queen that year, my father was his escort-guard. The entourage dined at Villa Zaragoza.

On that occasion, at the request of the governor who knew his musical talent, my father played *Matud Nila* on the piano. It was my father's favorite song and incidentally, it was also my mother's. He caught her eyes and that started their acquaintances and eventually fell in love with each other. Unfortunately, my father brusquely objected to the relationships. On finding it out, he kicked his daughter out of his house. With nobody to run to but my father, she had to live with him and eventually, what I knew of, they ended up getting married in a civil court. Then my father left for the Vietnam War. Then I was born. I woke up to the world in a country deeply troubled by a rising rebellion caused by the rampant corruption of elected officials in the government.

After having a mild stroke, Grandpa resigned from his post upon the advice of his doctor son. It was his alibi; the truth of the matter was he wanted to pull himself out of the ruling party that was smeared with bad reputations.

In the subsequent local elections, Uncle Benito tried running for mayor but lost tremendously. Since then, the name Zaragoza had become politically dead for nobody anymore in the family was ever interested in getting involved in politics.

Philippine politics had become dirtier than ever. It was sickening to learn that high- ranking government officials, who called themselves public servants, were getting rich or richer while serving the public. A sure vehicle to fame and fortune, it gave thoughts to the common man that people entered politics for money and power. Brazenly, they fielded husbands or wives, sons and daughters, nephews and nieces, cousins and cronies, and even mistresses, to various government jobs even if these lacked clerical know-how.

My grandfather finished Law with honors and topped the Bar. He had wide experience in politicization and handled his job with utmost sincerity; nobody could ever accuse him of nepotism. If he had appointed a relative, it was because he or she was the most qualified among the applicants. He promoted a friend because he or she topped among the next-in-ranks. He didn't appoint Uncle Benito as municipal physician and never lent a hand to Aunt Merriam's bookkeeping business; didn't give grandma any paid position in the municipal government. My mother, who finished her degree in Secondary Education with honors, got a teaching job in a private institution without my grandfather's influence.

During Grandpa's tenure as mayor, Sacandaya was transformed into a first-class municipality after it was adjudged the country's cleanest and most beautiful town of the year twice in a row. Grandpa was voted Municipal Mayor for five consecutive terms and left his job with pride and dignity after 20 years of service. After his retirement, while Grandma kept herself involved with civic and charitable organizations, Grandpa had his prowess in management applied in the farm.

One day, Aunt Thelma came home to inform her parents of her plan to marry, which was a great embarrassment to the family because the man was but a mere clerk in the company she worked with. Grandpa vehemently opposed it; he didn't think that an office clerk was worthy of the dignity of a corporate lawyer. Besides, he had committed his daughter to the provincial governor for his lawyer son.

"A highly intellectual lawyer is marrying a clerk. Where are your brains?"

"Love doesn't come from the brains, Papa."

"Love doesn't come all alone from the heart. You've to use your intellect."

"Your decision might be good for you but unfair to me," Aunt Thelma dissented. "What if your parents were against your marriage to Mama?"

"I picked the right woman for me. You're picking the wrong man for you!"

The will of Aragon Zaragoza prevailed. Right after the fallout, Aunt Thelma packed up and left without saying goodbye. That greatly hurt my grandfather. He turned despondent. His health deteriorated.

Nothing was heard of Aunt Thelma anymore since then.

When schools closed for the summer, I went with Mama to the city to look for my runaway aunt. We went to Aunt Thelma's working place and found out she filed an indefinite leave after she broke up with her fiancée, who had resigned from his job to work in the Middle East. Nobody among her officemates knew where my aunt had gone.

We checked on Grandpa's relatives. No one had seen Aunt Thelma for a while. She might have asked them not to divulge her whereabouts, my mother suspected. Even woozy with fatigue, we went to see Uncle Ralph at the bishop's convent. He was out of town. Mama left him a message.

Way worn, we returned home in the afternoon and found Santiago waiting for us with sad news: Grandpa was dying, and he wanted to talk to my mother as soon as possible. Upon knowing her father's condition Mama started weeping and kept going around inside the house like a dazed fly.

Santiago hurried back home because a heavy storm was coming.

The Philippines is in the path of storms. About 15 to 20 of them churned the islands every year. Some were mighty and dangerous like the tropical cyclone Amy which ravaged houses and crops and brought deaths and injuries in December of 1951. There wasn't a weather bureau then. It was in the early seventies when my mother heard about the Philippine Atmospheric, Geophysical and Astronomical Services Administration. The name sounds with impact and although it is incomprehensible to a layman, its acronym 'PAG-ASA' meaning 'hope' carries promise and trust to safeguard residents from the danger of coming natural calamities. Yet many times, the PAG-ASA failed to predict exactly the path of the storm and the amount of rainfall. What the agency predicted as Category "Five" came out as "One" or the other way around. It wasn't yet equipped with equipment that predicts correctly weather disturbances. Miscalculations were disastrous, but the government always had the same alibi whenever predictions went wrong.

That afternoon, a tropical storm "Marie" was coming. It was defined as having an intensity of 215 kilometers per hour. The Public Storm Warning Signal hoisted it to number four. Mama said it couldn't be as furious as "Amy", but the bureau wasn't accurate of the typhoon status as proven in many times. Nevertheless, we prepared a few personal belongings just in case the weather bureau was right; then we must stay a day or more in Villa Zaragoza. Mama, worried over our house which was of light materials, hoped the weather bureau was wrong again and prayed hard "Marie" won't ever come.

Sacandaya looked deserted that murky Saturday afternoon; the coming storm made it look like twilight had come but no light emitted from the houses we passed by; there was a brownout. Stores were closed except for one grocer where people were in panic buying household stuff. The store was using a kerosene lamp that town folks called *Petromax*, which was the name of the brand.

Public transportation plying to barrios had stopped, so we must walk to my grandparents' house which was some few kilometers away from the town proper. As we turned right to the provincial road, a black cat suddenly crossed our way. Mama said it was a foreboding sign that we won't reach Grandpa alive. She put the sign of the cross on her and cried out: *Oh Lord, not now. Thelma is yet nowhere to find.*

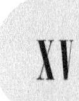

XV

Death at Heaven's Gate

His lips moved as he tried to say something
between his breathes that sounded
very strenuous and ragged.

An expanse of thick dark clouds was threatening to pour down. It was as if twilight was coming fast. I didn't see any vehicle running on the road and nobody was walking there but us.

Lightning flashed; thunder roared. The furious wind reminded me of my father's return. He was coming back home as Solvera predicted, on a boat one day when the wind was strong, and the sea was as restless as a mad dog gone wild. My mother couldn't be thinking the same - too worried about not reaching her father alive. The effort to reach the villa before the storm could strike down was probably what occupied her mind.

As the wind was getting stronger, it turned chillier. Against the wind, I could hardly forward a step while Mama was defying its wrath. Her skirt wavered behind her like how the flag in our school waver in the wind at the top end of a pole. Her right hand, holding the brown paper bag filled with our personal belongings was swinging rhythmically with the ticktack of her footfalls; her left was gripping my wrist so as not to lose me to the wind. Mama was dragging me at her side so I had to carry my wooden clogs to catch up with her strides for I could walk faster on bare feet even if stone aggregates on the roadside were hurting my soles.

The wind was getting more furious; it bent down the bamboo grooves we passed by. My grandmother had pictured to me how my ancestors, who stooped down for 333 years under the Spanish oppression and three years under Japan's persecutions, fought back and stood united like those bamboos after the wind had passed by.

We were almost there. I could see Villa Zaragoza holding dominion over the land that spanned down to the seashore. A line of shrubberies separated its backyard from the rest of the hill that was covered with a mantle of cogon grasses dancing to the wind's humming. The century-old house looked heavy gray at our approach, a silhouette standing still and stern but seemingly submissive to a severe storm.

Over yonder was in sharp contrast - a landscape of the western side where the sun was flaming red that threw red-orange sparkles rippling down to the shore that was desolate and gloomy. Two occurring circumstances antonymous to each other resembled to the virtual peace in my country and the pandemonium in Vietnam the day Saigon fell. That could be what Mama meant that life varies in other places and often changes with time.

Made of whitish sea coral bricks grayed with age and with a roof of imbricate brownish-crimson tiles, the manor defied catastrophes and outlived the oldest trees around. Its windows bore the vestige of 19th century elegance only affordable to the Spanish settlers. All the panels were of small squares of wooden frames that enclosed *Capiz* shells of even sizes in rows and columns forming into one whole rectangular structure. The walling inside the house was of deep brown wood; the floor was of black mahogany.

Formerly known as Casa de Torres, after the name of its builder, who was my maternal great, great grandfather, the house had been Sacandaya's watchtower, during the years when the town was often attacked by the pirates of the southern seas. It earned the moniker "Heaven's Gate" when an American troop used it as a garrison in 1944. Grandma got it back before the bombing of Hiroshima and renamed it Villa Zaragoza in honor of Sacandaya's returning hero, for surviving the Bataan Death March. Like Grandpa in the olden days, Villa Zaragoza was mighty and valiant.

"Santiago! Santiago!" Mama shouted when she reached the door, pounding the panel with her palm, looking scared as if a zombie was coming close to devouring her.

A heavy rain came rushing like a stampede of galloping horses.

Santiago opened the door and hurriedly locked it back before the pummeling rain had swooshed down. A blast of a thunderclap jerked me off in an impulse throwing me to the foot of the stairs that was fronting the doorsill.

Mama dashed in after me, reaching the foot of the stairs in one stride, and immediately climbed up the stairway of red mahogany slabs two meters in width. It was a flight of seventeen steps that hadn't been rebuilt as far as I can remember, but still sturdy although it sagged and creaked midway under a certain weight. Mama climbed up barefooted. I did the same. Shoes or slippers from outside shouldn't be brought upstairs - Flora's rules.

The housemaid announced our arrival. Grandma wailed on seeing us. Mama carelessly dropped the bag to the floor and opened her arms to her mother. Then both stepped into the room where my grandfather lay dying.

I had been to that antique house several times but that night, I was terribly frightened; the thought that the mansion was haunted was occurring in my mind.

Villa Zaragosa was believed to be haunted. Flora swore, seeing white spirits walking around inside the house past midnight. That sounded creepier with the thought that the century-old cemetery where Grandma's ancestors were buried was just nearby. That night, Sacandaya was dark and lonely as the century-old graveyard long-forgotten by time.

The whooping western winds whipping the windowpanes intensified. Its soughs sounded like a mournful moaning; it made the ambience eerier. Santiago closed the windows but still I perceived the flashes of lightning in the windows of *Capiz* shells which were without awnings.

Flora lit the Persian oil lamp that had been hanging in the same corner of the living room. Its yellowish light shaped up the shadowy figures; its melancholic tranquility complemented the permeating silence. I peeped through the slightly opened door of my grandparents' room out of curiosity on what's happening inside. The room wasn't well lit but the two candles on the headboard enabled me to see my grandfather lying on the bed which wasn't too far from the door. I heard his breathing; it sounded strenuous. With eyes closed, he was speaking to my mother in a halting manner. Mama was choking back her sobs so as not to cry aloud.

"She's here," I heard Mama's voice; she must be referring to me and I hunched she was to get me to my grandfather's bedside to listen to the dark secrets he'd be revealing.

Impulsively, I ran to Flora who was brewing coffee in the kitchen and hid behind her. Mama trapped me there. She said there was something that Grandpa wanted to tell me. I didn't want to know it. I heard from the old people that if a dying person could still speak, he'd divulge all the secrets and lies he'd been keeping in life for these would be heavy for his spirit to carry and most likely these wouldn't be nice to hear.

Like a dog, I was whining with fear, but my mother seemed not to care about it. All what she wanted was to bring me to her father's side to listen to what he was about to tell me. The words alone coming from a dying person would be tormenting and Flora even noticed the horror plastered in my face.

"Back off, Patricia . . . can't you see your daughter is terrified? Back off!"

The arrival of Father John with Miss Via and an acolyte diverted Mama's attention. She led the visitors to Grandpa's room. After a minute she came out of the room with the acolyte. Grandma and Miss Via followed leaving the priest alone with my grandfather.

The door was left slightly open; nosiness crept in me again. I heard Grandpa speak unintelligibly in a halting manner; I saw the priest nodding his head constantly. I heard Miss Via telling Flora that my grandfather had his last reconciliation with God.

Moments later, Grandma slipped back to the room with my mother and Miss Via. The acolyte followed them and shut the door behind him. I remained standing by the doorstep even though I feared what was happening. I heard nothing more from inside the room even if I placed my ear against the panel of the door. Only the recurring tic-tac of the old grandfather clock was stirring the eerie silence that moment.

Then came the trembling voice of Miss Via chanting in vernacular the prayer for the dying; it floated eerily like it was Halloween again. In my curiosity, I opened the door wider and saw the priest kneeling on the floor while anointing Grandpa's forehead with Holy Water. He was mumbling a prayer in the language he used in officiating the Holy Mass. I felt Flora's cold hands quivering on my bare shoulders. I heard her stifled cry.

"*Requiescat en pace,* Aragon Zaragoza," I heard again Miss Via's voice. "The Good Lord is waiting for you in Heaven."

Miss Via was reciting imploration for my grandfather's soul when Grandma passed out. She stopped her prayer and shouted: "some air, some air. We need a fan!" Mama was quick to run out of the room and immediately came back with a fan. There was a commotion. I never knew how Death could create a pandemonium among the living.

My grandfather passed away moments later amidst the warring of lightning and thunder. He would have to take to his grave what he wasn't able to tell me. I skulked in one corner whimpering in fear. Flora saw me shuddering and pulled me to her side. As old folks said later, Grandpa's soul couldn't rest in peace and might be coming back to tell me the secrets he carried to his grave.

The rain fizzled out save for its pitter-patter on the windowpanes. Lightning still flashed, and thunder still roared although faintly, but the scream of the wind as it raged across the trees was still as frightening as the shriek of a wandering banshee.

There was a moment of silence.

The priest was sitting on the rattan chair beside the grandfather clock silently reading the missal. Miss Via was praying the rosary at one end of the couch; on the other end, the acolyte slouched. Santiago was taking a nap in the family room. Flora was in the kitchen brewing another teapot of coffee. Even the housemaid burst into tears when she learned her master had breathed his last. Flora said that a day before my grandfather died, he let her promise never to leave Villa Zaragoza. The old housemaid gave her pledge.

Grandma was in the living room reposing in the recliner. Even with her eyes closed, even with graying hair, even with the wrinkles in her dried skin, her beauty was still eminent. Grandpa was right – Margarita Federica Torres Zaragoza looked as enchanting as the night of full moon. Gandma just turned 60 when Grandpa died; he was 63.

XVI

In God's Will

Life is just a passageway.
In our journey from birth to death,
we'd never know when God tells us to stop.

The bedlam was gone. There was silence again but only for a moment. The old grandfather clock roared and banged at the hour of midnight stirring the stillness that reigned.

After about an hour, the priest and the acolyte left leaving behind Miss Via, who opted to stay to help watch over Grandma. Flora posted herself in the kitchen. She must have spread earlier what was happening to my grandfather. Town folks started coming in to pay respects to the town's former mayor, but Aunt Merriam and Uncle Benito were still nowhere to see. Grandma had stopped inquiring about them.

By daybreak, when Grandpa's roosters started crowing, Aunt Merriam arrived with Madel, but without Uncle Fidel. Uncle Benito came with his sons and wife. More people from around town were coming in. Mama and Flora were getting busier serving them coffee.

Kibitzers were asking my mother if she had found her runaway sister. Mama told them the same thing she told my grandfather while Grandma couldn't stop asking her: "Is Rafael coming? Is Rafael coming?" and Mama kept nodding her head even if she wasn't sure if her younger brother was coming home.

Grandpa's dead body was yet to be transferred to the funeral parlor later that day.

After lunch, Uncle Ralph arrived in his new blue Toyota Corolla. I heard Santiago telling my grandmother that Aunt Thelma was coming with him. Everybody heard it. Excited as I was to see my uncle's new car or watch how Grandma would welcome her prodigal daughter, all went rushing down the stairs before I could.

Flora opened the main door. Aunt Thelma came in and wailed in her mother's arms. It had been months they had not seen each other. I also heard the sobs of Uncle Ralph. The three of them were crying as they huddled together. Grief is infectious. I was crying while watching them; so were Mama and Flora.

"Your father kept asking if you were coming," Grandma told her youngest child.

"He must've been so worried about me, Mama," said Aunt Thelma as she released her mother from her arms. Tears were streaming down her face.

"Long before yesterday, every day before the sunset could pass by your father would ask me if you were coming home. I couldn't help but lie to him, telling him that you were coming even if I didn't know. Patricia was in the city looking for you but failed. However, she lied to your father - that she had found you and that you promised to come home as soon as possible. Last night, before your father could breathe his last. . ."

Grandma held her words. Everybody seemed too anxious to hear what she'd say next, but my grandmother seemed to be out of breath. Mama gave her water to drink. When she was able to take a deep breath, she had her eyes focused back on Aunt Thelma.

"Your father, before he could breathe his last, told me to tell you that he was so sorry he went against your will to marry. Your father tried to say something more, but I could no longer hear his voice. It was then I found out . . ."

Grandma couldn't finish what she was to say; her words suppressed in her throat. She fell into her daughter's arms. Uncle Ralph wrapped his arms around them. The more they made me cry.

"So, had he forgiven me?" Aunt Thelma asked her mother afterwards.

"You know how dearly he loved you. When you were an infant, you were always the first one he looked for upon coming home. How he loved to carry you in his arms and how he laughed seeing you smile."

"I was missing both of you and how I wanted to come home long time ago, but I was afraid. I know it was hard for him to forgive," Aunt Thelma spoke in-between sobs.

"He was deeply hurt when you screamed at him. He cried when you left, the second time I saw him cry; the first was when he came home from Bataan after the war."

"I didn't mean to hurt him, Mama. You know how much I loved him."

"You'd been your father's baby. He considered you his good luck charm for you were born on the day he was elected municipal mayor for the first time. In his deathbed, he called out your name three times before he breathed his last."

"Did he? Did he, Mama? I prayed hard I'd reach him alive."

"You have come home and there's nothing more that I could ask for," Grandma told her daughter. She then turned to her son and wailed: "Oh, Rafael, I offered you to the Lord for it had been my ardent desire to have one of my sons serving God in His vineyard. And now that you are there, serving the Lord, He took your father's life, as well. What more does God want from me?"

"Hush, Mama. God's reasons are unfathomable. Who are we to question His wisdom? Please say the Lord's Prayer, Mama. Let me hear you say The Lord's Prayer."

In Uncle Ralph's shoulder, Grandma recited the prayer:

> *"Our Father, who art in Heaven*
> *Hallowed be Thy Name*
> *Thy kingdom come,*
> *Thy will be done*
> *On Earth as it is in Heaven."*

"*Thy will be done on Earth as it is in Heaven.* You say this every day in your life and now what are you complaining about? Don't let the devil move you to go against the Almighty. Save yourself from blasphemy, Mama, save yourself from blasphemy."

"Oh Lord, forgive me. I'm very sorry," Grandma said and released herself from her son's arms. "I just can't help it. It's painful, Rafael . . . it's painful."

"I feel your pain, Mama, but let me tell you that Life is but a passageway from birth to death. In this journey, death may meet us at any point we'd never know when. I feel your pain, but God's will, Mama, God's will,"

Uncle Ralph clasped Grandma's hand and followed Aunt Thelma upstairs. Some people already had gathered in the family room to watch them view their father's remains.

"Try to stay calm, Thelma," said Uncle Ralph. "Don't bother Papa in his repose."

"I'm here now, Papa. Look. I have returned home. Please open your eyes for me."

Aunt Thelma convulsed. Mama helped her to the couch. It dawned on me how excruciating the pain could be in losing a loved one, yet Aunt Merriam showed no remorse at all. She was standing without emotion as she watched her family in grief. She looked like the unruffled flames of the candles burning motionlessly at the head of Grandpa's remains; her eyes - as sullen as those of a dead fish.

During the vigil, I noticed Mama isolating herself from her mean siblings, cautious that another argument might come up between them. At one instance, I saw her talking with Grandma with hushed voices in the corner of the living room.

On my approach, she asked if I'd like to make Villa Zaragoza my home. That stunned me for it had been my fondest dream. I thought it over; that wasn't a nice idea. For sure, my cousins would be jealous because they would think Grandma was doing me favor again; the more they would hate me. Also, would Aunt Merriam be passive about it? It wouldn't be fine with her, but Mama had to stay there to take care of her mother and she could only cry for she must have foreseen we never could find peace living in Villa Zaragoza. Yet, we must move there in adherence to what her father told her. Mama promised him. It was irreverent to refuse a dying wish.

I could only cry. It had been my longtime wish to live in that big mansion and my greatest chance had come, but I felt afraid not only of Aunt Merriam but also of the white spirits roaming inside the house at the stroke of midnight.

"Your grandmother said it was but Flora's hallucinations," Mama told me.

"What if she really saw those spirits?"

Aunt Thelma had told me once that Flora had never lied in all her life. On the white spirits, the old maid swore to the high heavens that she really saw them. What if I see those spirits one midnight and my grandfather had come with them to tell me what he wanted to tell me before he died? Old folks said that the dead surely would come back to divulge the secrets they were unable to reveal while still on earth.

It could be true that a huge ancient house would be a favorite abode of souls that were refused entry into heaven. The sins they've committed while on earth obstruct their passage to heaven but weren't also enough to dump them outright to hell. Some old folks said that with nowhere to go, their souls stay in limbo and only the prayers of the living could save them out for they no longer have the power to pray and save themselves. Miss Via said that God would welcome my grandfather's soul to Heaven for his heart was as chaste as a saint's. He didn't need the prayer of the living to clear his way to heaven. He had nothing to contrite with the Lord. He was a perpetual benefactor for charities and devoted a good portion of his life to his Faith. My grandfather had been honorable and godly and that entitled him for free passport to the Pearly Gates, according to Miss Via. It was because of the Filipino Christian tradition that we should say a nine-day novena for the dead that we said the same for my grandfather.

Perhaps in some cases Miss Via wasn't right. My grandfather was bedridden for some time. Had he been sinful that God gave him time to repent?

XVII

On His Last Farewell

As if there was always a storm coming,
the twilight that witnessed my grandfather
breathe his last seemed to be staying forever.

The town council declared a day of mourning that Sunday my grandpa's remains were interred. A tribute for my grandfather was held at the Municipal Hall. People from all over the town attended. As it's a human nature to set aside personal differences on death, Grandpa's political friends and foes took turns extolling his virtues.

Grandpa's niche was a sepulcher of light gray marble, highly polished that its top surface mirrored the sky. An epitaph of him excerpted from the eulogy prepared and delivered by the Provincial Governor at the funeral was inscribed in the gravestone:

HERE LIES THE REMAINS OF THE GOD-FEARING MAN, WHO SERVED HIS TOWN WITH UTMOST DECENCY AND GENEROSITY: AN IDEAL HUSBAND, A LOVING FATHER, A WAR HERO, A

NOBLE STATESMAN, AND THE MOST HONORABLE, THE MOST BELOVED, THE MOST INVALUABLE CITIZEN THE TOWN OF SACANDAYA COULD EVER HAVE. HIS BENEVOLENCE MAY ALWAYS BE REMEMBERED.

Draped with Philippine flag, the coffin was placed on top of a steel stand flanked by Grandma and the rest of the family. The women wore solid black dresses; the men in cream Filipino barong with a black band wrapped around the right sleeve. The granddaughters were in white dresses; the boys in white shirts and black pants with a black ribbon pinned on the chest. Some of Grandpa's relatives from the city were there.

The Police Chief took the Philippine flag that covered the coffin, folded and handed it to my grandmother. He opened the casket for the people to take a quick last look at the remains of their former town leader while Father John was blessing the tomb to ward off evils. The municipal band played the Philippine National Anthem. Cops, seven of them, fired their rifles three times into the air. I heard my grandmother wail when Grandpa's body was interred. I also heard Mama's and Aunt Thelma's voices wailing and even Flora was crying hard for Aragon Zaragoza.

By noon, all had left the cemetery but me and my mother. Flora tried to stay with us, but Mama told her to go ahead so she can help prepare lunch for the visitors. My mother remained standing in front of Grandpa's tomb. She was in deep thoughts for about half an hour. All the while, I was watching her wondering what made her long to ponder. I was tired and hungry but couldn't complain; Mama wasn't in the good mood to hear complaints; she looked so exhausted and sick worried. I wondered how I could survive on my own if her time to leave the world had come.

The high noon sun was scorching when we walked back to the villa. Halfway, I saw Uncle Ralph's car coming in our direction. He stopped in front of us and told us to hop in. Mama turned him down saying it wasn't far anymore. Uncle Ralph perceived I needed the ride zealously as he saw me frowning; my face was drenched with sweat. His eyes glowered at the stubbornness of his elder sister. With anger in his voice, he persisted in us to get in so I hurriedly got into the rear for fear the priest would shout at me. Mama was still adamant. She only hopped in when her brother screamed again at her.

Uncle Ralph made a three-point turn and proceeded back home. Mama was tight- lipped. Then out of the blue along the way she said it wasn't my father's own decision to go to Vietnam. That was uncalled for those moments. Uncle Ralph's anger exploded and brought the car to a sudden halt so that I bumped my forehead against the back of his seat.

"You're torturing yourself," Uncle Ralph said; again, intense anger was in his voice.

"Even if I won't think about it, Rafael, I could feel Romulo is still alive."

"That fake psychic poisoned your mind. It's been six or seven years now since the soldiers came back home from Vietnam. If your husband were alive as you think he is, why hadn't he come home? Why can't you think of that?"

Uncle Ralph was right. I hadn't seen my father ever since I woke up to the world.

After lunch, while the visitors were still consuming desserts, Aunt Merriam called their attention and summoned them to come to the front yard where she dumped all her mourning dresses. There, she did a stunt by burning them all before the eyes of the guests. Speaking like she was drunk, she told them in her irritating way that wearing black for a year was stupidity for a long mourning would never bring the dead back to life again; that it was but a gesture of hypocrisy.

I thought Aunt Merriam was wrong with that. Mama had told me that wearing black is an expression of deep sorrow for the dead. The guests were whispering to each other while Grandma immediately went inside the house to hide her embarrassment. Neither Uncle Ralph nor Uncle Benito, Aunt Merriam's ally, persuaded her to calm down.

We moved to Villa Zaragoza with our belongings on Palm Sunday. Flora met us at the gate waving a bunch of palm leaves likening us to Jesus Christ in His triumphant entry to Jerusalem. Flora's gesture could have provoked me to laugh, but I felt bad that moment for I foresaw myself living in a place full of miseries.

For nine successive nights after Grandpa's burial, some folks keep returning to the villa by eight in the evening to pray with us for my grandfather's soul.

A month had gone by since Grandpa died but the mournful atmosphere stayed inside Villa Zaragoza like it was devoid of life. The twilight that had witnessed my grandfather exhaling his last breaths was staying forevermore.

As it is said that Jesus ascended to Heaven on the 40th day after His Resurrection, most of the town folks of Sacandaya believed that the soul of the departed stays with the living during the first forty days after death. I didn't hear Grandma and Aunt Merriam shouting at each other during those forty days as I didn't see them confiding with each other. Gone was Grandma's laughter. With eyes worn out and sullen from crying, she looked as mournful as the Mater Dolorosa of Holy Friday.

XVIII

Life Without a father

Life would have been easier
if I grew up with a father who
could've saved me from trouble.

I was born without a father, and it had been the talk of the town years ago. At one time in school, I heard from other children that I was like any other animal born without a father. Life would have been a lot easier if a father had been there for me; that could have saved me from those troubles that came on my way.

In May that year, while schools were closed for the summer, Sunday classes on catechism for kids of at least seven years of age were conducted under Miss Via's tutelage. I was a month shy of turning seven, but Miss Via couldn't refuse Grandma's request. It was also in May when we had floral offerings for the Virgin Mary, a yearly religious tradition of Christian Filipinos inherited from Mother Spain.

On the first day of that May, I prepared a bouquet of red kalachuchi flowers as my floral offering; Madel saw it; she wanted to have it. When I refused, she grabbed the bouquet from my hand and before my eyes smashed the flowers on the floor. That blew my top. A rumble ensued. Aunt Merriam rushed to the scene, grabbed my hair and immediately bumped my head against the wall several times addressing me with bad names every time she did it.

"That's enough!" Grandma shouted on seeing what Aunt Merriam was doing. "You have no right to lay a hand on Patricia's daughter! You have no rights to maltreat her for she didn't come out from your womb!"

"This devil's daughter needs discipline!" Aunt Merriam shouted back at her mother. Anger was all over her face.

"You're accusing without even knowing who's really at fault!"

"She started it! This *hija de puta* started it!" Aunt Merriam declared while poking my forehead with her fingers. "She had to be disciplined!".

"And what do you think Patricia's doing to her daughter? *Aber?*"

"That *consentidora* is consentient of her daughter's bad temper!"

"Patricia is imposing discipline much better than you do to your daughter."

"If that is so, then nothing can reform this daughter of the beast who died like a rat somewhere!" Aunt Merriam yelled with her nostrils flaring as if she was running out of breath. Terrified she'd hit me again, I slunk away from her reach.

"You're referring to a dead person. What harm had he done to deserve your wrath?"

"I'd say what I want to say. There's nothing good to praise in him, anyway!"

"Then say nothing of him!" Grandma's voice was tinged with so-much anger. "Judge not and you'll not be judged! What do you think of yourself, *una immaculada?*"

Aunt Merriam frowned at what Grandma told her. She pulled her daughter to the living room from where her henpecked husband was watching his wife's outrageousness. But he did nothing to calm her down. All the while, my mother was there too but didn't intervene. Instead of siding with me, she blamed me for having caused the incident. She seemed to please always her mean sister. That baffled me.

"If only you gave in to Madel's wishes, this wouldn't have happened. There's something I want you to do, Jinee."

I readily nodded, "What is it, Mama?"

"Go to them and tell Madel that you're sorry for what happened."

"What? Why should I? I didn't start the trouble."

"To appease them; it won't cause us pain, anyway."

"Yes, it does . . . lots of pain. Don't let me do it, Mama, please . . ."

"Just do it so that they'll stop oppressing us! That won't be too hard to do."

"I'm not listening to you for that's hard for me to do! I'd never do what you said. I'd never do it! The more oppressive they could be!"

Raising a voice towards the elders was strictly prohibited in the family; it was one of my grandma's commands. My mother ran out of forbearance when I refused to follow her order. She dragged me to the prayer room to contrite. And why should I apologize to the person who beat me up? That was so irrational! So weird! Is that what the bible means to offer your right cheek to whoever slapped your left?

That was a kind of foolish thing to do. The bible is imposing messages that are impossible to follow.

At the prayer room, I wasn't really praying but pondering on how my life had been.

Mama must realize that there are things worth fighting for. In the days to come, I won't let anybody oppress me again; nevermore. Grandma, who could save me from trouble is now very old; she might be following Grandpa to his grave. I don't have a father to stand by me and this mother I have is so submissive she doesn't have the courage even to defend herself whenever her mean siblings are trying to oppress her. And so, that leaves me alone to defend myself. I must not be meek like my mother. I don't believe what she said that 'blessed are the meek, for they shall inherit the land'. Miss Via is so meek that she didn't inherit even a square inch of land from her parents' wide landmass. Her sister got all the inheritances leaving her landless.

"Won't you say sorry to me?" Mama asked on seeing my resentment. I apologized for screaming at her but not for refusing her request.

Later that day, I asked her what Grandpa wanted to tell me when he was dying.

"You'd come to know it someday," she answered coldly. I stopped asking questions.

Life was hell in Villa Zaragoza. I begged my mother to go back to our old home. I begged the Holy Spirit to enlighten my mother's mind that she would find a good reason to come back to our old home. It was only proper that if my father had returned, he'd find Mama where he left her. But my mother had to take care of her mother. Grandma didn't like Flora to prepare her food because she was a tobacco smoker and forgetful of Grandma's time to take her medicine.

The old maid also suffered maltreatment from Aunt Merriam when she suspected my mother of selling an antique tapestry. She accused Flora of connivance, slapped her and bumped her head on the wall like what she did to me. If my aunt did that to my mother, she'd suffer my wrath. I'd been thinking of fighting her back when she'd come to the villa one early morning.

"Look at this piggish piglet," Aunt Merriam started another trouble by calling the attention of Uncle Benito. "She's consuming milk like she's drinking plain water."

"And she had her bread buttered as if she's used to it," Uncle Benito butted in.

"The next time I'd see you again drinking fresh milk, I'll pour it over your head! Did you hear me?" Aunt Merriam's ear-piercing voice was all over my face as she poked my forehead again; her eyes smoldered with anger. "Did I make myself clear? Do you understand what I'm saying?"

Before I could nod my head in response, Aunt Merriam grabbed the glass of milk from my hand. It slipped off from my hold, dropped to the floor and I could only cry watching the milk spill on the floor. My mean aunt was about to go to the kitchen when Mama forwarded and reprimanded me.

"Grandma said I could get anything I want from the ref if I get hungry."

Aunt Merriam heard me and came back in a second.

"Your daughter is a liar," she screamed at my mother. "A very good liar like you!"

"I'm not lying!" I screamed back at her in an impulse, turning like a provoked snake, hissing and forming to strike. "I'm not lying! You can ask Grandma right now!"

"Don't shout at me! Do you think I couldn't break your bones anymore?"

"Try it!" I was ready to fight back. Oh, God I was ready to fight!

"Please, don't mind her; she's just a child," Mama pleaded.

". . . A child! Were those words of a child? Or did you tell her to fight back?"

"My daughter didn't mean it."

"I mean what I said, Mama!"

"Did you hear that, Patricia?"

"Yes, I mean what I said!" I screamed out again. "Your sister had gone too abusive to us because you don't fight back. This time, we must fight back!"

"I've never heard of a child talking like a demon!"

While my mother was admonishing me, her sister was staring fiercely at me. Without fear, I stared back at her. That was enough to let her know I was no longer afraid of her.

I must not be always afraid; must overcome my fear; must defend myself so that by the time that my mother had left me, I was ready to take care of myself.

"You raised a beast. She'd kill you someday!" Aunt Merriam said, pointing her finger close at my mother's face. She glared at me and said that her blood was boiling at the sight of my face. I glowed back – staring sharply at her. That gave her a sense that I was ready to fight back. Then she moved towards the China closet where all the Spanish silverware were kept on her suspicion that we stole some of those. Finding nothing to prove, she left.

Mama's mean sibs were gone. I squirmed to one corner when Flora mopped the floor. She had heard Aunt Merriam's tirades.

"She won't stop oppressing unless you fight back," Flora whispered while I was moaning in pain. "I'll back you up. We need to stop that devil. She needs to be stopped; she's getting worse."

Mama had fathomed what I'd been through; didn't scold me for going against her wishes and for shouting back at her sister.

I was turning tough, was no longer a blade of grass that stoops down when trampled upon, but a blade of glass that would slice the soles of those oppressors. I promised myself to get back at them someday. There would come a day when those mean siblings of my mother would beg for something from me on bended knees, but I'd be having the kind of heart they had. I'd lash them with their kind of harsh words. They would realize by then that I wasn't always afraid of them. They had to be sorry for what they did to me in the past; they'd curse the day I was born.

The "*Flores de Mayo*" culminated by the end of May and so were our catechism classes. Our First Communion was scheduled for the first Sunday of June. I told Miss Via I didn't deserve to receive "the Body of Christ" for I thought of fighting back my aunt. Knowing the kind of person Aunt Merriam was, Miss Via told me that it's not a sin to wage a war against a Satan's apostle. Nevertheless, I apologized to God for what I had done and took my first Holy Communion.

XIX

The Banishing

I always wished to live in Villa Zaragoza,
but when I had the chance to live there
I found out it was full of nightmares.

One early morning a loud banging on the door to our room roused me from a deep sleep. Mama opened the door and what met my eyes was the horrid face of Aunt Merriam. With dilated eyes, she called us thick faced. Fresh from her mahjongg session where she must have heard talks that raised her hackles and heightened with a streak of bad luck, she burst out all her fury on us that very early morning. The grandfather clock was chiming for the hour of four.

"Pack up your things right now and get out of here!" Aunt Merriam screamed at my mother's face. Mama pled for a day to look for a place to stay in, but with her face drawn closer at my mother's, Aunt Merriam screamed again, "*Hora mismo*, Patricia, pack up all your things and get out of this house!"

Moving out of Villa Zaragoza had been one of my earnest prayers for it had been like hell living there, but at the same instance, the thought that we would end up homeless scared me. What if we couldn't find a place to stay.

"You can't drive them away!" Grandma's voice rang out from her room made me sigh in great relief. "Patricia's taking care of my needs which you hate doing."

"And in return she's inheriting this house . . ."

"In return for her services. That's what your father promised her!"

"That's not possible! Patricia hasn't all the rights to inherit this house. There are five of us who have the rights to inherit!" Aunt Merriam shouted back.

"This house is my inheritance, not a conjugal," Grandma said while coming out from her room. "Disposing this is my prerogative!"

"You don't have to shout about it! The entire world knows that . . ."

"Then, what are you complaining of?" Grandma put more force into her voice.

"I have the right to protest!" Aunt Merriam was screaming her lungs out with eyes nailed at her mother's face. "You forgot I'm also your daughter!"

"It's you who forgot that I'm your mother!"

"Well, if that's what you think, you got what you deserve!"

"Deserve what? You're the one who's bringing trouble here! As the wise Solomon said, '*he who brings trouble in this house shall inherit the wind*'."

Aunt Merriam rolled her eyes and responded in the same raised voice: "Whatever!"

"I'm sure I was never wrong in imposing discipline to all of you and I don't know how you grew up like that. You said that Patricia needs to discipline her daughter . . . do you discipline yours? You never teach your own daughter good manners."

"I discipline my daughter in my own way!"

"Huh? What way? By following what you say and not what you do? Tell me: How can a drunkard father tell his son not to drink?"

Aunt Merriam gave her mother a quick sharp glance. She got a cigarette stick, placed it between her lips and lit the cigarette stick with her fingers trembling.

"And how could a chronic smoker tell her daughter not to smoke? You can never instill kindness into your daughter's heart because you, yourself, are hateful! Why do you hate Patricia that much?"

"She brought shame to us, her family!" Aunt Merriam screamed at her mother.

"Your sister stumbled. You should've helped her get up, but what did you do? Instead, you stepped on her back."

"Whatever! Nevertheless, she brought us shame!"

"If Patricia brought shame, did - you - bring - honor?" Grandma enunciated the last four words that had piqued Aunt Merriam's ego very badly.

"I'm married to an honorable and prestigious lawyer not to a so-so soldier."

"Prestige and honor are in the person's image and reputation, not in his profession. There are many lawyers in the world that are not worthy of their profession's dignity. Don't pride yourself on what you have. And don't be proud of your husband because somebody up there knows what kind of a lawyer your husband is."

"You're referring to a closed case!"

"Nevertheless, it left an ugly stain on what you referred to as your husband's prestige and honor. That winnable case should have won him his spurs."

"You don't know what you're talking about!"

"Via Cruses let her sister get all their inheritances because, aside from not having a family of her own, Via despises wealth but what did you and your husband do? You persuaded the *pobresita* to claim her share and to donate it to the church. You encouraged her to bring it to court with your prestigious husband offering his modest services as her counsel. Now, what is it that I don't know?"

"That's a blatant lie!"

"When his client was about to win her case, your honorable husband double-crossed her. He made secret arrangements with the judge and the defendant's counsel. Via lost her case and then, you built your dream house in cash, so quickly like a mushroom that suddenly popped up in the morning after a night of lightning. That house of yours is a memento of how your husband sold his prestige and honor. *No puera delicadeza!*"

"Those are all false accusations!"

"If there's smoke, there's fire!" Grandma flared up. "You were able to build a mansion when your husband seldom gets clients. People wondered about it. It echoed all over the town, a great embarrassment to me and to your father. I pretended not knowing about it and it made me feel too stupid pretending unaware about it."

"They're just envious because I have this house they could never afford."

"*Tu esposo* sold his case for *dos cientos cincuenta mil,* a huge amount that was enough to buy a mansion that time."

"You're talking nonsense!"

"*Misma la hermana de Via* spread the rumor. She tarnished your husband's name as a public defender and that made him a pettifogger. If this isn't true, why did you not accuse her of slander? Huh! Nothing's left of your husband's prestige and honor! *Nada!*"

"How dare you to say that, Mama!"

"Don't call me Mama! You're not respecting me as such!"

"Don't drag my husband's name unto this!"

"I was telling you what I know that you thought I didn't know. Don't ever think that in Sacandaya, a little burst of scandal isn't too loud to be heard around."

"Let's not talk about it!"

"Then, who are you to cast the first stone?" Grandma said haltingly, mouthing the words distinctively that made Aunt Merriam's blood boil.

"Why do you always side with Patricia?" Aunt Merriam was trembling with anger. I could tell she was about to cry; her voice was breaking.

"You're jealous because you think that I care for Patricia more than I care for you. You're awfully wrong. I treat all of you equally and fairly."

"You'd never feel what I feel because you don't have a sister of your own!"

"You don't see it because you're blinded with envy. There's no more room in your heart for a love towards your own sister because all you feel is hatred."

"And why do I feel that way?"

"You resented without bothering to know why there were times I must focus my concern and attention on any one of you. The fact is I've spent more time and attention on you than any of your siblings because you were my first child."

"Baloney! When Patricia was born, you've forgotten me as your other daughter!"

"That's totally inane. She got an attention distinct from what I was giving you. I'm treating all of you equally. A mother's love to each of her children can never be divided."

"Then, why did you always side with her whenever we quarreled and even now!"

"Not to mention that it was always you who started the trouble. Patricia, at that time being the younger one, had a lesser understanding of the situation. It's a parental instinct you should've known if you have more than just one child. If you only loved your sister, took care of her being your younger sister, you'd never have envied her, and you wouldn't have been an impolite daughter."

"You're calling me impolite? Did I ever run away from home? Where was your favorite Thelma when Papa was dying? She was nowhere to be found!"

"And you were here in town fully aware of your father's condition, but did you ever bother to see for yourself if your father was still breathing? Did you?"

Aunt Merriam stayed mum – couldn't disprove what her mother asserted. She could just roll her eyes as she placed another cigarette stick in her mouth.

"It was only Patricia who came with her daughter while you were playing mahjongg," Grandma continued her verbal assault. "You preferred to listen to your friends' gossip rather than your father's last words. Like Benito, instead of coming here, he was in the cockpit watching the roosters fight for their lives rather than watch his father fight for his own life. In the evening, when Patricia called to inform him that his father was dying, the doctor-son said he couldn't come because he was having a drinking spree with his guests in his house; didn't even tell his wife and sons to come ahead. And you – you should have told your daughter and your lawyer-husband to come here. Your father had been dead for hours when you and Benito finally came in the morning, five hours after your father breathed his last."

That was the last thing I heard. Mama pulled me down to Santiago's quarter which was under the stairs so I could no longer hear them arguing. Fear gnawed inside me – the fear of repercussions – that we would suffer my aunt's indignation. Mama whispered her prayer, her sanctuary whenever fear besets. In her arms, I was a little chick seeking safety under its mother's wings whenever a hawk soars by.

"Mama, I know Jesus doesn't love us."

"Jesus loves all the people in the world."

"Does He love everybody in the world equally?"

"Of course, He does – nothing less, nothing more."

"If it were so, why is it that He's making some people rich and other people poor?"

Mama freed out a little laughter and pulled me closer to her side.

"If God makes all the people in the world equally rich, then life gets stagnant. Nobody wants to work for anybody. Can you imagine the situation here in the villa if Flora were as rich as your grandma? Or if Santiago were as rich as my father?"

"Mama, I don't understand what you're saying."

"Who will work for my parents if all the people around were as rich as they were?"

I gave Mama's thoughts a thought. She was right. I couldn't even imagine how the world goes on if everybody were equally rich.

"I have another question: If Jesus loves me, why is He ignoring my prayers?"

"What are your prayers?"

"I'm praying for my father's return. If my father were here, nobody could be oppressing us. I had been praying that my father would come home but until now. . ."

"If you ask God of something, you must have patience because He won't answer your prayer instantly, but sooner or later, God will."

"But it's been a long time that we waited for his return . . ."

"Patience is virtuous . . ."

"He's not coming home anymore. Maybe Aunt Merriam is right. My father died somewhere like a rat. Or maybe, he already had another family to take care of."

I noticed Mama wiping her tears. I made her sad. I changed the topic.

"Mama, Miss Via does not want to get rich. Why?"

"It's because she believes that it's easier for a camel to pass through the eye of the needle than for the rich to pass through the portal of heaven."

My mother's reply was way over my head.

"I don't understand it, Mama."

"Then stop asking questions."

"Can I ask one more? Why did Aunt Merriam call you *puta*?"

"Your Aunt Merriam said that?"

"You heard her, Mama . . . you were there when Madel and I had a fight."

"Ahhh . . . it was only her expression. She'd say something bad when she gets mad."

"And what imperfection did Grandma say about you?"

"I don't know. I have what I need to have. It's your Aunt Merriam who needs perfection. She doesn't have compassion. I pity her for having an unkind heart."

"Even with her unkindness to us, you pity her?"

"Bless those who curse you and pray for those who abuse you. 'If someone slaps your left cheek, offer your right', the Bible says."

If that's the case, I think I couldn't follow what the Bible says. It says lots of things that I don't understand. To me, it's a matter of getting even. As the saying goes: an eye for an eye. Aunt Merriam deserves my spite. Her daughter is doing to me what she's doing to my mother. In a few years when I get bigger, I will fight her back. If Aunt Merriam slaps my left cheek, I will surely slap her right.

"Why can't you hate them, Mama?"

"Every night, I always ask God's forgiveness for the mistakes I may have done that day. How could God forgive me if all I harbor is hatred? If I don't have love in my heart, do I deserve God's mercy? God gives grace to the meek and the humble and opposes the proud and the mighty. If I hate those who despise us, do I deserve God's grace?"

I didn't understand my mother's virtues. She said she got them from the bible. As I didn't understand the bible, I also couldn't comprehend my mother's reasoning. She claimed to be blessed with her virtues of humility and simplicity. People thought she was too humble to be mistaken as a domestic helper. Flora told me that when my father was escorting the Governor to the villa and she was serving the table, Mama was doing the same. Probably mistaking my mother for a housemaid, my father dared to woo her.

Miss Via said that Mama would've been an oblate in the nunnery hadn't she met my father. God must have reasons for bringing me out to the world; that I'd be born to Patricia Zaragoza, the woman with a kind heart.

Yet, despite Mama's kindness, her sister hated her. Probably, it was envy because Aunt Merriam wasn't born with the same kind of heart that my mother had.

"Why did Aunt Merriam say you're a shame in the family?"

"It was because I married a soldier."

Is it a shame to marry a soldier? Grandma said that there's nobility in being a soldier and serving in the military is an honorable career. Was Mama hiding something? Perhaps, Aunt Merriam was just excessively mean.

Grandma didn't want us to move out, but we did to avoid further trouble.

When we were packing up our things, Grandma wasn't around. Aunt Merriam demanded that she'd inspect our boxes and bags to make sure we were taking only the things we had when we moved in. As if everything we got was hers, she took away the old kerosene lamp that Mama found abandoned in the attic. She didn't miss the old Barbie Doll that Aunt Thelma had given me; she said it was already promised to Madel. She noticed that the antique Persian lamp was gone from where it was hanged. When she couldn't find it among our things, she slapped Flora without investigation. She thought we hid it and suspected Flora of conniving. It turned out that Uncle Benito had it, but she neither apologized to Flora for what she did nor retrieved the lamp from her brother.

Aunt Merriam closed us the door, but God opened us a window. The bamboo house Mama was renting before was still available. We moved out of Villa Zaragoza that Saturday before sundown. We didn't have the family get-together the next day. The younger Zaragozas weren't coming over for some reason.

I was deprived of a good sleep in Villa Zaragoza; the house was full of nightmares. At any moment, Aunt Merriam and Uncle Benito would come to scold me for any mistakes I might have committed unknowingly. Those were all nightmares. They scared me like they were the spirits haunting the house and I'd lock myself inside our room, crawl under the bed, count the ticktack of the grandfather clock until I had fallen asleep.

XX

There's No Place like Home

Back at our old home, I had a good sleep again,
dreamed with nothing to be afraid of
and nothing to worry about.

The old bamboo house we had before was a shabby one. It was the same house Mama had shared with my father – until he left for the war and until I was born. I grew up in that house; lived there in peace - could sleep and wake up to a pleasant morning with nobody barking at us – me and my mother. "Any house can be a home if harmony reigns within," said my schoolteacher; I didn't find that harmony in Villa Zaragoza.

After we left my grandparents' house, Aunt Merriam's family moved in without Grandma's sanction. She rented out her property at the town proper, making her richer by thousands of pesos every month and the mightier she'd become.

One Sunday morning, Flora dropped by. With her face frowning, I could tell she was bringing some of her miseries and was to unload them unto us. She said she could have poisoned Grandma's 'new boarders' if killing weren't a sin.

"They're as if they were the First Family living in the Presidential Palace. Pweee!" Flora spit out of the window in sputtering her repulsion.

"They're the thick faced after all," I interacted.

"Shut up, Jinee. You're still too young for this."

"The little girl's right. Santiago is even quitting because of them."

"Santiago's leaving? My good Lord! Can he afford to leave you?"

"What do you mean?" Flora's voice tone changed; her face turned grim.

"Well, I think he had his eyes on you."

"Well, Patricia, what I think is this: there's a cockroach crawling inside your head."

"After the many years of living together under one roof, I think . . ."

"You think not only roaches but spiders and flies and maggots."

"I'm speaking of possibilities. I need to know the truth."

"You need Raid for those maggots," Flora scoffed. "Stop talking nonsense. Santiago's too young for me and besides, I'm not his type."

Mama laughed. "Okay, let's get serious. What's your plan?"

"I also thought of leaving but where shall I go? I have nobody to run to."

"You're very much welcome to live with us, but look, if Santiago leaves, the more your *senyora* needs you. Those intruders would never care to cook for her."

"Your mother doesn't want me to cook for her . . ."

"That was before . . . because you were smoking tobacco."

Flora jolted me with her long loud laughter; eyes were moist when she spoke.

"I used to smoke cigars before, and your mother told me I was like the ogress she saw one midnight smoking under the mango tree. I switched to cigarettes, and she said I looked like a washed-up street hooker. Now, in your honest opinion, Patricia, would any man pick me up if I were a street hooker?"

"Careful, a child is watching," Mama cautioned when Flora cupped her breast with her hands right before my eyes, while laughing off Mama's warning.

"It was because she wanted to stop you from smoking. You never listened to her warnings that smoking can cause lung cancer."

"I don't want to die; I haven't experienced yet having a boyfriend," Flora said and laughed boisterously. Then she leaned against the wall and exposed her right thigh.

"Anyway, the *senyora* taught me her secrets in cooking and that was only when I gave up smoking. Now I'm ready, willing, and able to serve a husband. Patricia, do you think I still can find one?"

"Who knows? Maybe, somewhere out there someone's waiting for you--"

"Butterflies pay no attention to wilted flowers. When a woman's face starts shrinking, men just pass her by. Anyway, I've promised Mister Aragon not to leave Villa Zaragoza. You know how I serve the *senyora* faithfully, but we got new boarders who only sleep and eat. Those lazy pigs can't even wash their dirty plates."

"Of course, they can't. Have you ever seen pigs washing dishes?"

"And you know what? Merriam and Dr. Benito are now managing the farm."

"Do they? Does Mama know about it?"

"I doubt if the old lady knows . . ."

"Are the peasants not complaining?"

"Merriam told 'em to move out if they didn't like her policies. She does the accounting of the coconuts harvested quarterly and calculates how much money the copra makes. The old mango tree in the middle of the peanut farm is fruiting again. Your sister wants all fruits wrapped and numbered, so she can tell if some are missing. All the windfalls should be accounted for. Can you imagine that? Merriam's practicing what she learned in college. If she could only count every grain of rice harvested, she would do it."

"Did she not tell you to count the grains one by one?" Mama asked and laughed.

"I would've killed her!"

"Papa used to share the tenants two-thirds of the harvest . . ."

"Merriam wants fifty-fifty. I wonder what she can do if the *Senyora* gives up her land to the government. Have you heard about this Agrarian Reform, Patricia?"

"It's the 'land for the landless' program. A person with more than seven hectares of land should sell the excess to the tenants at market price but that would never prosper unless the First Couple's cronies follow this program."

"If this program is implemented, Merriam and Benito would lose their gold mine,"

"What gold mine?"

"Patricia, be sensible of what's happening around you. Doctor Benito hardly has a patient and yet he smokes, drinks and gambles a lot. Like the doctor, all Merriam could do is gamble. Where do they get money to play? You know, I'm tired of your sister – tired of her laziness. She can't cook for her family; always leaves the cooking to me."

"What time do you cook for lunch? Your crocs must be hungry by now."

"Let them starve . . ."

"They would eat you raw."

"That's their end. I'm poisonous when eaten raw."

"Would you also starve your *senyora*?"

Flora hurriedly got her basket of groceries and walked straight to the door; she turned around before she could get out.

"There's something you forgot to tell, I guess," Mama jested.

"I know that Merriam didn't let you take the old electric oven your mother gave."

"You know a lot of things. What else do you know?"

"I also know that Merriam's furious about the villa. If the *senyora* gives you the house, get it. It's a landmark and the government would pay millions for it."

"If I'd have the villa, I'd never sell it. It's the only memento of my ancestors."

"Merriam doesn't love mementoes; she loves money."

"She could never sell it. It's in my name as stated in my parents' will."

"Then you have all the rights to live there if it's yours."

"Someday, but not now," Mama said. Flora twitched her mouth and left.

Not long after we moved back to our old home, Grandma told Mama that the house we lived in was entwined with curse because the main door was facing sunset and the stair had six steps that when grandma counted *oro, plata, mata* for the first three steps successively and went back to *oro* on the fourth, she ended with a *mata* on the sixth which means death or bad luck. It must have caused my father's fate. Mama said there was no harm in believing so we moved out upon Grandma's advice.

Mama bought a small house at the Teachers' Village along the border of Grandma's farm. It had a five-step stair that ended up with *plata* which means silver; not as good as *oro* which is gold but not bad as *mata*. It was facing the morning side of the day. Per Grandma, the early morning sunrays that would stream through the main door and windows could bring us good luck. It was also facing the rear of the ancestral house which I long had wanted to be my home. We had lived there for over a month, and only then did I find out that the most magnificent house in Sacandaya wasn't at all a 'home'.

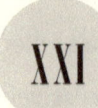

XXI

The Transition

Beautiful feelings started to evolve in me.
I was at the age when talking about
boys had become very exciting.

On the seventh of April in 1978, the regional elections for the interim National Assembly were conducted. Some political prisoners were still languishing in jail, but the government allowed any political prisoner to run for a seat. Mama said that was only to show to the US President that the Philippines was still a country of democracy, so America won't stop sending us aides.

Benigno S. Aquino Jr., a political prisoner, ran for a seat in the Greater Manila area. Random surveys had him at the top followed by his party mates, but election results showed the contrary despite the militants' noise barrage on the eve of the Election Day forewarning the administration not to resort to fraud. Aquino lost the political race.

In October 1980, after Aquino suffered a mild stroke, the Marcos administration allowed him to leave the country for a heart surgery in America with the understanding that he'd return to the Philippines as soon as the surgery was done and if he was fit to travel. He didn't return anymore. With Aquino gone from the country, on January 17th of the following year, Ferdinand Edralin Marcos lifted Martial Law through Proclamation 2045.

I graduated from elementary with the highest honors. As there was no middle school in my country at that time, I was a high school freshman when schools opened in June of 1981, which was rather late because of the "presidential election" conducted that month. Constitutionally, elections should be in November but must have to be done that early upon America's order according to my mother. With the opposition boycotting those forthcoming special elections, the administration allegedly drafted a nonentity in politics to run against the incumbent President. Unsurprisingly, the incumbent won.

Meanwhile, Aunt Merriam and family were back in their old house. She had ejected her tenants who failed to pay the rent for a couple of months. The same tenants spread stories that the house was twinned with a curse and with Aunt Merriam imposing many 'don'ts', nobody anymore wanted to rent it.

The bad Karma that Aunt Merriam long deserved had started. She found out lately that her husband, who was spending some days in the city was living there with a young mistress. Her bookkeeping business slowed down; Chinese businessmen had learned the trade. She busied herself doing accounting of the produce from Grandma's farm which Uncle Benito administered without their mother's knowledge.

There were times that the family Sunday affair was not held because Uncle Ralph and Aunt Thelma were busy with their respective careers. Uncle Ralph, a newly ordained priest, joined a congregation that was building Christian faith and churches in Africa. Aunt Thelma was getting busier as a business lawyer for a foreign company. Like Aunt Thelma, Flora had become busier than ever doing the jobs that Santiago left.

Santiago tried his luck in Mindanao, the biggest island in the south dubbed as 'the land of promise' and home to a large group of Filipino Muslims. When the conflict between Muslims and Christians arose, I didn't hear any more of it called as 'the land of promise' as I haven't heard of what had become of Santiago Bantilan.

Mama kept going to the Villa to check Grandma's health and I had to go with her. I couldn't care less if Aunt Merriam's blood seethed on seeing my face: the more she suffered, the more I enjoyed it. I was growing up – sensibilities were transforming – I was turning dauntless.

Strange things evolved in me as days passed by; I was shaping up gradually. I loved watching myself in the mirror - practicing how to poise nicely, smile exquisitely and laugh modestly. Shirts and denims and sneakers were my Sunday's best, my hair in ponytail with powdered face. I found morning blossoms refreshing and the soft cool wind on a sunless morning soothing and the gentle rain on a sunny afternoon very entrancing. I wondered about these but never asked my mother why I was feeling that way.

Subjects about boys my age were exciting; their glimpses thrilled me. I didn't make a fuss about this transition until after I told Aunt Thelma about the cute boy in school who kept eyeing me. At one time, that boy offered to walk me home. Although I was a little flirty, I got scared when he asked if I already had promised myself to somebody.

One morning, I woke up bleeding. That scared the hell out of me, but Mama wasn't worried a bit; she laughed about it and said I was no longer a child.

Butterflies flutter around when a flower blooms, Aunt Thelma said when I told her about what was happening to me. She laughed hard when I told her that the boy in school who kept staring at me asked me again if he could walk me home. Aunt Thelma warned me never to let any boy kiss me or I'd get pregnant in no time. That was shocking! Anyway, I never let that boy walk me home. And how would Mama react seeing her little girl walking along from school with a boy?

Mama filed leave of absence from her job in the last week of August 1983 to see the president's wife with the hope that the First Lady could help her find my father. I asked my mother if she still believed my father was alive.

"I'm giving it up," she said with drooping shoulders. "I just want to find his remains."

"What if he were alive?"

"It's enough for me to know his whereabouts and how he had been."

I doubted my mother was serious of what she said. It was hard to figure out what was going on in her mind. It had been over a decade since my father was declared to have died. All the traces that would've led to the recovery of whatever was left of my father could've been gone by now as the name Saigon had been erased from the world map. She wanted to find out if my father really died in Vietnam and if so, find his remains.

Mama informed her mother of her plans to go to Manila by the end of the month for her much-awaited appointment with the First Lady. Grandma was against it and called her daughter stupid when she insisted on going.

"How can she help?" Grandma sounded upset.

"Any way she could," Mama responded with hesitance. "She has the means."

"Do you think she personally wrote you to come and see her?" Grandma's voice tingled with sarcasm. "Who are you to deserve her attention? She's much busier than the president of the United States. Attending to your needs would be the last thing she'd do."

"I told her in my letter that Romulo was the son of her first cousin."

"She wouldn't care. Forget everything, Patricia. Don't be stupid."

"This is a chance, Mama. I'm the only one that Romulo could hope for help."

"Why can't you accept that your husband is already dead --?"

"What proof do I have? An obituary isn't enough. Besides, I received a letter from Romulo a week after the ambush supposedly happened. That led me to believe he was alive. Maybe, the obituary that was sent to me was a mistake. I mean maybe, Romulo was able to save himself when the group was ambushed."

"If he's still alive as you believe he is, why did he not come home?"

"When Papa failed to return from war, when he failed to come on the day you expected, did you ever think he was already dead?"

"*Por Dios, por santo, Patricia* . . . in all those years your father was away, he was just within the country fighting against foreign invaders, and he came home in three years. Your husband was in a foreign land fighting in a foreign war, and it had been forever since he left. If he were alive, why hadn't he returned when the last Filipino soldier from Vietnam had been pulled out a decade ago?"

"I'm sorry, Mama if I have to go against your will."

"And why did you set the meeting on the day of our town fiesta?"

"I didn't set the date. It was in her letter."

"You should have asked for postponement. Aside that it's the day we're holding our town fiesta, Manila is in red alert nowadays."

"It's already set, and I have to be there that day, or I'd lose my chance forever."

"Granting your husband's alive and you found him, can you persuade him to come home with you? Do you think he doesn't have another family by this time?"

Mama was silent. She had her eyes focused outside, but I believed she heard clearly what her mother said, and she pondered about it.

"The more you'd hurt yourself. Think about it. *No seas tonta.*"

Grandma vehemently opposed our trip; it gave Mama an afterthought – often threw blank stares as we packed up our things - as if her life was hanging on a balance in her decision. At one point, she asked: "Shall we go?"

"Everything depends on you, Mama."

"Your Grandma could be right. Manila is in chaos due to the assassination of Aquino. But what if the First Lady had waited for us and we hadn't come?"

"Then let's go," I said authoritatively.

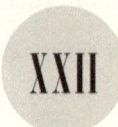

XXII

Across the Dark

It was to be the Dark Age for my country.
Like the boat we took that night we left,
it was crossing an ocean of darkness.

According to the media, the First Lady, herself, had warned Aquino in person that it wasn't safe for him to come home because somebody wanted him dead on his return.

China Airlines Flight 811 from Taipei that landed in Manila International Airport in the early afternoon of August 21, 1983, brought a very memorable event in my country. Benigno S. Aquino Jr., a political prisoner, was on that flight all the way from the state of Massachusetts on a mission: to save his people from possible despotism.

Aquino took a flight from Boston to Manila with a brief stopover in Taipei where a certain Rebecca Quijano boarded. Aquino was using an alias name of Marcial Bonifacio, yet the administration learned all about it. A task force of a thousand military and policemen was organized to meet the returning self-exiled statesman right at the airport that day the plane he was boarding on would arrive and to escort him back to his prison cell in Camp Bonifacio. 'For his safety', according to the administration spokesman.

Ironically, while in the custody of the military who were supposed to guard his safety, the returning statesman was shot the instance he was about to step down to the tarmac as witnessed by Rebecca Quijano, whom Aquino had conversed with. Horrified, the lady screamed out. That invited the attention of the military.

Quijano watched them from her seat by the window. In her account as published in several local and national newspapers, when Aquino and his military escorts were about three steps to the tarmac, one of the escorts pulled a handgun and executing a distasteful act of traitorousness, immediately shot Aquino point-blank at the back of his head like he was shooting a rabid dog, according to a local reporter. The returning statesman fell to the tarmac. After a few seconds, another man, who was to be charged later as Aquino's assassin, was gunned down near where Aquino fell.

Rebecca Quijano had to run for her life thereafter.

Per media, the military men loaded Aquino to the ambulance like they were loading a carcass of an 'animal' although at that moment he was still alive. At the hospital, he was pronounced dead on arrival. What else could be expected when 'a somebody' wanted him dead on his return, as the First Lady had allegedly warned him.

The dead body of the fall guy was yet to be identified. Nobody among the soldiers knew his name even if he had been around in the area having friendly conversations with them before Aquino came down from the plane and got shot. If nobody among the soldiers knew him, how come he was able to penetrate that heavily guarded area?

Later, he was identified as Rolando Galman, the name embroidered in his underwear.

That heinous event happened on a Sunday when the Zaragozas had their usual get- together in Sacandaya. The family watched the episode played over for so many times in the TV channel of the Catholic Diocese of the Philippines. Grandma got sick watching it.

Nevertheless, we went to Manila by boat crossing the sea for 24 hours only to find out that Mama's appointment with the First Lady was canceled; it wasn't rescheduled. It was a day before Aquino's funeral and the palace was heavily guarded by military soldiers in anticipation of street demonstrations. Vans blocked the front street and rolls of barbed wire barricaded the gate. Also, the palace was preparing a party to honor a visiting U.S. senator, the unsmiling guard said. Grandma was right; the First Lady was always busy.

"I should've listened to your grandmother and not followed my intuition," Mama said. I bore part of the blame; I shouldn't have made my own decision.

We idled the day at the Luneta Park that was formerly known as Bagumbayan, where the most brilliant Filipino of all time was executed on December 30, 1896. The park had become one of Manila's finest attractions. Cops were posted here, twenty-four hours every day to guard tourists and strollers from harm but ironically some cops were themselves the culprits; Uncle Benito had personally witnessed it. It was while jogging around the park before dawn break, when he saw two cops apprehending a man at a dark alley behind the Congress building. The cops only freed the man after he handed them some paper bills.

I saw homeless folks around the park begging for money from passers-by; I'd seen lots of miseries in many instances, enough to tell me that people aren't created equal.

Darkness was falling when we headed to Santo Domingo church where Aquino's remains were laid in state.

The queue of people wanting to get inside the church was long. After a long wait we were able to get inside the church and view Aquino's remains laid inside a coffin. He was wearing the same safari suit he had on when murdered, stained with his own blood that had dried black. The atmosphere was very remorseful in contrary to what was going on at the Presidential Palace those moments where some selected people were carousing in honor of a visiting American dignitary. Mama was right in saying that 'Life is like the weather; it varies in other places and changes with time'.

Mama decided to go home the next day without seeing the First Lady.

The dark clouds that hovered over Manila forewarned a heavy rain. It was the day when Aquino's remains would be laid to rest. The streets where the funeral was passing by were closed to traffic, so we had to walk to the Quiapo church to pay homage to the Black Nazarene and from where we could flag a taxi to North Harbor. But then, it started to rain so Mama and I sought shelter under a building's overhang where some people had gathered. In a few minutes we were stranded there, the flatbed truck that carried Aquino's coffin was passing by amidst a heavy rain followed by an enormous crowd mightily cursing the Marcos Administration.

"Heaven is crying for the lost democracy," I heard an old woman say.

The rain subsided; people dispersed. We headed to the church of the Black Nazarene. Inside, Mama dropped to her knees at the foot of the huge crucifix. *Please, Lord, let peace reign once more in our country,* I heard her say before she touched the bloodied knee of Christ on the Cross. She put the sign of the cross on her and uttered the Lord's Prayer.

I didn't pray; forgot about it when I saw the image of Christ hanging on the cross and crowned with thorns. I noticed the bruised knees, the wounded ribs and the red patches all over its face and body. Was that what they really did to Him? How excruciating were His pains! Wasn't Christ scared when the Roman soldiers arrested Him at the garden of Gethsemane? Did Aquino feel the same fear when military soldiers picked him up from the plane and had he intuited it that his life was about to end?

Lots of questions were bothering me that night we were heading home. In many times I heard people say that Christ was meant to suffer to save the sins of mankind, yet people still breathe out hatred and destructions. War is always around. Once I asked Miss Via if there would be another Christ to suffer again to save humanity from hell, but the old woman, who was visiting the church every day in her life, didn't know. All she told me was 'Christ is coming back to the world not to save mankind but to render judgment'.

It was drizzling when we hurried out of the church. Mama hailed a taxi. On our way to North Harbor, I wanted to ask my mother why God, the Almighty God, let His only begotten son be tortured and crucified. I wanted to ask her the questions that bothered me while we were inside the church. I kept those in my mind. Mama would just tell me to read the bible again if I asked.

"There are events on Earth that we don't know why those happened," Mama answered the question I raised a while ago which she ignored. At that time, we were already inside the boat sitting in our cots. "I can't tell you why the grass is green, and the cotton is white, why flowers are red or yellow and why there are white, orange or blue."

Mama didn't know the whys and wherefores. She said that there are happenings in the world that are hard for humans to comprehend; God let it happen.

Neon lights were dazzling all over when darkness was about to cover the city of Manila. The continuous drizzling was making the city look so sad – in deep mourning for the death of a patriot that left chaos among the living.

The boat was now leaving the harbor, heading across a dark path that covered my sight. I asked my mother what was there over yonder where the boat was heading to, but instead of answering my question, she said it was better for me to go to sleep. It could be that she, too, was wondering where her country was heading to after the death of Aquino.

In a little while, the boat had covered a quite good distance. The dazzling lights of the city were fading from my sight. I heard Mama say it was time for me to rest; her hand tapping my shoulder.

My mother was telling the beads of her rosary when I lay down in my cot and forced myself to sleep. The places we'd been to and the scenes I had seen in the two days we were there in that big city were recurring in my mind. Yet, those two days of my mother's vacation leave, not to mention the hard-earned money she spent on that trip, had gone to waste. She failed to see the First Lady and I felt sad for her – so sad that I wanted to cry. What could be the next move she'd take in her endless search for my father?

I looked around. Most of the boat passengers seemed to have fallen asleep on their respective cots. Except for the roaring of the boat's engine, everything was silent. I looked back at the city we left behind; my mother could be thinking of the darkness she was facing in her search for my father. I felt sad for her. I couldn't help feeling sad for my mother.

XXIII

The Bloodless Revolution

People marched onto the streets,
stormed the Presidential Palace, ransacked.
the volumes of wealth the First Family had left behind.

The man that was gunned down seconds after Aquino fell was later identified as Rolando Galman. Strange, but nobody from the military knew his name even if the man had been there in that restricted area of the airport having conversations with some of the soldiers.

What was he doing there? How was he able to penetrate that restricted area?

My mother's family had been discussing this. It was a huge puzzle to many, but the question was left unanswered. That made the whole thing smell fishy. As collateral damages, people suspected of having knowledge about the planned assassination of Aquino disappeared one by one in a few days. They were never seen again.

Human life had become a cheap commodity in my country. One could be slaughtered even in broad daylight, and no one was made to answer much less if the person had no recognition of human dignity. Foreign entrepreneurs, already unsettled by the government's high debt load, had moved out their investments to other Asian countries. Touring foreigners cancelled the Philippines from their itineraries – a big blow that defaced the Tourism Industry and badly affected the Philippine economy.

Mama didn't regret marrying my father but was dejected on the belief that Aquino's assassin was a soldier. Getting wary of this circumstance, and learning from her own experience, she told me to be a nurse and never marry a soldier because between a wife and a war, he'd abandon the former for the latter.

Things changed and so were my aspirations. Finding my father and reaching America someday were my childhood dreams. Those went off like smoke. My American dream hooked on me again after graduating from high school. I finished second honors due to bad conduct. I was no longer a meek lamb. As a high school salutatorian, I got a 50% scholarship to the government-owned school of nursing. I took up BSN.

I will finish the course with highest honors. I can see how my success makes Aunt Merriam more resentful. If my failure is her pleasure, my victory is her misery.

Education is basic for success, my mother kept telling that to me and I must achieve it while she was there to help. I was living in the city, far away from her like a newly weaned chick. It was kind of hard to be away from my mother, but being free from her beck and call was kind of exciting.

I joined student demonstrations sparked by Aquino's assassination. I was inured to the brutality of the cops in dispersing us. I was into the Korean Tae Kwon Do to be adept in fighting and joined the street parliaments of Inday Nita Cortez-Daluz, a radio personality who'd become a political figure. We were fighting for the less privileged and against government corruptions, shouting on the streets: "To hell with tyrants!"

It was when I met this prominent student leader named Vernon Vergel.

The rally that Vernon organized at the plaza was dispersed by cops; many of us got injured for while the police officers had their shields and truncheons, we had nothing to defend ourselves; we could only fight back with our voices. This invited the attention of religious organizations. A priest of the Redemptorist Order named Father Rudy Romano earned the ire of the military when he led street parliaments and rallies.

On July 11, 1985, on a broad daylight, the arrogant military displayed (again) their abuse of power by abducting the priest before the eyes of passers-by. Father Romano was never heard of again. Various organizations joined forces in searching for him, but the fate of the lost human rights advocate had never been known anymore or not that I knew of.

The widespread loss of confidence in the government made the President call for a snap election on February 7, 1986, to ease political pressures. More than a million signatures pushed Aquino's widow to run for the presidency against the incumbent. In the evening on election day, even with the election tabulators staging a walkout because of ballot-rigging, the National Assembly declared Marcos the winner.

That instigated civil disobedience. Realizing the immeasurable havoc that Martial Law brought, the former Secretary of Defense, together with the other Martial Law confreres, led the people's uprising that broke out on the 22nd of February 1986 while Cory Aquino was in the city of Cebu campaigning for the civil disobedience movement. Enrile revealed that the ambush done to his car in 1971 and the bombings in public places allegedly by the NPAs were preplanned by the government to justify military takeover.

The renegade group huddled at the Camp Aguinaldo along Epifanio De Los Santos Avenue. When the Marcos loyalists were about to attack the Camp with war tanks, civilians and religious orders led by the then titular head of the Catholics in the Philippines joined the revolt. They formed a human chain across EDSA to block the passage of the tanks. Helicopters hovered to fire down at the rebels on the instruction of the army general, but some pilots turned around to join the rebel troops who were raging to overthrow a government that had caused miseries to majority of citizenry for twenty solid years. It was exhilarating to see the little sparks we ignited turning into a hell of fire.

Aware of the imminent danger, in early morning of February 25th, the US ambassador Stephen Bosworth sent two military helicopters to whisk away the First Family, some cronies and 'blue ladies' and the last of the loyal troops, to the state of Hawaii where America offered them asylum.

Later, revolutionaries ransacked the Presidential Palace. It opened to the public eye a room filled with the First Lady's three thousand pairs of shoes. The First Family left behind not only precious mementoes but a country's debt to the World Bank in billions of dollars which the next generations of Filipinos would have to pay.

Corazon C. Aquino was proclaimed President. A Revolutionary government was imposed, and incumbent government officials were summarily dismissed.

At the wave of the anti-Marcos sentiment, the acquittal of the men from Task Force Alpha who were involved in Aquino's assassination in 1983, was overturned discarding the principle of double jeopardy. Convicted, they were all sentenced to double-life imprisonment. However, no mastermind was ever indicted. The 1973 constitution was rewritten; democratic institutions were re-established but there was so much to make up to bring the country back to what it had been.

At the revival of normalcy, the Manila International Airport was renamed Ninoy Aquino International Airport. Allies were appointed to major political government positions. My grandmother was appointed temporary municipal mayor of Sacandaya but in the local elections she offered the opportunity to the younger generation.

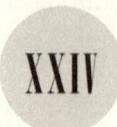

All about Vernon

Good looks weren't the only factors I was after of.
Vernon wasn't only famous and good-looking.
There was more in the guy that met the eye.

My mother had stopped hoping for my father's return. She no longer mentioned it whenever she gave me a call. I was living about a hundred miles away from home. Mama would call me on Sundays to ask if I'd been to church, reminding me to avoid student rallies, and not to get involved with a boyfriend.

It was my junior year in college; lessons were getting tougher, and more time was devoted to hospital duties. I told my mother I couldn't have any extra-curricular activities with boys – said it with laughter that gave her doubts considering that at one time I had mentioned to her I had a crush on a guy named Vernon Vergel.

Vernon was a popular campus figure; his name was a byword among girls at the main campus of the University of San Carlos where I took my pre-nursing course. The guy was a junior in the school's college of engineering which was situated far from the university's main building. Vernon got the qualities that I admired in a man – his advocacy of human rights foremost of all.

I got myself involved in the student organization he co-founded that raised protests on government ills. I couldn't deny how infatuated I was the first time I saw him in person. We acknowledged each other with smiles; mine was wide and cheerful, his was faint and dry. He didn't offer a handshake which I ardently expected; would have done it first if I didn't misconstrue it as improper.

It occurred to me he was unappreciative to people he regarded below his standard; hang out only with campus coeds who were displaying bags and shoes with brand names, their sexy figures and overly made-up faces. The man I admired most looked down on me as a plain and simple Jean.

For all I care!

Vernon Vergel was insufferable – the most presumptuous person I ever met. He must know that a guy with unkempt hair and with a ring in his ear simply turned me off. Worse was that he could have a tattoo on his butt. How I wanted to tell him he didn't look terrific at all but terrible.

I didn't stay long after that first meeting with him - I left without excusing myself; couldn't care less if he thought I lacked "GMRC". Well, he needed it more than I did.

But Good Heavens! My bad impression of him was my resentment for being ignored. Deep inside me, I wished to see him again; that faint smile stuck in my thoughts.

My wish was granted.

During our campaign against the hiking of college tuition fees, I ran onto him again. We were in the same car. He was already inside when I came in and greeted me first with his usual smile. That was enthusing. If I were sitting beside him, it would've been easy to start the gear and drive him to topics of interest to make him interested in me; I had lots of intellectual ideas to share.

Darn it! I totally forgot that I had wanted to snub him.

It was me who got ignored. I didn't get a second look. That was quite piquing, and I must discourage myself about him - the egotistical, the egoistic, the egocentric, and all the *egos* put together that would best describe that narcissistic egomaniac!

With the change of administration, student demonstrations eventually stopped but just when street parliaments had died down Vernon's group started another movement: the removal of American bases in Subic Bay and Sangley Point which was presumptuous because the legal contract for those bases was yet to expire in 1991. To Vernon's group, the US government was controlling the Philippine economy through the bases. They didn't consider the benefits our country was getting from the US government not to mention the number of Filipinos making a living inside American bases.

I stopped associating with Vernon's group. Good riddance! In a few days, I stopped thinking about him. I realized that my feeling for Vernon was just an infatuation, a wisp of smoke that vanished in the open air.

When I moved to a boarding house nearer to my school, I shared a room with Laura, a high school classmate who, I wasn't aware of, was Vernon's second cousin. One afternoon, Laura told me that Vernon was coming for her and I've to open him the door for she might be coming home a little bit late.

Seeing Vernon again after many years was kind of exciting. I thought I've got to be easy on his eyes that he'd wish seeing me again. It wasn't in defiance of his arrogance but to catch his attention – him, the immensely popular guy among the girls I was associating with on the main campus. That could be my last chance, or I'd be losing him forever.

My heart flipped when I opened the door. I almost didn't recognize him. Vernon Vergel had become handsomer – fleshy in cheeks and burly in build with well-groomed shorter hair sans the silver round ring that used to dangle in his left lobe. I noticed he wasn't wearing old worn-out rubber shoes but a pair of clean white Nike sneakers, not the old baggy dirty-looking denims but tidy faded-blue Levi's that gracefully fitted him well and blended perfectly with the dark blue shirt he wore. I noticed that he had grown taller and added weight proportionate to his height that made him more attractive. He'd grown matured physically as evidenced by his muscular build. I managed to compose myself and even pretended he was a stranger to me. He didn't remember me.

"You must be Laura's cousin. She's not here but she's coming."

"How did you know it's me?"

"She mentioned your name," I said casually as I glanced at the left side of his breast where a double "V" in upper case was embroidered in white.

"Ah, this stands for *Vig and Vold*," he said pointing at the initials. Carelessly, I laughed at his joke as I motioned him to the hallway.

"Have I seen you somewhere before?" Vernon asked after taking a seat. The sudden twist of mood in his face almost caught me off guard.

"An overused catchphrase sounds corny," I replied, suppressing a good laugh.

"Oh, yes! I've seen you in Sacandaya! Your name's Jinee, right?"

Ignoring his question, I asked him if he'd been to my hometown in a kind of tone like saying: *I haven't noticed you there.*

"We saw you one afternoon strolling in the shore with your mother. Laura said you always stay close to your mother."

"Yes, that was me!" I said it on an impulse. Darn! I forgot that I must pretend he was a stranger to me. "My mother always wants me to walk with her when I'm in town."

"And your father...?"

"He died in Vietnam during the war."

"Sorry to hear that."

"It didn't really matter to me for I haven't even seen him in person."

"He was fighting the war with the Americans. Did your father know why they were fighting a war in Vietnam?"

"I don't know. He died before I was born."

"Do you have siblings?"

I shook my head slightly without taking off my eyes on him.

"Then you are your mother's most precious treasure, and she could be so over- protective of you. Did she know that you were on the streets?"

"On the streets . . .! You mean a hooker?" He freed out an upsetting laughter.

"What I mean is that you were with us in those street parliaments."

"You recognized me! How stupid I was to pretend you were a stranger."

"I know but I still recognized you even if you looked frail and girlish back then with your straight long hair. You were sporting a name that sounds like of a nymph who used to stand by a stream on nights of full moon waiting for a lost lover who's said to return to her if she could hum all the waters in the stream to the sea."

"You're a budding poet! Grandma got my name from Roman mythology changing C to X to signify the tenth day of June I was born. Where did you get that story?"

"I just thought of it now when I saw your face in the light of the full moon."

"There isn't any moon tonight."

"Pardon the poet – he tells lies," Vernon said with his naughty smile. "Can we talk more about the American bases in Subic Bay and Sangley Point?"

"Definitely, you noticed me!"

"Who'd fail to notice one wolf from a herd of lambs?"

"That's rude."

"I mean one pro-American from a group of all anti-Americans?"

"You're trying to imply I was a pain in the neck of the organization."

"We were wrong. We realized you were a vital factor to our movement."

"You only realized the importance of a thing when it's gone. I was offended with the organization's advocacy for the immediate removal of the US bases."

"You left the organization, and nobody knew where you went to. We realized then that we needed someone who had a scale and balance of a Libran."

"I'm a Geminian."

"And you got that ability to make a good quick decision. With Laura's help, we found you in Sacandaya but then it seemed you were evading me."

"How could you say I was avoiding you? I wasn't."

"Because you thought I was arrogant; I wasn't. I waited for a chance to talk to you, but after the people's revolution our group dispersed. I never thought I'd meet you again. You're still as wonderful as you were --"

"And you're still as brassy as you were --"

"I only say what I see --"

His praise elated me, but he was bluffing.

Vernon Vergel had the gift of the gab: an orator, an excellent debater and spokesperson of student demos against government ills. I remembered him gathering students in the plaza to protest the hiking of tuition fees. A phalanx of riot policemen dispersed us. We fought back and we fought hard against those abusive police officers. I noticed a cop hitting a girl with his truncheon. Ready to fight to death, I darted at the cop, wrenched the stick from his grasp, and kicked him off balanced to the ground. I turned to the girl, her face bleeding.

"Good Heavens! It was Laura!"

"Yes, it was Laura who told me about you – that you are sharing a room with her. She also had mentioned how you rescued her from a cop's brutality that day when we had that unpleasant encounter with the police force."

"After that day, I didn't hear from you anymore."

"I lay low - felt guilty of inciting students to fight but then the abduction of Father Romano happened. I just couldn't sulk in a corner and wonder about it."

Vernon joined back with our group and helped us search for the lost priest. After a month that we didn't find the good comrade, we gave him up for dead as it happened to people the military abducted.

We held a prayer for the lost priest for nine successive nights at the Redemptorist Church. On the last night of our novena, Vernon gave a message. Being candid and daring, he won admirations from the audience, including several nuns and priests. I thought of congratulating him for that. I moved nearer to where he was and waited for a good time to approach him but then, I inferred he didn't have any interest in knowing me better. He left the place without saying goodbye.

I always thought of Vernon Vergel since then. I realized he had lots in common with Aragon Zaragoza. If my grandfather was an SBO president in college, Vernon was once chosen "campus king" during his school's university week celebration. Both graduated summa cum laude in their respective degrees. Grandpa was one of the top achievers in the bar, so was Vernon on the board.

"Hey, Jinee," Vernon said snapping his fingers. "What are you thinking?"

He had no clue I was comparing him to my foremost hero, my grandfather.

XXV

Little Silly Thoughts

What I had in mind was to be enchantingly lovely
the very first glance he'd cast on me that day.
He held me in his eyes, I was enthralled.

Vernon may have achieved academic excellence in college parallel to what my grandfather did but bore a sharp contrast to Grandpa's personality. Grandma said that my grandfather was fashionable when he was younger. He had a well-groomed hair, whereas Vernon loved wearing baggy denims, T-shirts and sneakers, and was sporting a disheveled hair down to his nape but short in the ears that revealed a silver earring on his left lobe - the fad prevalent among young boys in the early eighties which the Zaragozas regarded with disgust and indecency. Yet Vernon still attracted many-a-girl of my contemporaries and won admirations from his male buddies.

I met Vernon again in my junior year. Laura asked if I could have him as my escort in our J-S prom. Of course, I'd be too proud to be with him, the popular campus figure who was now a freshly sworn civil engineer. College girls would've wondered how I got the man they raved about. While some were pleased watching us with smiles of approval, others were whispering to each other while throwing us glances frowned with envy.

It was about midnight when the prom was over. Vernon took me and Laura home but said nothing about seeing me again, which I highly expected.

Surprisingly, he called me the next Sunday to ask if he could come to visit. That thrilled me no end; it was my first time to have a man paying me a visit.

Laura let him in while I fidgeted in front of the mirror studying which angle, I look nice and pretty. I mused on what we could talk about. Knowing how sagacious Vernon could speak, would I be dumb with my answers to his inquisitions?

Vernon stood up as soon as he saw me coming out of my room and greeted me with his usual fascinating smile. When I greeted back, my words muffled under my breath; it came out guttural sounding like a cluck of a goose. Surely, he noticed it and that made me move more awkwardly. Although it wasn't my first time with him, the situation was different. I was speechless in the next moments in front of him.

"Be gentle, coz. My friend knows nothing about birds and bees," Laura said and left. The more I blushed with Laura's tactlessness.

"How are you today?"

"I'm doing fine," was my instant reply. I asked him the same question.

"I'm okay. Did you have a nice dream last night?"

I didn't like to answer that question but coyly, I replied, "I had . . . Did you?"

"I had but I slept late last night."

Vernon said staring at me effusively. Momentarily, I realized that a girl could be tongue-tied when infatuated.

"Why?" I asked even if I was anxious for what he was to say.

"I couldn't sleep right away . . . I couldn't sleep thinking about you."

Bull's eye! This guy is a quick gunslinger.

I didn't know how I reacted. He must have noticed the blush in my face.

"Is it wrong to tell you how I feel about you? It's no longer martial law. The freedom of speech had been restored years ago."

"Of course, . . . of course there's nothing wrong with that but . . ."

"It's your first time to hear it."

I was so dumb to admit that at my age nobody had ever told me of something cute and nice. I nodded without really thinking of a good reply, yet that sent me an inexplicable kind of gladness. I shied away from his gaze yet wanted to hear more of his feelings about me. I was excited. I was thrilled. Oh my God, I chilled!

"Laura said you know nothing about birds and bees. Give me a hand. I could tell your future by the lines in your palm."

"So, you're the male version of Solvera."

Vernon sniggered. "Who's Solvera?"

"The psychic who told us that my father was alive and well. My mother believed in her, but I thought she was a fraud."

"The psychic could be right. The lines in your palms indicate your Fate."

"Solvera wasn't into palm reading; she did it with cards."

"It draws up the same results. Give me a hand. Don't be shy. I had held your hands during the prom."

"We were dancing that time. We were in different situation . . ."

"Well, we can dance while I study the lines in your palm . . ."

"Silly. People think we're crazy dancing without music."

"That makes us not different from anybody. Everybody is getting crazy. The world itself is crazy; it keeps turning around like a whirligig. When does it stops spinning?"

". . . At the turn of the century . . ."

"What do you think will happen if the world stops spinning?"

"It could be the end of everything God created."

"Do you really believe that the world is ending at the millennium?"

"As many do believe," was my quick reply.

"The world will never end, Jinee. If God wants to punish people for their sins, He could have done it during the Second World War when the heart of mankind was laden with wrath. Or He could have stopped the growth of humanity after the first sin was committed. And think about this: Why did God let it happen when He had all the powers over what he created? Then He banished Adam and Eve to the outside world to multiply and dump the world with more sins when He could have ended the sinning right there in the heart – in the Garden of Eden."

I loved how Vernon talked. I adored how he carried himself during our conversation. He was like a best-seller book, a page turner. Thinking of those things, I got lost in my thoughts and perhaps Vernon noticed that he asked if I were following him. To avoid embarrassment, I readily answered: *Yes, I am.*

"Okay. Where were we?"

"In the Garden of Eden -"

My spontaneous response was so amusing to him that he laughed so hard. His reaction amused me too and both of us were laughing aloud carelessly.

"There you go," he said.

He took my right hand and I let him trace the lines in my palm.

"Wait a minute . . . this line says you're going abroad. Are you serious with this?"

"Really? Am I really destined to live in another land? My mother dreams of it."

He looked up at me and asked, "To where . . .?"

I mentioned the word America. He gazed deep into my eyes. That left me offhanded. For a moment, I thought I heard my heart beating loud and fast. I should have taken my eyes off him, but strangely, I stared back like I was hypnotized.

"You're leaving me here? What will become of me when you're gone?"

Vernon's words took my breath away. It seemed my heart was throbbing faster. Reflexively, I pulled my hand from his hold. To change the topic, I asked him about the engagement ring he used to wear.

"What engagement ring?"

"You had it in your left ear."

Vernon had a good laugh again. "That wasn't an engagement ring."

"It wasn't?"

"It was simply an earring. It was the vogue – the *'in'* thing."

"Oh, but did you think that made you better-looking? No, it did not!"

"Well, I have outgrown that fad. How do I look now?"

I shrugged his question off. He held my hand again, sending me a throbbing sensation that was inexplicably beautiful. Enthralled, I almost responded on an impulse. Gracious! I didn't think about pulling off my hand and he might have thought I was consentient to what he was doing, he pulled me closer, closer to his face that I was now breathing his breath. Knowing what he was up to, I released myself from his hold.

In many times I kept recollecting that situation. I had it for the first time and that was beautiful – extremely beautiful.

There was that inexplicable joy talking with Vernon. We spent quite a long time there talking of various things like politics, the Cory Aquino government and the many coup attempts the President survived; the unstoppable corruption of government officials and employees; economy, the shrinking of the Philippine money against the U.S. dollar; and the exodus of oversea workers to the neighboring Asian cities as domestic helpers or entertainers, and to the Middle East as construction workers or drivers if not nurses or engineers. When we reached a topic about America's military bases in our country, we changed course for both of us realized it would only bring us to unpleasant situation. Except for that, Vernon and I were very compatible with each other.

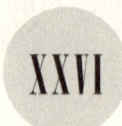

XXVI

The Joy of Loving

I enjoyed all those times with Vernon,
But it seemed the hours were passing fast.
That left me yearning for more time with him.

I found the man I wished to be with my whole life through, but I mustn't be flirty. Grandma kept telling me that women should be demure and highly refined to earn respect from the opposite sex. Women in her time would test a suitor's sincerity by accepting him only after a year of courtship. If he can't wait that long, then he is not the right kind to get married with.

That was passé.

I followed Grandma's advice, anyway, to avoid upsetting her – she, the ever prideful of having a wider experience in life.

Laura jested that Vernon was a marrying kind; he had an executive job in a big construction company. I wasn't ready for marriage but not the type to be relentlessly pursued. I couldn't just let this chapter of my life end without getting involved with a prize catch like Vernon. I wasn't dumb not to know the man's sincerity after a quarter of year. Two months of courtship was already long for westernized people – very unlikely if compared to Grandma's time when a woman pondered about it for a year or two.

It was different in my time.

I grew up when TV sets were already colored. Computers and cellular phones were a fad. People were adapting to new needs and habits, ways and views. Vogues and fashion changed and so were customs. Lovers holding hands in public were no longer smeared at. The principle of sexual equality had been accepted - my country was now ruled by a woman, the first in my country's history.

But when can women court men without humiliations?

It was the late eighties. The world was changing. Alternative rock music was rising. Communism was falling. The USSR was disintegrating. Berlin's iron curtain went crumbling. East met west. 'Cold War' was over, but doomsday was coming near. It was the end of the world that people feared most.

I didn't believe that phenomenon, but my friends' derisions embarrassed me. Each of them had a boyfriend and I was always the butt of their jokes that if I remained unattached at the crack of doom, Saint Peter wouldn't let me enter the pearly gate of Heaven. What if the world had really ended and I died without experiencing a boyfriend?

That was pathetic.

With Vernon Vergel getting into my life, I could have the last laugh.

Vernon and I used to stroll in the rotunda park uptown or watch movies on Sundays but most times, we stayed at my place and talked about anything that came up. Vernon had an excellent sense of humor that kept our conversations alive.

One Sunday that he didn't come, I was overly worried. I kept looking out of the window hoping to see him coming or kept staring at the phone like crazy wishing it would ring for me. I was about to give up on him when I heard a knock.

So excited, I rushed to the door with just a couple of long steps.

Yes, it was Vernon!

Astounded, I pulled him into my room and fondled him as if it had been a century since I had seen him the last time.

He responded to my emotions. It invoked a kind of sensation. An extremely wonderful pleasure surged within me sending wondrous thoughts about how beautiful love is. I closed my eyes as I ruffled his hair, ran my fingers down to his nape wanting him to kiss me passionately. I felt his face coming closer - his breaths wrapping me in raptures - that was too exciting. I controlled the sound of my breaths, yet my heart was panting, heard it beating as I waited zealously for him to kiss me but when his lips touched mine, I woke up from mesmerism.

I withdrew myself from his grasp.

Vernon grabbed me back and immediately locked his lips in mine and even if I smelled liquor in his breath which I didn't sense right away, I clung to him ready to melt in his arms. When I felt his hand crawl under my skirt, I realized he was up for something. Impulsively, I resisted. He persisted. I asked him to calm down, yet he went on with his advances like a demoniac; his manly strength overpowered me. When I had the chance, I gave him a good hard slap on the face that awakened him from his frenzied excitement. He moved a step back looking embarrassed.

"You're a monster!"

"I'm a man, Jinee…"

"It was a wrong concept to prove your manliness."

"Did you want me to be unresponsive like a statue?"

"Gentlemanliness is what measures virility."

"What's your point?"

"I'm not as easy as the other girls you have had."

"Come on, Jinee. It's the eighties; everybody's doing it."

"What everybody? Make me an exception! Pre-marital sex is taboo!"

"Pre-marital sex . . .!" Vernon reacted. "What are you talking about?"

"As if you don't know where it leads to, smart guy--"

"It depends--" Vernon muttered casually, squaring his shoulders, raising his hands. By his gestures, I suspected how badly he behaved with other girls. I have assessed him the other way. He wasn't of the likes of my grandfather at all.

I was catching my breath that hinted to him of my seriousness.

"Better leave me alone this time and the next time you come here, be sober."

I let him go. He apologized but I let him go.

Realizing it was my fault I thought of calling him back, but pride held me. I watched him walk away until he got lost in a corner.

Deliberations of thoughts: Was I too flirting that pushed him to be insolent. I should have subdued my emotions; he was only responding to my actuations. God must have wanted to scorn me for lying to my mother. Mama didn't know I already had a boyfriend while in college. I had to lie for all I heard from her was to study hard and avoid boys for having a boyfriend only distracts studies. Having a boyfriend wasn't a distraction; it was an inspiration.

I started missing the first man ever to have kissed me. I couldn't deny it that he brought a bewitching sensation that I longed to have his kisses again soft and sweet as the breeze at twilight blowing gently across my face while watching a sunset over Sacandaya Sea. I drove him away without giving him the chance to reason out for what he did. I resented holding him in contempt but maybe he deserved my wrath. He had turned rough and daring. Vernon Vergel deserved to be driven away!

But would he be like that if I didn't wake up his demons?

I couldn't focus my mind on one thing, couldn't settle in one place. I thought of the incident repeatedly and regretted driving him away. There was no use for ruing. I picked up the phone but couldn't dial his number due to tension or was it pride? I hung up.

Vernon and I had become intimate with each other but what if he wouldn't be coming back, if something tragic struck him at those moments he was walking out there?

I roused up, dashed through the door and fled into the streets. I found Vernon lying in the middle of the road: bleeding and breathless. I saw nobody around to help me. I wanted to scream. No voice came out.

I woke up, sweating and panting like I was reaching a peak. It was a nightmare, but fear was gripping me on the thought that some bad dreams could come true.

Fear intensified.

I swallowed my pride and tried to call Vernon. Just when I heard his voice, I hung up, but he would have intuited it was me. Now, he must be thinking I felt bad for sending him away and that I was willing to give up everything just to have him again.

How I wished Vernon would think of calling me at that moment, but when the phone rang, I ignored it. After the third ring, it stopped. I counted the seconds that passed and wished it would ring again. It did. I lifted the phone but didn't say anything; had the hunch it was Vernon on the other end. I was right!

"I know you called. I came home safe. Thanks for your concern, Jinee."

I didn't respond - disgusted at what I did made him believe I wasn't a bit different from any other girls he had had; he was showing that insolence.

I hung up again.

The phone rang again.

My intuition was strong: it was him again!

I let the home phone ring three times or maybe four. I thought of locking myself inside my room, but still, I could hear the phone keep on ringing. It was getting on my nerves. Vernon could be stubborn. *I must stop him from calling me.*

"Stop it, Vernon! What else do you want?"

"Vernon . . .? It's me."

"Mama . . .!"

"Yes, of course. Who's Vernon?

"Why did you call?"

"You didn't answer me. Who's Vernon?

"A friend . . ."

"What kind?"

"Mama, do you think I ought not to have a friend?"

"Well, you can, but what kind of a friend?"

"An ordinary one, Mama . . . nobody's special. Why did you call . . .?"

"Why did I call? Did I surprise you?"

"It's not a Sunday."

"Yes, it is! Anyway, Sunday or not, I'd check you up whenever I want to."

"You don't have to worry about me, Mama . . . trust me."

"Jinee, always remember to follow what I say . . ."

My mother couldn't be a perfect one, but she was what a mother should be. As I didn't want to hurt her, I must deny Vernon. *I'd tell her when the time comes. She'd understand. She also had experienced loving a man.*

Everything was fine again with Vernon and me. We agreed to stop seeing each other often. I needed more concentration on my studies; I was graduating that year and Vernon had a job to attend to. It was much better - as the saying goes: absence makes the heart grow fonder. We had petty quarrels as usual - normal happenings that measured how deeply we cared for each other.

In my graduation day ceremony, I wished for the presence of the three people I cared so much in my life that time. Grandma couldn't come to the city due to her failing health, but how could Vernon afford to ignore my invitation?

Speakers came to the podium one by one. None of what they spoke about got stuck in my mind. I kept on thinking about Vernon. It would be impossible if he forgot what that day could mean to me. Where could he be at that time?

Came the turn of the guest speaker. I heard the audience roar for the distribution of diplomas coming near.

Then names of graduates were called alphabetically. Cheers and whistles followed every time a name was called. I was the last to receive my diploma, greeted with the loudest applause being the *summa cum laude.* Vernon could be staring at me those moments. If he were nearer to the stage, I would've seen how his face beams with pride having me, the graduate with the highest distinction, as his girlfriend.

My mother pinned on me the sash of highest honors and the school principal handed me a gold medal for topping the class and two certificates of excellence.

There was a loud uproar when I stood before the podium for my valedictory address. While waiting for the applause to subside, I scanned again the rows of faces, widening the scope all the way to the farthest corners hoping to catch sight of Vernon. He promised to come even quoted a catchphrase from the movie *Mahogany: Success is nothing without someone you love to share it with.* I wanted to share with him the joy I had in those moments and to see how his eyes could tell me he wasn't wrong in loving me, but where was he?

Mothers are the most wonderful gift the Lord has ever granted to humanity.

My first statement brought the house down. I chanced to survey the crowd again while waiting for the cheer to subside; I didn't see him. *Maybe, he's seated too far from the platform,* I consoled myself. *He's here. He cannot afford to miss this occasion.*

I ended my speech with emphasis on the parents' duties and responsibilities of shaping up the younger generation to be better citizens of the country. A loud applause broke out again. There was a standing ovation. Exalting. Deep inside me those cheers and praises weren't so much entrancing as the sight of Vernon who was nowhere to see.

XXVII

The Pain in Parting

Losing him was a pain to bear.
It hurts to leave but it pains
more to be left behind.

Vernon called to see me after work at the Fuente, an uptown rotund park built in honor of a Cebu native who was the country's President during the American period. We used to stroll there on Sundays. The place was only crowded on weekends or whenever there were student rallies against government ills.

That Monday afternoon, few were strolling or passing by from the Robinson's Department Store to the opposite block where adjoining square-faced little shops stood. Across the street at the west side, few men were hanging out for bottles of beer and skews of chicken and pork barbecue at a place habitué called Larsians. Vernon used to while away his time here with officemates after work.

I waited for him on a bench fronting the building where the construction company he worked for was occupying the seventh floor. It was only a year since he was hired. Now I heard from his friend that he was slated for promotion. I guessed it was why he wanted to see me – to brag about it and celebrate.

A beady-eyed boy of about six walked toward me and asked for coins. After I gave him four quarters, he ran to where another boy was waiting: both vanished from my sight.

I noticed a young couple nearby playing with their toddlers, a son and a daughter.

A middle-aged woman peddling fried shelled peanuts passed by. She asked politely if I wanted some; I smiled and shook my head. She rested on the next bench some meters away. I heard her asking me about the time. It was five – the time when office employees were getting off work.

The streets were now congested with vehicles plying here and there. I recognized Vernon pulling himself away from the bulk of pedestrians crossing the street. He must have noticed me already; he was hurrying in my direction.

The guy looked superb in a long-sleeved sky-blue shirt accessorized by a light-blue tie with black diagonal stripes that matched his black slacks and black leather shoes. Gone were those days when Vernon used to wear what he described as the shaggy hippie look of the eighties. His hair was neatly trimmed this time but at a closer look, the hole in his left earlobe where the round silver earring used to dangle was still visible.

He showed a wide grin. He stood there for seconds before me with his usual fascinating smile. In his hands were a bunch of red American roses and a box of Hershey chocolates. I gestured to him to sit beside me.

"I thought you don't like any American . . ."

"Look. America had long granted us independence but until now, it's still meddling with our country's affairs," Vernon responded after settling beside me. Then he laughed sounding like a naughty boy amused by his own pranks.

"I thought you hate America . . ."

"I don't like America minding our country's affairs, but I love its chocolates," Vernon said with a light laugh. "These roses are yours; we'll share the chocolates."

He placed the box of chocolates and the flowers on the bench between us and took out from his shirt pocket a small black box. He opened it close to my eyes. The box revealed a gold ring of tiny diamonds that were embedded around a mother pearl.

"Is this real? You don't have to buy me an expensive graduation gift."

"Of course, this is real but not a graduation gift. This is an engagement ring."

"What engagement ring? Do we need to have it?"

"Yes, of course so that nobody anymore would be making a pass on you. These twelve tiny diamonds surrounding the pearl stand for the number of kids we're going to have. The more, the merrier," Vernon jested and laughed at his own joke. "Don't you think I deserve a kiss for that?"

In my country that era smooching in a public place was immoral. I looked around. Nobody was watching but the peanut vendor who was looking enthusiastic. Who cares, I thought and gave Vernon a quick peck on his lips. The woman cheered. Vernon glanced at her in askance and raised a thumb-up sign.

"I know your point," I told him.

"Do you think I won't ever marry you?"

I didn't respond but was gaping at his face while he took out the ring from its box. He held my left hand and said, "Jin Xeres Zaragoza, do you take Vernon Vergel as your wedded lawful husband for better or for worse till death do you part?"

My response was a loud laugh. The peanut vendor laughed with me.

"Just say 'I do'."

"I do," I responded by repeating his words, but with a mock that excited the peanut vendor; she cheered again.

Vernon slipped the ring onto my finger and gazed into my eyes. He looked very serious; I was about to laugh again. "Now, repeat after me: With this ring, I thee wed."

"Vernon, this is just a joke -"

"Yes, it is, but don't you think of making it real? I'm now a junior executive in my job and I'm now ready, willing and able to raise a family of my own. Don't you think so?"

"I do but not so soon."

"Of course, we need months of planning."

"I'm counting years."

"Years . . .? You already have finished your studies -"

"It doesn't mean it's time to get married. My mother doesn't even know about us."

"For how long shall we go on like this, Jinee? I respected your decision when you told me not to show up on your graduation -"

"You got me wrong. If you only knew how I wanted to see you there . . ."

"I was there, hiding in the crowd."

"You were? Why were you hiding?"

"I thought you didn't want me to be there."

"I wasn't yet ready to let my mother know about us but that didn't mean . . ."

"And why can't you tell her about me? What's wrong with me?"

"I'm not ready for this. My mother thought I never went out dating and only concentrated on my studies."

"And you've proven it."

"When it comes to studies but how about not having a boyfriend?"

"You've finished your degree and old enough to decide on your own."

"But I still need my mother's decisions and advice on what's good for me."

"You and I can decide things together after getting married."

"It would be disastrous to her. I'm the only one she must dream for."

"You're the only one she has now but if we got married and have a dozen kids, we're giving her twelve more than she had."

"This isn't a time for kidding, Vernon. I must fulfill what she aspires for me, I can never forget what I promised her."

"And that's reaching for the pie in the sky. There's no place like home, Jinee."

"If you were living in Vietnam during the war, can you say the same thing? People in the world want a happy and beautiful life; it's everybody's dream."

"Our country needs the talents and skills of young graduates to help make our country a better place to live in. If only what we learned here are applied here, our country would have prospered, and nobody anymore wants to go to America to seek a beautiful life for that happy life can very well be found here."

A great enthusiasm glistened in his eyes. I measured how patriotic he was, and I realized we were aiming life in different directions. I was dreaming of reaching America while he was building a dream of making his country great which I didn't think possible. My country was neck-deep in debt - in billions not millions and in dollars, not pesos. It had lost its chance to be great again unless we could eradicate corruption, that social disease affecting our government officials which to me was a very impossible thing to happen. I didn't want to crush the dream Vernon was on, but at the same time, I didn't want to give in to his ideas. I thought I found in him the man to dream with and die for. I was wrong. How I wanted to cry upon realizing we weren't made for each other after all.

I fell silent; didn't find a good response but I was waiting for him to say more of his patriotic ideas. He, too, fell silent. When the young couple with two young kids were passing by, he asked something like *'isn't it nice having a family of your own?'*

I looked around on pretense I didn't hear him.

I noticed more people had come to the park. The peanut vendor was gone.

In Vernon's face, I saw hopelessness but a Virgoan with the gift of the gab, he loved to argue. He said America isn't a paradise; racial discrimination still exists, and one must work hard to make both ends meet because bills and taxes are too much and many. But reaching for America wasn't only my mother's aspiration; it was mine too.

"I took up nursing to chase that dream," I broke the silence between us after a minute. "Also, I can't afford to fail my mother. It's not the end between us, Vernon. We're still young, anyway, with lots of time to make up what we lost in the past."

"But if we can avoid losing time in the past . . ."

"Marriage needs thorough planning. It isn't a spoonful of food that you easily spit out if bitter to your taste. Marriage is for life."

"You better tell me straight to my face that you also dream of having an American husband. Tell me to set you free and I will do it without hesitation."

Vernon's insecurity was irritating. I've loved him so dearly and never would trade him for any American man, but I could never trade my mother for him.

"Love alone isn't enough to hold a marriage strong," I said my words softly, but it seemed Vernon wasn't listening; he kept looking in different directions. "Love needs trust and confidence from both of us. If you don't have both, then what you feel about me isn't love at all."

"But the twist of fate is uncertain," he said without looking at me. "Unexpected events may come in the years of waiting. What if you'd never come home anymore."

"Even death cannot prevent me from coming home. I give you this promise, Vernon: I'm coming home. Just give me a few years . . ."

"Sorry, Jin . . . You can't blame me for getting insecure."

"Then we aren't made for each other if you can't wait."

"You just can't decide because you're hoping to find a better one in . . ."

"I hate it when you say that", I snapped at him for his childishness.

"Let's get it through right now – go and come back whenever you want but don't make a promise; it would be more hurting once you break it."

Thinking my silence was acquiescence to break up; he stood up suddenly and walked away like in a hurry. I didn't want to stop him because of pride, but I did. He stopped and turned around. He moved closer.

"Please, don't leave me here just like that . . ."

"Does it hurt to be left behind? How'd I feel when you leave me for America? I'd feel more pain," Vernon said with hand gestures like he was delivering an oration.

"You're catching people's attention. Please, sit down and listen . . ."

Vernon sat back but kept his head moving; his eyes shifting in different directions.

"What is it?" Vernon asked without looking at me.

"Stop looking around and listen to me . . . please. . ."

He clasped his hands, his elbows on his laps. "I'm listening . . ."

"Love isn't a one-way thing. One needs to sacrifice for the sake of the other. When you were on your job-training in Japan, I didn't hear a word from you. You sent no letter, not even a card. Every night, I looked forward to another day seeing you in my thoughts. That gave me hopes and consolations that you were coming back for me."

"That situation was different. I was sure of coming back."

"But I wasn't sure if you were still with me because you never communicated with me. I consoled myself that you wanted to write or call me, but you were too busy with your training. I made up that situation for I didn't want to entertain thoughts that you were forgetting me. My friends said it was impossible if you weren't having an enjoyable time with a geisha. If I were to believe in that, it would have destroyed the trust I had in you. I ignored those insinuations although it could be possible. I kept on hoping that you'd honor the trust and promises we kept for each other. When you returned, you didn't hear me complaining. I never asked who was with you when I was away from your eyes because it only hurt me if I found out you were lying. It was a situation where a lie is more appreciated and better to leave the truth unspoken."

"There never was a lie," Vernon cut in.

"I never accused you of lying; I never complained because as I said, I had my trust in you. Now I'm asking the same favor: If you truly love me, Vernon, have faith in me. I'd never ruin the trust you're giving me."

He gazed closely into my eyes but said nothing. He must have perceived in my face how much I desired for his permission to leave for America.

"Do you know that you're more precious than all what I've achieved in life?"

"Then I'm worth waiting for."

"I'll die of waiting . . ."

"Patience is virtuous . . ."

"But Fate is uncertain. What if you won't be coming back anymore?"

"That's a very impossible thing to happen . . ."

"What if it becomes possible?"

"Why do you refuse to understand me?"

Upset, Vernon sprang to his feet. "It's you who don't understand!"

"I don't want to lose you . . ."

"I don't want, too . . ."

"Is it not enough assurance?"

"A person's mind changes many times in a day. How many times more in years?"

"Oh, Vernon . . . how can I follow a dream without losing you?"

"You must free yourself from that dream. It's not the right place for you. You'd find nothing there but frustration. Forget about it and think about me. If you can't forget America, then you must forget me completely."

"How could I make myself forget those moments with you? How can I make myself forget you when a thought of you makes my day, when everything about you is keeping me alive. I seal every sunset that passes by with prayer for another sunrise, for another day of having you in my thoughts. I'm neither a prolific writer nor an impressive speaker but I wish I were, so I can say more explicitly how much you mean to me."

"How good are those words when you're gone? What would become of me without you? If I can only give up what I have achieved to prevent you from leaving, I'll be willing to give up everything."

I have reached a crossroad. It was tearing me apart. I didn't want to lose the first man I ever loved but I didn't want to destroy the dream my mother built for me.

To have the best of both worlds was impossible. I thought I'd suffer less pain in leaving Vernon. I would survive without him; it was just a matter of trying.

Tears were swelling in my eyes when I took off the ring from my finger, placed it back in the box and slipped it into his shirt pocket. He kept himself silent.

"Why do we have to part?" I whispered but got no answer.

He gave me a fleeting embrace, released himself from my arms and left - leaving me the pain of being jilted. My heart bled as I heard his footfalls on the concrete pavement fading away. I closed my eyes and my tears fell profusely.

The night closed in. Vernon was gone. I tried to look around for him thinking he must just be around waiting for me to call him, but I didn't find a trace of him. He had completely vanished from my sight.

Everything happened so fast that I couldn't think of what to say or do that could have stopped the breakup. I remained seated in the bench for long, counting the seconds passing by and recollecting those days I spent with the very first man I ever had loved.

Then I came to wonder how my life had been. How I got that obsession of seeing my father at an early age and of coming to America to have a taste of a beautiful life. I had those thoughts on most nights I was about to sleep. I felt joy thinking of those and made it my escape from the miseries I was going through. Then I lost those dreams when I reached adulthood. I didn't care anymore about seeing my father and forgot about reaching America. I never thought that my mother was carrying that dream for me.

The night was getting deeper. The number of people in the park was reducing. In the sky, stars were fading. A wide expanse of clouds was hovering. It was about to rain, but I remained seated on the bench hoping for Vernon to come back.

The boy who asked for coins earlier came back tugging another, perhaps his younger brother. Both were staring at the box of chocolates; I felt their hunger. I gave them the box and they looked surprised as if to ask why I gave away those expensive-looking chocolates. I wondered how their parents could afford to let them beg for alms in late hours, to scavenge for something to satisfy their hunger. What could be their future and how would their lives end up? How could people afford to sire children if they aren't ready to assume parenthood?

The night turned colder with the winds of March sweeping in. It ruffled the leaves of the trees, the mute witnesses of the promises that Vernon and I made the first time we were there. I told him then he was the first man I ever have loved, and I was afraid to lose him - afraid to feel the pain of losing. He kissed my eyes and told me he'd never ever look at any other woman's eyes but mine. That was a beautiful promise I treasured so much that it kept resonating in me in my solitude.

It's beautiful to be loved but woeful to be jilted. If it occurred to me that every beginning has an end, I might have shut the thought off my mind whenever I was with Vernon. On those moments, I forgot that nothing in the world is lasting but its endless spinning that causes the phenomenal evolution of sunrise to sunset, the transfiguration of darkness to daylight that makes the comings and goings of the seasons a forever.

Vernon came into my life like a sweet dream that vanished upon awakening. How true was it that it's better to love and lose than never have loved at all? Losing him was unbearable. I wished I never had met and loved him. But what's wrong with loving?

I had been in love with a man, and I know it by heart there's more joy than pain to have loved and be loved. It's much better than not to have loved at all.

But . . . . . .

Love must not be just a lust in the hearts that ebbs out after consummation. It's not only a want for satisfaction or a need for water to thirst and food to hunger. It could be a vital factor in strengthening the union of a man and a woman – the loyalty towards each other for better or for worse.

Therefore, marriage can't be perfected by just loving each other. It's the union that should be measured with confidence and trust, coated with respect, and strengthened with fidelity and sincere devotion. So, marriage must be built firm with strong knots to make it sturdy, solid, and stable for marriage is an eternal communion with God.

XXVIII

The Psalm 139:9-10

I ride the morning wind to the farthest oceans,
and even there Your hand holds me,
Your strength supports me.

With my mother's persuasions, I got interested in taking up nursing in college, which was an expensive course in our country that an average family could hardly afford. During those years, my mother and I kept nursing our hearts with the hope that I would successfully hurdle my dream to finish the course. It was my mother's surest way, her way of getting us out of the hell we're living in.

Uncle Benito laughed about what I dreamed of saying I was too ambitious to tread on a medical field unaffordable to my mother being a mere schoolteacher. He didn't believe or might not have known that I was offered by my school a fifty percent discount on the whole course on my tuition fee for finishing salutatorian in high school. Aunt Merriam said I'd never finish the course and would never reach my dream in life for I was born 'jinx'.

Those jeers defied me to strive hard to succeed. I took those negative comments to my advantage. With prayer and my mother's constant encouragement, I maintained my scholarship throughout the entire course. I had promised myself to give my mother the happiest moments in her life.

Thanks, God! Those moments came!

I received my diploma for finishing RN-BSN, took and passed the board and in the same year passed the CGFNS. I was ready for America.

It is said that all the people in the world are created equal. In the eyes of God, maybe we are, but different from one another in some respects. People from a third world country must have to suffer in securing a visa to America. On my first attempt, I failed. It was when the American bases in my country were facing ejections.

The American Embassy was getting stricter in screening visa applicants, yet it didn't discourage hopefuls to queue up at early dawn, skipping breakfast and lunch with only a bottle of water in hand to endure the long wait. I was one of those hopefuls.

I had suffered lots of pains already, had gone through miseries while growing up. I had one more will to survive, to achieve the dream my mother had for me. I must show my detractors what I was capable of. I knocked on Heaven's door with sincerest prayers I ever did. It pays to pray; the Lord opened the door for me the next day.

I was scheduled to leave for America the day after my 22nd birthday. Grandma held a party for me. Aunt Thelma came and Uncle Ralph, too. He was temporarily the parish caretaker of our town. Father John had retired and had returned to his country home.

Aunt Thelma was the luckiest of the brood for inheriting Grandma's beauty and Grandpa's intellect. She was a lawyer like her father, but with her status, no bachelor in Sacandaya dared to court her. The Governor wanted her for his lawyer son, but the two never got the chance to get acquainted. At an old age, she thought of marrying an office clerk, but Grandpa disfavored it; she dropped her plans of marrying for fear of bad Karma. She chose to become a nun. She advised me to do what I think is best for me because it's better to regret doing what I wished to than to regret following what others wanted.

Uncle Ralph and Aunt Thelma celebrated with me for what I achieved; the older siblings grieved it. They didn't come to the party that Grandma held - both suddenly got sick. They heard before of my plans to go abroad and laughed about it saying I was daydreaming. Now, they must have eaten their words and that had made them sick.

Monday morning. Uncle Ralph drove us to the airport together with Aunt Thelma. Some relatives of Grandpa met us there. Mama told them that her sacrifices for me had paid off. But the fact that I wouldn't be with her anymore made her remorseful. Even if her tears were meant for gladness, I saw distress. She often told me to be brave in crossing a dark path alone because she'd be leaving me someday. On the contrary, I was the one leaving her – leaving her all alone. I knew how it felt to be left alone; I'd been there.

Your attention please! This is your final call for Philippine Airlines flight 215 service to Manila. Passengers should now be boarding at Gate . . .

In the stream of passengers flowing out of gate, I drifted away from my mother's reach. I saw in her the passion to hold me again that on the spur of the moment, I thought I should not go for I would be leaving my mother all alone and for how long? I felt guilty, but I was already at the point of no return and must cry to ease out the guilt that was surging me up. Even then, I must be dauntless and daring at this point to soar through what's ahead of me: I must not cry. Mama had told me that crying isn't a good gesture of someone leaving. When tears started in my eyes, I didn't let her see my face again. Inside the plane, I was sobbing silently for leaving the people who were dearest to my heart.

I had mixed emotions: happy to reach my dream and sad for leaving behind the people I loved. *Did I give everybody a hug? I missed one! Vernon!* He could be there and was hiding again in the crowd like he did during my graduation ceremony. Oh Lord, I wished his face was the last I saw before I left.

The plane forwarded. Two flight attendants demonstrated how to use the emergency kit; checked seatbelts then settled to their respective seats.

The plane was speeding down the runway getting ready to take off. I prepared myself for my first plane ride. Outside scenery was flashing fast. The plane ascended. I gripped the armrests. My toes curled; my legs were as stiff as my neck. I felt a hollow inside my belly like I was about to throw up my guts. I closed my eyes and leaned back. I prayed: *Please Lord, support me with your strength; hold me as I fly in this morning wind.*

A great expanse of the city that had become a part of my life with Vernon came into view when I opened my eyes. In the glory of the morning, the city's panorama was breathtaking. I tried to look for the park down below where Vernon and I met for the last time and had an unpleasant argument. What if I gave in to Vernon's persuasion? Was it worth more than reaching for my dream?

I can't be happy with your achievements because deep within me, I felt I'm dying. If you really want to leave, then forget me completely . . .

How can I? How can I forget you, Vernon?

Casting him out of my thoughts wasn't even easy at all. I'd always remember him. It may be a pain in my heart but casting aside memories is quite hard. At times in my solitude, recollecting memories – whether sweet or bitter – is a beautiful thing to do.

The plane mounted to a higher level and took wings towards the Northern firmament across layers of cumuli clouds. Those weren't so different from the thick mist that Mama and I came across on our way to the villa when Grandpa had his second stroke. That time, I heard a faint roar of a plane and saw it emerging from behind the clouds looking like a tiny black bird in that great distance flying westward towards where I always thought America lies beyond. I dreamed of riding on it someday.

Dreams do come true; we just can't tell when.

Like a migrating swallow on a summer day, I was riding in the winds over a great ocean of bluish gray that looked teal trimmed with patches of white strips stretching wide as far as my eyes could see; as vast as my mother's dream for me.

When I was suffering the wrath of my mother's sibs, I had become like my mother who kept searching Vietnam by the eastern skies believing that my father was somewhere there in the land beneath. I searched for refuge on the opposite side to the furthest horizon where the sun had gone thinking that beneath the western skies, I would see the dream I had been searching. Mama said it was where I'd find America - too far away - half the distance that covers the world.

The engine's monotonous roaring was deafening. I forced out a yawn to ease my sense of hearing. Although I only had forty winks the previous night, I didn't feel sleepy. The excitement of riding a plane for the first time kept me awake.

I saw nothing now but an ocean of clouds. The pilot's voice speaking about altitude came over while my mind wandered back to the days when I'd resort to fantasizing about life in America to escape from the miseries hounding me.

The plane crossed in an hour the 360-mile distance between Cebu and Manila, the two biggest and most populated cities in my country. We landed at the Ninoy Aquino International Airport past noon about ten hours ahead of the schedule for my international flight. It was Mama's idea never to fall behind schedule because time is a very important element in a journey. I had to follow her words even if to me, being ahead of the schedule for ten hours sounded crazy. Arguing won't do any good; she'd always end up saying: "Mother knows best".

XXIX

The Lady in the Plane

"I'm also scared of flying," the lady said.
"But wherever you are, when God calls you,
You've got to follow for you can never say no."

Passengers were crowding the Manila airport terminal that early afternoon waiting for their respective flights to somewhere. I was thinking what fate I would be having when I'd be on my own in a far-away land. It could be like I was lost in the middle of a thick forest that showed no trail to follow.

After lunch, I found a copy of Philippine Inquirer on a bench left by a passenger in a hurry to board his plane. I read the newspaper until I was sleepy. I got a cup of coffee from a store nearby to get rid of my drowsiness and spent the rest of the hours musing about what could be happening that time back home - worrying about my mother, my grandmother, and thinking about Vernon. I thought of calling him; pride held me back.

Five hours had gone by since I came to the NAIA terminal. Twilight was coming. I thought of the sunset I used to watch in my hometown. I remembered the one I spent with Vernon -the most beautiful sunset I ever had watched in Sacandaya.

Evening came. Passengers in waiting were getting fewer as the night was getting deeper. We of the last batch were supposed to board by eleven but for some reason our plane from Vancouver arrived past midnight.

The boarding started.

I didn't realize how huge that PAL plane was until I stepped inside: It had three seat rows separated by two aisles. Seats were pre-assigned; mine was by the window on the right side second to the rearmost.

I was putting down my hand-carried things underneath the seat in front of me when a robust middle-aged lady stopped in the alley across from me caught my attention. Her mumbo jumbo about the size of the overhead compartment where she jammed her bags reminded me of Solvera's conjuration at the height of her fake trance.

The woman dropped herself on the aisle seat that looked small for her butt; she fitted anyway. Nobody was between us, so I could see her even if I didn't intend to. She wasn't wearing cosmetics - dowdy like my mother - couldn't care less about fashion. Strapping her seat belt, she kept on jabbering; maybe, just having a ritual which I found amusing. Our eyes met. She greeted me with a sweet wide smile and a nice hello.

"You're alone? Going where?"

"Raleigh," I replied.

"North Carolina? But your point of entry is L.A. New York is closer to Raleigh," the woman said with dilated eyes and gently nodded her head.

"I'd be late with my appointment if I fly via New York because of its schedule."

"Why, what's your appointment?"

"What's RDU?" I asked instead. "Somebody's meeting me there."

"It's the airport in Raleigh. Who's meeting you? Your fiancée...?"

She jolted me! Like Flora, the lady was extremely nosey.

"What fiancée?"

"Never mind; you may think I'm nosy, I'm not. So, from L.A, you'd take another plane to Raleigh. Is this your first time in going to America?"

She didn't see me nod; her eyes were on her shoulder bag from where she fished out a black rosary. She gave me a quick squint.

"I always have this whenever I travel. Praying frees me from fear."

"My Grandma does the same. By the way, Madame, how far is Raleigh from LA?"

"About five to six hours by plane. You change flights in Dallas then a brief stopover in Baltimore. Your next stop should already be Raleigh."

The lady said of my itinerary with familiarity; *had she been there?*

"I'd been to that state a couple of years ago," she answered the question I had in mind and chuckled, a prelude to what she was about to say. "I almost missed my flight on my first time going there." She sniggered off what she thought about. Missing a flight isn't funny to me. "Is this your first time to come to America?"

"Yes, my first time. Have you gone to Middletown?"

"Did you say Middleton?"

"Middletown."

"There's a Middleburg, a Middlesex and a Middleton in that state but never heard of Middletown. No, I don't know where that is. My cousin must have heard of it."

"Uh . . . you have a cousin in North Carolina . . ."

"In Wilmington; she'd been around the state like a fly with a red butt that couldn't stay long in one place. She's lucky to have found a man who follows her wishes. Her husband is luckier. He got a domestic helper and a bedmate for free." The lady followed her words with a boisterous laughter that invited the attention of the man across the aisle.

"Is your cousin a nurse?"

"A mail-order bride," she whispered aloud what was new to my ears. "It's the woman ordered by an American for a wife. It had been in the market like breast implants and nose-lifts. Now, this American was old and looked sickly. My cousin thought she'd soon be a rich widow but until now this husband of hers is still alive and kicking."

"How did she know him?" I asked on remembering Marissa who had gone to America on a fiancée visa but came back on a crate – black and blue and dead!

"Are you familiar with the Freedom Park in your city? My cousin was a flower vendor there. According to her, this old American tourist was passing by. Their eyes met. He winked at her, and she winked back. They introduced each other. After a conversation, he bought a bouquet of rosebuds right from her store and offered it to her as marriage proposal which she readily grabbed in a heartbeat. The man went back to America and not long after, my cousin got a fiancée visa and presto! Everything was woven into like a fairy tale."

"Wow! Like Cinderella."

"Yes, but this Prince Charming is as old as Cinderella's grandfather. He was the water boy of the Wright Brothers when they did their first flight in 1903. . ."

"Are you serious?"

"Just kidding. . . and you know what, North Carolina even manifested it in car plates. It says, 'First in Flight'."

"What's that supposed to mean?"

". . . so, no other state could claim it."

The lady was going out of topic, so I went back to asking about her cousin.

"Had your cousin been home?"

"She had, looking so proud of herself she thought she was Nancy Reagan. She didn't talk in our language but in English, a broken English with a very heavy accent. Now my cousin lives happily in Wilmington, North Carolina, United States of America," the lady said her words amusingly that made me laugh with her. She reacted with more laughter and the man over the aisle laughed with us so hard it turned into a whooping cough.

"Are you going there now?"

"No, but to San Diego. I have a daughter living in San Diego. She's a nurse. Are you? If you're not a mail-order bride, then you must be a nurse. Married?"

"Nahhh, still single. Is your daughter married?"

"She is. How old are you?"

"I just turned twenty-two . . ."

"You're still young. Don't be in a hurry. Marriage comes at the right time, you know. My daughter was also 22 when she came to

America in 1985; got married a year ago, and now has a son, you know. I'm going there again to be my grandson's nanny."

"What about her husband? I mean how's it having an American son-in-law?"

"Michael's a marine; a very nice black guy, but the first time we met, he just shook my hand," the lady said twitching her mouth.

"I've heard that Americans don't address their parents-in-law properly."

"Yes, they don't. Michael doesn't call me Mama but by my name, you know as if I were his contemporary. *Good morning, Berta. What're you cooking, Berta? Hey, big Berta, what's up?* And I'd answer him: *'Nothing's up, everything's down'*."

"American culture is very different from ours," I told the lady while freeing a good laugh; her words and gestures kept me in stitches.

"Our countrymen are the best husbands in the entire world. Well, American men are loving husbands too, you know. They're fond of loving and losing their wives."

"My Grandma said that in America, if a housewife died mysteriously, the prime suspect would always be the husband and most often than not, he did it!"

"Your granny was right. Have you heard of 'battered wives'? No, you haven't. But if there are 'battered wives' in America, there are also what they call deadly wives."

"What does that mean?"

"They'd kill their husbands for money, you know what I'm saying."

"Are you serious?"

"My dear, wake up. There are still lots of things you've got to know about America. That country may be rich and generous in giving out aides to the third world countries, you know, but would you believe that there are also beggars there?"

"What? Doesn't the government do something about it?"

"In America, you can live by your style. A few prefer to beg. I've heard that there was once a Filipino in California who earned a living by begging and was able to send his son to a medical school in the Philippines. You'll see these beggars at the highway entryways, displaying a cardboard that says: HELP the HUNGRY and the HOMELESS."

"How come they're homeless?"

"Most of these mendicants are ex-convicts, abandoned by their families or war veterans, you know, who couldn't find their families upon returning home from war."

"That's so sad. Why do Americans love to go to war?"

"Americans love war. They can smell where war's brewing. They were here in the forties, Korea in the fifties, Vietnam in the sixties and seventies, and now in Kuwait. They love guns. In America, guns are like toys which are sold in toy stores. My son-in-law loves guns; he's brave and not afraid of death. He's now in Kuwait looking for it." The lady laughed out her words and so did the man across the aisle.

All passengers had boarded in. A flight attendant locked the door while one came up for an emergency kit demonstration in our aisle. They checked the passengers' seatbelts then settled to their respective seats. The robust lady beside me began counting the beads of the rosary she had in her hand when the aircraft started to move, very gently at the start. Then the plane turned right, stopped at one point for a few seconds. Moments later, it taxied on the runway. Gaining momentum, gently it took off. The fear of flying crawled in my flesh when it ascended. I felt like throwing up my guts; my stomach seemed empty. I did my own prayer: *Dear Lord, you're guiding my destiny, please, let me follow you to safety.*

The plane tilted to its left and glided towards somewhere across the dark leaving below the dazzling city of Manila. *How long would it be before I'd see my country again?*

I dozed off and woke up to the plane's incessant hoarse roaring. Nonsensical thoughts came and went off my mind. What would be my life in America? Would I return home after I'm through with my contract? What if I meet somebody worth loving? Would that be enough to make me forget about coming back to the country where I belong? In the vast expanse of darkness, I lost count of the hours that passed. It never occurred in my mind that I would be cruising a long agonizing journey.

Turbulence, the robust lady would mumble the word whenever the plane rumbled. It was her third time riding a plane but still scared as I was. She said that if a basket hanging on a nail in the wall could fall, how much more of an airplane hanging in the sky holding on nothing. She followed her words with a shrug as if to say everything's in God's will. I responded with a dry smile to her hypothetical rationale, but the lady was laughing boisterously. Her plump figure rumbled as she laughed, yet fear was in her face when air pockets occurred.

"If God calls us, we can never refuse. We won't know anymore what happens next for dying is like falling to a dreamless sleep, uhm, forever. But I'd never thought about that. Just pray, young lady, pray whenever fear comes in."

She'd never think of dying moments but had just said it. She gave me goosebumps: my hair stood on end; my eyes watery. I felt relieved when she fell silent. Then she started to snore and the more I couldn't put myself to sleep while some passengers were nodding off in their seats unperturbed by the whirring sound of the plane's engine. I kept stretching my jaw to ease my deafness caused by the plane's continuous burring.

I would have thought the flight was endless if it had not been for the captain's announcement that we were arriving in LA by midnight. I was praying when the stewardess announced that we needed to adjust the time in our watch to something about nine hours back. Counting back the time, I realized we'd been hanging in the air for a solid thirteen hours! Gosh!

I caught a glimpse of a huge city glittering like a set of diamonds in the distance. The lady said it was the city of our destination. Los Angeles was ravishing – more dazzling than the city I left behind. I could hardly believe I was about to step down on the country that millions of Filipinos were dreaming to reach. Overwrought with an inexplicable kind of joy, I felt I was a bird perching on a steeple ready to soar across the skies. Mama's dream of a good life for me was coming to reality. I dreamed of it rather differently: The time was coming near when I could get back at them who treated me and my mother very unkindly.

XXX

Memoirs of my Grandmother

"Life is a continuing journey," Grandma said.
"Those wonderful moments that pass by
are simply turning into memories."

It was a little past midnight when the plane I was on was hovering over the city of Los Angeles. Bathed with extreme brightness that added radiance to its festival of fluid lights, it reminded me of the phenomenon that once in every score a super full moon comes and most likely during the month of June. Los Angeles that evening was sparkling like Grandma's necklace that was embellished with crimson rubies and yellow topazes – exquisiteness the British Mother Queen would adore.

On the eve of my departure, Grandma told me that after her death this very precious necklace would be gifted to the first grandchild to achieve a degree.

"I'd rather not have that necklace than not having you, Grandma."

"Humans aren't immortal. Yes, the journey of life starts at birth, but death ends it."

"Why think of that? Anxiety only drives you to depression. Forget about it for as you said, Life's too beautiful to be enjoyed to the fullest while being young."

"But I'm already old, Jinee and I couldn't stop the world from turning. Every day that passes by is one step closer to my grave," Grandma said. I watched her eyes as she looked around as if wondering how many years more, she'd be sleeping there alone in the room she had shared with Grandpa for 35 years.

"Life is in the heart and as you said, hearts don't grow old. You'd be as young as you are now when I return. I'll come back to take you and Mama to America and . . ."

". . . And what?" Grandma's voice turned cheerful. "What will we do in America?"

"Lots of things to do like visit the White House, see amusement parks . . ."

"My knees couldn't work anymore as they used to."

"What are wheelchairs for? Grandma, amusement parks are for all ages. We'll go around New York. And around LA, we'll visit Hollywood to see your movie idol in person! Isn't that exciting, Grandma?"

Grandma sniggered. "Clark Gable had been dead forever, Jinee."

"Well, there are lots of younger ones to choose from."

"You're trying to make my heart young again."

"Hearts don't grow old; you said that. See, you don't even look old at 53."

"*Cincuenta y tres?*" Grandma laughed heartily. "Jinee, I'm 73!"

"What? Look at yourself in the mirror." I nudged her closer to the dresser. She stared at her reflection. "Now, don't you think you look as if you're just my older sister?"

She forced a smile that implied more hurt than joy. "Time left its footprints on my skin," she said while fingering the brown spots in her face. Her eyes caught mine. "See these blotches? My skin had turned like crepe paper. Time is robbing off my looks – turning me old and ugly. When I was your age, people said I looked pretty like a rose."

"Of course, you couldn't be Miss Sacandaya if you were not. Grandma, you still look as pretty as a rose as on the first-time Grandpa laid his eyes on you."

"You're flattering me again. I'm susceptible to flattery."

"Didn't he tell you that you're as beautiful as an immortal song?"

Grandma looked again at herself in the mirror as if to study how those spots became eminent. She glanced at the necklace laid in her dresser. It stayed elegantly beautiful through the years. She shifted her gaze to the picture when she was at the prime of her youth. That was about half a century ago. As I gazed at it, I couldn't help but ask myself: *How do I look upon reaching Grandma's age?*

"A blossom won't stay beautiful forever. I was twenty, maybe 21, in that picture and never thought of how I would look after fifty years; never thought of growing old. I married at twenty-three. *'A newly bloomed pretty rose in the Torres Garden of Sacandaya that nobody among the town's bachelors dared to nip but the gentleman from the city named Aragon Zaragoza'*, the article said of me when my marriage engagement was announced."

"So, you married Grandpa in three years after knowing him --"

"Almost three yet people dubbed it as a whirlwind romance quite embarrassing that time, but Aragon was in a hurry for a church wedding; war was coming."

Grandma fell silent for a few seconds. A dainty smile formed on her face while staring at herself in the mirror, perhaps recollecting some memorable events she shared with my grandfather.

"Your Grandpa was a charming man. Many-a-lady fell for him, but I didn't give him any reason to go unfaithful to his vows."

"What was your secret?"

"It wasn't at all a secret," Grandma replied. She was sitting in front of the mirror staring at her reflection as if tracing back the years she shared with my grandfather.

"If men are polygamous in nature . . ."

"Who said that?" She asked impulsively like it was the first time she heard it.

"Somebody I don't know," was my instant response.

"A wife should take care of her husband's needs but shouldn't stop taking care of herself. I always made myself look nice to your grandpa's eyes as on the first time she saw me. Whenever we had misunderstandings, I kept my temper. I did whatever it takes to let him know that he was never wrong in choosing me his partner in life."

Mesmerized, I wondered if I could ever follow Grandma's footsteps. I let myself stay silent while waiting for her to continue her monologue about my grandfather. She then shifted her eyes to her framed picture.

"He was fond of surprising me. He had this blown-up and framed. This had been here since our first wedding anniversary, reminding me every morning when I faced the mirror that I was taking one step further from my youth every day that passed by."

"Okay, let's face it that youth had left you that far, but your beauty stayed. Grandpa was right. You're eternally beautiful, Grandma."

"The first time I met your grandpa was during our town fiesta in 1937. I was crowned Miss Sacandaya; he was my escort. He kept seeing me on Sundays since then."

"In 1937. Was it not in 1937 when the Second World War started?"

"People were talking about the possibility of the Second World War after Japan's attack in Nanking, China in 1937 a month before we had our town fiesta here. Young draftees were then in a hurry to get married. I tied knots with your grandfather in 1940 but war was still over a year away. Aragon continued his studies in the city. I stayed here for my job. One morning in December of 1941, Japan bombarded America's Pearl Harbor."

"Was that the start of the Second World War?"

She looked up at the ceiling as if listening to the droning of warplanes passing by. In her face, I perceived the sorrow and the fear, the grief and the pain my countrymen suffered in the hands of Japanese soldiers during the war.

"*Si estaba*. The Second World War erupted that year after Japan attacked America's Pearl Harbor. The following morning Japanese planes attacked Manila, then the city of Cebu. I lost contact with your grandfather and for the next three years, we didn't see each other. I placed his fate in the hands of God, but every day of those years I begged the Lord to let your grandfather return to me safe and sound."

Grandma took off her glasses. I reached for her a tissue and she dabbed her eyes dry. I drew her to my arms; she needed a hug for comfort.

"After this night, do you think we'll see each other again?"

It hurts to leave. Vernon said it hurts more seeing someone leaving. I felt both for grandma. I had intuitions she was leaving us in the not-so-distant future.

"Are you not happy for me, Grandma?"

"Of course, *yo estoy feliz*. But I wish I could pay you in dollars to have you stay and take care of me. When you're far away from me, will you always remember me?"

Grandma's words exhausted me. I felt guilty leaving her to serve Americans of her age when she herself needed me. But it was Mama's dream.

"I thought of staying to take care of you, but Mama assured me she'd always take care of you. You'll never be alone, Grandma . . ."

"*Vete a los Estados Unidos*. Pursue a dream that we never had in my time."

Grandma moved closer to the window and looked up at the skies.

Stars were blooming. They added radiance to the most beautiful night I ever had seen in my life that complimented my grandmother's smile when she beckoned me to her side.

"My mother said that for every person born on earth, a wishing star was also born in the sky for the newly born person to wish for. She pointed out which one was mine and although I didn't really know which one, I made three wishes: for good health and happiness, for success in life, and that I could take care of my parents when they grow old. That would be the time when they'd need me most. My third wish wasn't granted. I stopped wishing on my star ever since I lost my parents. Now, I'll wish on it again."

She held my hand tightly and closed her eyes: *I wish you'll be back to Sacandaya while I'm still alive.*

It hurts to leave but it hurts more to be left behind; I felt her pain. I stepped back when tears shimmered in my eyes. Grandma sensed I was about to cry; she turned around.

"I didn't mean to offend . . ."

"I just couldn't help it. I, myself don't know how long I would be away."

"Come here." I moved back to her side, and she placed an arm over my shoulder. "Point to me your star. Every night, I will wish upon it for your safe return."

"I don't have a wishing star in the sky, Grandma. I carry it with me, in my heart, so that I can wish upon it all the time wherever I am. Every day while I'm far away from you, I won't stop wishing on my star to see you again."

She drew my head closer to her breast I could almost hear her sighs. I wished she wasn't about to cry. I didn't want to see old people shedding tears of pain; they mustn't suffer any longer for they already had had so many miseries in life.

The moonless night had brightened up with more stars blooming like the flowers of *kamuning* and sparkling brighter now that evening had completely fallen. Grandma watched the night with nostalgia to the good old days in Sacandaya.

"The world is forever spinning; never would it return to what it had been."

"How was life back then?"

She took off her arm from my shoulder and let her eyes wander outside.

"When the world was younger, people seldom got sick; food was safe. These sicknesses we have now were unheard of. Grasses were evergreen; skies were glorious blue. A daybreak promised a wondrous day with the chirps of the birds and the blooming of blossoms. The winds from the hills smelt fresh, untarnished as the air we breathed. Sunrises were refreshing; sunsets were captivating. The kiss of twilight was soft as the sea breeze, tender as the touch of a baby's lips, sweet as a dewdrop on a petal of a rose on a summer day. How beautiful was the world back then! How glorious were those days!"

The wind that swept in was getting colder as the night went deeper.

Grandma took a brief respite, embraced herself and smiled. How joyful it was to see her smile. Shifting her eyes back to the outside, she inhaled the essence of the night.

"Deep in the night, young ladies were thrilled with the serenades of their suitors. Their songs drifted to silence as the night deepened and once again time sailed for another morning. Those wonderful moments had simply turned into memories."

"Did you have any other boyfriend before you met Grandpa?"

"Your Grandpa was the only man I got involved with. When I was a student, all I did was to study and pray."

"That was quite boring. Didn't you ever dream of reaching America?"

"Reaching for a dream isn't boring, but reaching for America was never dreamt of during my time. Once I asked my mother what was there beneath the western skies. She said it's where I'd find America, a far-away world so, I never dreamed of reaching for it."

"What did you dream to reach for?"

"To finish college and be a teacher . . ."

"As simple as that . . ."

"A teacher isn't a simple profession."

"Of course, it isn't but why not a nurse or a doctor or a lawyer?"

"Teaching is a highly respected profession. Teachers are helping parents mold their children into great achievers. I loved teaching as much as I have loved your grandfather."

"You're right, Grandma. Teachers are primarily important in a community as doctors are. Aside from Grandpa, did you have other suitors?"

"Yes, I had, but I only have one heart which was meant for your grandfather alone. He was the first and the last man I would have ever loved and married."

Grandma took out her wedding dress and proudly showed it to me. It was wrapped in plastic stocked with naphthalene balls to ward off bugs and molds. But it still bore elegance which I thought could have cut a big slice of Grandpa's savings.

"I wanted a simple one, but your grandpa insisted on one from Pining's Elegance, the most sophisticated dressmaker in the city at that time. Your mother didn't have a chance to wear this. Merriam refused to wear this saying it smelt ancient."

"But it still looks fresh . . . fresh as a daisy . . ."

"You'd be the next to wear this for Thelma decided to enter the nunnery. If possible, Jinee never marry an American; you'd end up a divorcee. Americans are fond of loving and losing wives. An American husband would leave you if you can't come up to his expectations. Because of culture differences, we couldn't reach their standard. Marry a Filipino who's as ideal as your grandfather was."

She returned the gown to her dresser and turned at me with a query look.

"What is it?" I asked, anticipating what she was going to say. I was right. She asked if I already have a boyfriend. I nodded but she could have perceived the prosaic look in my face; her brows were scowling when she asked what kind of a man my boyfriend was.

"As you'd have wanted it – he's just like what your Aragon Zaragoza was."

Like a star in the sky, excitement sparkled in her eyes.

"Then you're a lucky girl. The likes of your grandfather are one in a million. There's an old song that says: 'Once you have found him, never let him go'."

I stared at Grandma's face. She'd grown so much older. Time left more wrinkles and age spots on her face. She didn't deserve to be lied at her age.

"I'm sorry, Grandma - I lied about my boyfriend . . ."

"He doesn't have the qualities of your grandfather."

"It's not that. He broke up with me when I insisted going to America."

"Sorry to hear that. Come here . . ." She wrapped her arms around me and kissed my forehead. "It's alright, Jinee. He's not the only fish in the ocean."

"Yes, he is to me as Aragon Zaragoza was to you."

"You weren't made for each other. God has other plans for you . . ."

"Do you mean to say I might be staying a spinster in all my life?"

"Of course, no," Grandma replied and freed a little laugh. "There's a man who's meant only for you. He may not be like your former one but can be much better."

"But when does he come into my life? I'm getting old, Grandma. In another year, I'd be 23. Were you not at that age when you married Grandpa?"

"The ideal age for a woman to get married is at least 25."

"But I still must go to America. How many years more should I wait?"

"Pursue the dream your mother built. Marriage comes at the right time. I didn't want your mother to marry early. I, myself, didn't want to get married at that young age but war was brewing. Young draftees married their girlfriends before leaving for camp training. Your Grandpa was a reservist bound for active duty, so I agreed to tie the knot with him before the war could break out. But that was during my time. Your time now is very much different; you don't need to hurry. Enjoy your single blessedness. Now, wear a happy face because it's your birthday. Our visitors must have been waiting for you to come out. Go and meet your guests, blow your candles and make a wish."

The guests started leaving before midnight. We were the last ones to leave. Grandma walked with me to the end of the driveway. We stopped by the gate.

"*Vaya con Dios*. Will I be seeing you again?"

Grandma hugged me so tight as if that was the last time she could. In her eyes, I discerned lonesomeness. She released me from her arms, wiped her tears with her fingers then turned around and slowly moved away. She didn't look back anymore until she got back inside the house. Flora closed the door.

Uncle Ralph drove us home. While Mama was talking to her brother, I was recollecting the things that I and Grandma had talked about that night. She hinted at wanting me not to go abroad but at the same instance told me to follow my mother's dream. That put me in quandary like I was at a crossroad and didn't know which way to follow. But everything had been set for my trip early the next day and I must go for it. That even cost me losing Vernon.

We reached home past midnight. Uncle Ralph drove back after promising to return early in the morning to drive us to the city. I was fully confident that all my things were packed up; everything was going well. I went to bed musing if I had said goodbye to everyone. I did except my mother's mean siblings; they didn't like grandma's idea for holding a party for me and so, they ignored Grandma's invitation.

Then, I realized I had left Grandma's question unanswered.

In the Middle of Nowhere

All I thought back home was New York was America,
Los Angeles or San Francisco or Chicago
was America, but Middletown?

It was still dark when our plane landed at LAX terminal. The lady I conversed with in the plane was gone from my sight. I got confined at the terminal while waiting for my flight to Raleigh.

By daylights, boarding time came.

We were flying over the "Tar Heel State" before the sun had risen. I could see a panorama of luxuriant vegetation with patches of ponds and lakes. In my country, North Carolina isn't as popular as New York and California are.

Intense excitement was all over me when I disembarked at the RDU International. I was breathing American air – breathed it to my contentment. How I wanted to shout out to the world that finally I'm here; I had reached my dream.

I got my luggage and walked up to the waiting area where I saw a white guy holding a placard with my name. Presuming I was the person he was waiting for, he introduced himself as Brendan Cameron. There were two other Filipina nurses with him: Catherine Pascual was from the province of Albay and Dalisay Marasigan was from Pampanga; both nurses came via New York.

We rode on a minivan marked 'Saint Jude Nursing Care', going east along Interstate 40 and got out onto US 1 Highway passing by the city of Cary. In 1991, this highway was a two-lane road: leading north and heading south; we were going south.

I thought that in America I'd see more buildings, not trees; more glasses, not grass or weeds. The scenery we passed by wasn't much different from what we have in our country. The few houses in between corn and tobacco farms made me think the state of North Carolina was thinly populated - never thought about it. Houses were getting fewer and farther between as we got closer to Middletown. As its name implied, the town seemed in the middle of nowhere although not far-flung from the capital city of Raleigh.

We were directed to the only hotel in town; stayed there temporarily prepaid by SJNC with meals included. All expenditures were accounted, however.

Each of us got a thousand-dollar cash advance after two days and we moved to a small two-bedroom house, a walking distance from SJNC.

We reported for orientation the following day. Brendan Cameron was driving us to the facility when we started working regularly. We were getting off at three and had to walk back home because Brendan was working until five. A 'Jack of All Trades', the guy was working activity assistant, handyman, company driver - all rolled into one: Certified Nursing Assistant which didn't fit well to his build and talents and skills.

We were also working as CNAs while waiting for the results of our state board and were paid $7.50 an hour, about half of what was stipulated in our contract. It was too late to back out; we didn't know of any place to go and had nobody to depend on for help.

It wasn't easy bathing heavy grandmas and grandpas every day. Brendan said I'd be used to it after a week; I hadn't even after a month. I worried about the frail Catherine Pascual. Dalisay Marasigan was fine; she used to wrestle cattle on their family farm. The two ladies were working on the same shift in the same hall. I was partnered by a black lady who hardly smiled. We talked to each other rarely because most times, each one of us could hardly figure out what the other was saying.

Muscular pains were all over me, the same sore I felt after my first lessons in Tae Kwon Do. I'd drop myself dead on bed as soon as I reached our rented home. Quitting wasn't an option. Daly had a more fundamental problem. Mount Pinatubo, the volcano in my country that was dormant for five centuries, erupted and destroyed the family's farm and crops. I heard nothing from Cathy but her sobs.

Those 'sumo wrestlers' seemed to be getting heavier every day. I've heard that obesity has become a national epidemic in America. The government should pay attention in battling against obesity rather than minding the wars in foreign countries. Out of ten people I saw every day, six or seven of them were overweight. Someone said it was anabolism or catabolism, but I didn't think it was. With lots of bills to pay and taxes are high and many, people are always working and have no time to cook healthy food for themselves. Anyway, people could eat much more than what they pay in buffet restaurants which were all over the place and there's no law that prohibits overeating.

America is a country of freedom – had long been the sanctuary of people escaping poverty and political persecution from their own countries. We came here for the dollars, bearing in mind that wealth is easy to achieve in America; that life here was satisfying.

We weren't the first Filipinos to come to Middletown. I've heard there were three others before us, who moved to other states after getting their green cards without finishing their contracts. Nurses were paid higher in other states and were afforded with benevolence. In SJNC, nurses were paid $14 an hour doing undignified jobs such as wiping sagging and shrinking butts, washing diapers, and disposing garbage. In the later days, the extra-nice administrator was gradually taking off her mask. She made us work like we were felons and kept our passports to ensure about finishing our contract.

Vernon said it was hard to live and work in America where there are lots of racists. I dismissed his warning merely as his speculation. I thought of America as the most wonderful country to live in. Immigrants came here for the great opportunities the country offers. Nurses are in-demand and highly paid and that was my mother's foremost reason for wanting me to be a nurse and come to this country.

Following my mother's desire, I chose America over Vernon, not knowing that I would end up in a kind of town I never imagined existing. All I thought was that New York was the America, Los Angeles was the America or San Francisco or Chicago, but Middletown? Gosh!

After the many days of hard work in a facility, I was getting bored with my life but didn't tell Mama about it to keep her from worrying. In many times I was missing Vernon, I tried to get in touch with him hoping for a chance to have him back. From my mother, Laura got my home phone number and through her, I learned that Vernon was working on a construction project of his company in Manila. I got his address; sent him letters but none was ever responded. I realized later that I didn't write my return address in the envelopes; I lost the reason why I did it. So those letters would have ended up as dead letters in the Post Office if they didn't reach Vernon's hands. At one time I reached him by phone, he hung up. Realizing he was eluding me, I resigned to the thought that we were not really made for each other.

There were times I felt terribly homesick thinking of the great distance separating me from my homeland. It seemed worries and depressions were ongoing factors that made me continuously sick. I had had a miserable life, but I had the will to survive. If I weren't determined and strong enough to face miseries, I would've ended up 'dead ball'.

I tried to associate with the Americans, talk to them with efforts of getting rid of my accent: twitching my lips and opening my mouth wide to say my words clearly and yet how frustrating it was to hear some of these white Americans say 'I didn't understand what you're saying. Will you say that again?'. It seemed to tell me I didn't belong here. If I thought that Brendan Cameron, with his prowess, was misplaced to work as a CNA in the facility, so was I to work in this country.

America wasn't at all the paradise that I thought of. I could hardly believe it but as the lady on the plane had told me: there are also mendicants in America. And not only that; there are also vagrants and looters. Mass killings and protest demonstrations were ordinary happenings. Fate must have misdirected me, like how the mail carrier had stuffed our mailbox with letters that were neither for me nor for Daly or Cathy.

In less than a month, I learned the American way of greeting which I heard every day at work, like *"How are you doing?"* or *"How have you been?"* or *"How are you today?"* As usual, my reply to these greetings was always *"I'm fine, thank you."*

Lots of Americans are fond of using the phrase *"you know"* in the middle of their speeches. In many times during my conversations with them, I often heard them say, *"Do you know what I'm saying?"* or *"you know what I mean"*. In the long run, I learned how to riddle my speech with *"you know"* and *"ohms"* amid my *"blah-blah-blah"*. But my foreign accent was still there. For years, I didn't learn how to get rid of it.

I had lost my sense of belonging, yet I couldn't deny where I came from. My ancestors' footprints - the shape of my nose, the form of my eyes, and the texture of my hair and skin – were visible. If I'd have a transfigured nose, blue contact lenses, and a peroxide blonde hair and bleached skin, I would have had a funny look.

"When you're already there in America, don't ever change your ideals and your looks," Mama told me the day before I left. "Be proud of what you are; God made our race beautiful. The Lord made us the most special people in the world."

"I'm proud of what I am, of what I have. I never change anything on me, Mama . . ."

"You know, Jinee, 'though you're the only one I have, I'm so thankful to God for having you; you're worth a dozen more."

"I'm also glad for having a mother like you. You're the best in the world, Mama, you know that. You know how much I love you . . ."

"If only your father were here . . ."

"Can't you stop thinking about my father? If he were alive and living somewhere, do you think he worries about us? I don't think he does."

If my father were alive as Solvera said, why did he never come home? Was it because he already had another family that allowed him to forget us forever?

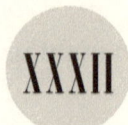

XXXII

Life is Worth Living

Kitty's lonesome days were now over.
She was like a dying plant that bounces
back to life after a thorough nourishment.

Middletown may be near to the capital city of Raleigh but far from its razzle-dazzle. The town seemed stagnant; its residents come and go like years forgone. It looked deserted on weekdays because most of its working population were commuting to the neighboring big cities.

An ideal place for the senior citizens, the breeze in Middletown was rejuvenating, its ambience heavenly. Only the tweets of the tiny birds, the honks of wild geese and the rustles of the trees dancing to the whistles of the wind could stir its celestial serenity.

Wal-Mart dominated the tiny shopping center. Nearby was Lowe's Foods. Between them stood side-by-side the Burger King and McDonald's. There was also the Dollar Tree store where prices of goods weren't higher than a dollar. No mall. There wasn't a movie theatre. There were no big houses but the abandoned white two-story building the neighboring people called the 'Plantation House' in the middle of a vast tobacco farm bordering the town limits.

Built during the pre-Lincoln era, owned by a white master with a ring of slaves, the 'Plantation House' had four concrete columns at the frontage. Its ancientness visualized to me the old Casa de Torres of my mother's ancestors. My great, great maternal grandparents didn't own slaves. Their farm workers and house helpers were fairly paid. Slavery was non-existent in my country during the Spanish era.

A quarter of a mile away from the plantation house was the SJNC and across the street, Jaycees Park sprawled. This was where people held picnics, hiked or jogged around.

Not all residents of SJNC were from Middletown. Those from nearby places always had visitors on weekends. The out-of-state residents were occasionally visited. A few that I referred to as *The Forgotten Ones* never had visitors in years.

One of those was Kitty Brown, the black woman who greeted us with a bitter smile the first time we came there. In her eyes, I saw the too-much desperation she had had like she was on the brink of giving up her life. She followed us with her hands clutched at her belly, bending at the waist imposing an awful posture.

Thinking she was hungry and needed coins for the vending machine, I took some quarters from my pocket, but when I turned around for her, she had walked away. My companions said she was just confused but the woman was completely sane. I talked to her later that day and it came to me that God might have sent me to this facility to console and take care of this poor soul.

Kitty had been a resident of this facility for a decade, and nobody ever paid her a visit since she was brought in by her daughter who never came back anymore. Her smile, despite her pains and frustration made me think she deserved someone's attention. I knew how painful it was to be all alone in the world with nobody to turn to and care for. Once she asked me if God had abandoned her, I told her that God sent me to take care of her. Kitty Brown was getting closer to me and in confidence, told me her life's story.

Kitty's daughter was born out of wedlock. After finishing high school and realizing her sleepy hometown couldn't give what she wanted in life, she left the town to chase dreams in other places. Kitty was too old and heavy for her to carry.

The old woman retired from her janitorial job due to physical disabilities. Afflicted with diabetes mellitus, her daughter brought her to SJNC and thereafter, that daughter was gone from Kitty's life. Her daughter's disappearance was a daily torture to her. I could hardly imagine how the sickly Kitty survived through the years. It reminded me of the days when pain and frustrations were daily occurrences to my mother. Kitty's world brightened up again when she found in me the kind of love she lost from her daughter.

Kitty was an expert knitter; learned the trade from her grandmother's master who ran a small knitting business in the '40s which little Kitty helped cope with orders when knitted shirts and shawls were in vogue.

I brought her yarns and needles to occupy her thoughts. Her first piece was a closely- knit pink shawl for me with my initials 'JXZ' woven in crimson red at the back. I often wore it at work that fall and winter and spread words about Kitty's exceptional skill. Soon, she was getting busy with orders so that she didn't have time anymore to ponder over the miseries she'd gone through. Like a dying plant, she bounced back after thorough nourishment. Thereon, Kitty Brown didn't cry anymore for her lost daughter.

One morning, a fair-skinned woman came looking for her. It took Kitty a long time to recognize her; she broke down when she did. There was a long tight hugging. Both were sobbing but no one uttered a word until Kitty announced to me that her daughter had finally returned. How beautiful it was to witness a mother seeing her daughter after a decade of not knowing her whereabouts.

"You ran away from me but God brung you back! Where have you been, my child?"

"Far from here, Mamma. I didn't run away from you. I searched for a good life for both of us. Hard days are over. I promise I won't ever leave no more."

"I never stopped storming the gates of Heaven begging for your safe return. Let me look at you." Kitty let her daughter turn around. "You look very different now; a full-grown woman," Kitty said laughing. "How have you been?"

How sweet Kitty's question was. I wanted to take off my eyes from them for I didn't want to look like crazy - crying and laughing out the joy I had in my heart on those moments I was witnessing their meeting. Yet, I was nailed where I stood and let my tears stream down my face while I laughed carelessly. It proved to me again that crying and laughing were human emotions not far different from each other.

"Oh, Mamma . . . it should be me asking you of how you've been."

"God's taking care of me . . ."

Kitty was a housekeeper at an inn in the east coast where four drunken white American truckers, staying for a night, raped her. That one-time incident bore her a child. The government ignored her pleas to run after the perpetrators and her own people suggested abortion especially that her child, according to her relatives, was sired by a "honky". But she could feel the heartbeat of the fetus in her womb, begging to spare its life. *My baby has the right to be born. Why should my child suffer for others' mistakes?*

God wanted her to be a mother. She accepted it despite humiliations. It could be her last chance to motherhood. Preferring to be cast out from the society she'd been with than aborting the life in her womb, Kitty Brown ran away from her family, from her community, from her hometown. She eventually got a janitorial job in a state agency while on the family way, then gave birth to a daughter, named her Tabitha and suffered countless miseries in raising her. Yet, Tabitha left her mother when she was eighteen and that pained Kitty miserably more than what she'd been through while carrying this daughter in her womb.

"I never had forgotten you, Mamma. I left you in the hands of the Lord."

"For many years, I longed to hear your voice again."

"I did too. I missed those times when you'd ask me if I wasn't hungry; when you told me not to lapse hunger for it would result in bad health. I always had your words, Mamma. While I was far from you . . ."

"Shush. Tell me no more of it. It's enough that you've come back."

"No, Mamma. You must know you were never wrong in giving me life. I left to chase my dreams and I got them – got them for you - to lift you from indigence, to end your sufferings and I won't ever leave no more without you. I'm taking you home."

"But I'm home. This place had been my home . . ."

"Home is where your family is. Come with us; wherever Duane and I go."

"Duane? Who's this Duane?"

"He's a nice white. He told me to find you thinking I abandoned you. No, I would never do that to you, Mamma. I searched for a good life for the two of us. Please forgive."

"What's there to regret? You're back with your dreams fulfilled. If you only told me of your plans, I wouldn't have thought otherwise." Kitty Brown chuckled. "I never thought of making you suffer the same life I had. Now, where's this Duane?"

"He's in the car with your granddaughters."

"What!" And Kitty laughed again, harder this time. I never saw her laugh that loud. "I have grandchildren. I have a family!" She turned to me. "Did you hear that, Jinee?"

I shouted back, "I heard it: You've got a family!"

Kitty ran inside the facility and came back with a bag of personal belongings. I walked with her to the door. We stopped to see her daughter walking towards us.

"Tabitha, the Lord sent someone's daughter to take care of me while you were gone," Kitty Brown declared.

"Words aren't enough to pay for your kindness," Tabitha said and gave me a hug.

"I found my lost daughter, but I'm losing my newfound one. I want you to know how precious you are to me, Jinee. Will I ever see you again?" Kitty asked the question that reminded me of my grandmother the night I left her. I responded with a smile that spoke more of sadness than joy.

"We'll find each other someday. I pray for that day to come soon, Mother Brown."

She stared at me like how my mother did the moment I was about to leave for America. The anguish in Kitty's eyes seemed to ask me if I'd let her go.

"Don't cry, Miss Kitty. Tears aren't good sign for a wonderful journey."

She poured her sadness on my shoulder. Then she walked away from me; didn't look back anymore. I watched Kitty and her daughter disappear into the whirring car.

Gradually, the car moved down to the ramp. In the next moments, it was gone onto the highway, and I was left there weeping. Nobody saw me weep for losing Kitty Brown.

Serving Kitty Brown for some time was like I was serving my own grandmother. I was sad the old woman had left me but at the same time, overjoyed by the sudden turn of events in her life. Indeed, Life's full of surprises; they come when they are least expected.

XXXIII

Letters from Home

On the day I expected
Vernon's answer I sent Grandma
a letter and she wrote back; Vernon never did.

I got a letter from my mother once a month updating me on the latest happenings back home. I learned that my cousin Madel had been a fiesta queen. Because of high pride, Aunt Merriam loaned her house to the local bank to make Madel win. Now she's three months behind the payment of her house mortgage. Worse is that Uncle Fidel abandoned Aunt Merriam for a younger woman from the city. My mean aunt had been so poor that Mama asked if I could send financial aid to her sister.

"That would be the last thing I'd do with my money. Your sister deserves my spite."

"Don't be so proud of your money. God is only lending it to you temporarily and He can get it back in any way at any time. Forgive those who'd mistreated us. It comes easy if you recall unpleasant memories without anger. In forgiving you'd find peace."

It's easy to forgive but memories, no matter how bitter, cannot easily be forgotten. I didn't have my mother's kindness. With what I'd been through, I'd become a windfall in the storm - blown away far from its mother tree. I told my mother I wasn't ready to forgive. She hung up on me. But as I couldn't have reasons to harbor a grudge against the person who took care of me through thick and thin, I wrote her my apology. Mama wrote back.

My dear daughter,

Thanks for the money you sent. The current exchange rate per dollar is twenty-five pesos. I let your Aunt Merriam use the whole amount. Imagine the immense help you've given her. She's so happy and thankful to you for the big help. My friends said I'm so lucky to have a daughter, and a kind one at that, working in America.

Talking of friends, Laura won't be returning to Saudi anymore. Life there has got worse. She plans to come to America and is thinking of taking the CGFNS. Laura mentioned Vernon Vergel. If he's your boyfriend, that's fine with me. Honestly, I don't want you to marry an American; he'll just dump you for another woman if you can't come up with his expectations. In America, marriage is a very easy thing to break; in our culture, family is of utmost importance.

Your Grandma is now forgetful and hard of hearing. Will you be here for me when I get old? You're the only one I have. Your grandma has five children, yet it's only me who takes care of her. If only Thelma and Ralph were here.

However, your aunt's attitude is getting better while Benito is as mean as ever. He believes that Ralph and Thelma are sending Mama financial help and Benito is suspecting me of keeping the money, even spreading his words to my co-teachers. He's suspicious because it's what he had been doing like cheating our mother with the income from her farm. You know that Madel had been a 'Queen' in our town fiesta. Your Aunt Merriam's pride was so high that she loaned her house to make Madel win. Now she couldn't pay the mortgage.

Don't ever miss your Sunday obligations. Always pray. Write to Laura. Help her find a job in America. Take care.

Mama

I heard that life in Saudi Arabia for foreign workers was getting worse. When I got a chance to talk to Laura, I asked if she wanted to work in America and how I could help her. Instead, Laura asked me to help Vernon rebuild his dreams.

Reconciliation with Vernon seemed impossible. I had written to him twice, but he never replied. I shouldn't have been writing to him anymore, but then, I did!

Dear Vernon,

Hope everything is fine with you. You're right. There are lots of bills and taxes to pay in America but it's still better than in any other place in the world although prejudice still exists in some parts. An old male resident, who was a war veteran and had experienced severe maltreatment from Japanese soldiers during the Bataan Death March, told me pointblank I must not work here. He thought I was Japanese. Like the law which extenuates guilt because of mental illness, I forgave the old white man for insulting me.

I'm serving old Americans while my own old folks there are on their own. Grandma hinted at the irony on the eve of my departure, but everything was already set. I was ready to go, challenged by what Aunt Merriam said, that I would never achieve success in my lifetime for I'm a daughter of misfortune.

I hope you'll find someone who can give you what you really need in life.

Sincerely,
Jinee

I also sent Grandma a letter that day. Grandma wrote me back; Vernon never did.

Dearest Jinny,

Many years had passed and every day that passes brings me closer to my end. I'm afraid of the coming of nights I might not wake up anymore. I hope we see each other before I'm gone.

How's life there? Your Mama said that in the state of North Carolina racial discrimination still exists in some cities. Just be nice and humble, and you'll make lots of friends.

Careful with the food you eat. I've heard that many additives are added in the food Americans eat. Additives may cause cancer and heart problems. Your health is your own responsibility.

Don't forget your prayers. God is always taking care of those who call Him for help. Also, keep your wishing star shining in your heart. Always feed it with wishes.

Your abuela,
Lola Marga

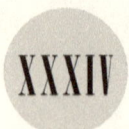

Impressions

I pictured Cathy as sweet and demure,
Daly as loose and wild, but I was wrong.
I haven't been good with first impressions.

One Sunday when my mother called, I told her that I passed the state board. Mama screamed out her excitement so loud her neighbors might have thought something bad happened to her. I heard the building up of noise caused by the neighbors rushing in.

"Jinee made it! My daughter made it! Saint Therese granted my prayers!"

"See . . . blood is thicker than water!" A woman commented. "Did you say that this Saint Therese was the aunt of your great grandmother?"

"That was Saint Therese of Avila." Mama's voice spluttered. "What I mean here is Saint Therese of Little Flowers. If you do the nine-day novena for her and during that period receive flowers from somebody, I mean from anybody, it means your petition is granted. Saint Therese didn't fail me."

Addressing me, she asked if I remembered Mr. Solano.

"Of course," I replied. "He's now retired and a widower. What about him?"

"He gave me flowers," Mama said and laughed, "three red roses one afternoon right after I came out of the church. I thought he was asking me to give those to Miss Cruzes, but he said those were for me! I should've rejected them if not for my novena to St. Therese. Those flowers were really meant for me," Mama said freeing out a loud laugh.

"Is the old man courting you? You're too old for that."

"He is, I'm not."

"Yet, you accepted his roses," I said with a chuckle.

"Yes, the flowers, not him. I told the old man to find someone his age."

"Mama, that was rude."

"I should have said it in a nicer way. I told him that he and Miss Cruzes would make a very wonderful pair. Do you remember Via?"

"Who could ever forget Miss Via? Mama, were you making fun of them?"

"No, I was doing them favor. They were 'on' long time ago, but Mr. Solano's family wasn't in favor of Miss Via because she was . . . hmmm, never mind."

"Mama . . . are you gossiping? People might hear you."

"They know about it. I'm just telling you that I can't trade you for a husband."

"I know. You know what, Mama? I have secured my green card, and I can get you and grandma soon but don't tell anybody about this. Pride is a sin."

"I couldn't help it; you're my pride and joy. God will forgive me for being proud of you. The Lord is an understanding being."

"For sure the Lord is forgiving you. He's a kind God, didn't you say so?"

Mama came from a religious fanatic family. Since the Spanish era, the reenactment of Christ's Last Supper every Lenten season was always held at Casa de Torres. Grandma inherited the patriarchal home and so this tradition. Excessively religious, she urged Mama to do a nine-day novena to San Antonio de Padua, the patron saint of lost things when she learned that my father was missing in Vietnam. Yet my father was never found. I believe the saint was only good at finding lost things and not lost people or Mama's faith wasn't strong enough to compel the saint.

Daly passed the board on her second try. As full-pledged nurses our hourly wages were doubled but disposing garbage and washing disposable diapers were still part of our responsibilities. Moor couldn't tell American nurses to do the job. They'd shout back at her: *"Do it yourself!"*

Cathy flunked again. One day, she was gone. She left a note that she was safe and was considering fixed marriage with a white guy from Pinehurst to acquire citizenship even if she had a fiancé back home. I was wrong to think of Cathy as sweet and demure, Daly as loose and wild. My first impressions weren't always lasting.

I got the job of assistant nursing director; Daly was the Medication Administration Records Officer. We were made to sign another three-year contract, which we did outright. I hated to be fooled by someone who wasn't better than me intellectually but there I was, like a mouse baited into a trap. We could only laugh at our weakness to resist the half-a- dollar raise to our hourly wage.

Daly and I knew each other better. I learned that she never had a suitor yet probably because of her tomboyish behavior.

I often saw Brendan Cameron in Daly's station. He told me of how he felt about her and asked about the Filipino way of courtship.

The first time Brendan paid my friend a visit, it took her a long time to fix herself. I also had that sensation on my first time with Vernon. Poor Mama didn't know I had a boyfriend while in college. She kept on reminding me that having a boyfriend could ruin my studies, but I regarded my relationship with Vernon with a positive trait: having a boyfriend was an inspiration, not destruction.

Daly and I were of the same age, but I was more mature in deciding things. When Brendan started dating her, I imposed house rules so that at one time when Brendan brought Daly home after midnight, I gave them a whip of my tongue. I didn't let them in until I heard Brendan's apology. They abided by my house rules since then.

The promise of Mrs. Hax to raise our salaries never came to pass. Daly decided to do a part time job; her take home pay wasn't enough for she was paying a monthly amortization of her car and was sending her three half-brothers to college. Also, her parents needed much financial help because their farm was heavily damaged with the eruption of Mount Pinatubo in 1991, a few days after we left for America.

Mama's loan was fully paid so I sent money to her and Grandma irregularly. I was apprehensive over my mother being alone at home.

I urged her to return to the Villa especially that Grandma needed constant attention.

"Take care of Grandma but don't leave your job if you don't want to. It keeps you from getting bored, and besides you need that long-distance walk from Grandma's house to school and back. Don't worry about financial matters; I'll take care of that."

I told Mama that in America finding money was as easy as picking wild guavas in the peripheries. I lied. I was working hard and seldom took a day off to save for the rainy days, but I could only save a little in a month for the so-many taxes and bills to pay.

XXXV

Sizing up Bandy Moor

Don't judge a book by its cover, goes the saying, but that wasn't applicable at all to Bandy Moor, whose attitude was as undesirable as her looks.

"*Do not judge a book by its cover*", goes the adage, but that didn't hold true with the despicable Bandy Moor. That woman's attitude was bad as her looks. She was the kind of supervisor that could make an easy job hard. I found it out after a month of working with her.

Bandy Moor had a daughter born out of wedlock. Her live-in partner left her for good before this daughter was born. She wore black dresses since then and only discarded them after getting acquainted with Joe Bower who was managing the afternoon shift of a convenience store. Bandy Moor used to spend some nights there sharing with Joe Bower nonsense things over a bottle or two of Budweiser and a pack of red Marlboro.

Joe was a family man, yet Bandy Moor kept flirting with him. Then Brendan Cameron walked into her life. Knowing he was looking for a job, she offered him to work for any available job in the facility which the young guy unhesitatingly grabbed.

Rumors had it that Miss Moor was always in a good mood if Brendan was around; the gaga had a special feeling for the guy, thirty years her junior. Everybody who heard this rumor couldn't help but sneer.

Bandy Moor was widely known in the facility as a mean inconsiderate person. Everybody knew how unapproachable the woman was, but at one time when I saw her talking to Brendan, I asked if she could give me a two-day off. As I said, she was a person who was hard to please and deal with, but perhaps to impress Brendan, she granted my request without further ado.

How would Miss Moor react on knowing that Brendan and Daly were dating?

One day, Bandy Moor asked me if we could talk privately in her office. I hunched we could be talking about Brendan and Daly. She must have heard it already that Brendan often came to our apartment.

"How are you today, Miss Zaragoza?"

"I'm pretty good, Miss Moor, hope you are . . ."

"Sure, I am but there are times that I can't help getting upset, you know, because of the problems we have here. No doubt you'd be doing the same thing if you were in my shoes. Don't you think so, Miss Zaragoza?"

"Of course, I would, Miss Moor."

"You know, I appreciate it better if you just call me by my first name."

"Same here, Bandy. Just call me Jinee – it's music to my ear, you know."

"Glad to know that Jinee. Please have a seat and if you care for something, maybe tea or coffee . . ."

The subtlety of the woman gave me discomfort that we'd end up our conversation with something displeasing.

"Thanks, I'm fine. Do we have any important matter to be discussed?"

"Yes, Sugar. Don't you have any problem with your work schedule?"

How she addressed me was kind of tickly. She never had called me like that.

"No, Bandy. We don't have a problem with that. Why did you ask?"

"I'm thinking of transferring you and Miss Marasigan to the afternoon shift because the newly hired nurses from India will be working in the morning."

"Is that so? Wouldn't it be fair if you consider seniority?"

"I wanted to but as you see, Brendan is car-pooling them in the morning while those poor ladies don't have cars to use."

"That's understandable, but suppose you transfer Brendan to the afternoon shift . . ."

"That's not possible. Brendan, you know, is badly needed here in the morning."

I knew my suggestion was unacceptable to her for she'd be seeing her crush lesser. I was highly suspicious that Brendan's constant coming to our apartment after working hours had come to her knowledge and that was the probable cause of the rescheduling.

"There's no other way then."

"Sorry, honey, I only want to be fair to everybody, you know."

"Then there's nothing we can do if that's the case."

I walked out of her room and was about to close the door behind me when she said something prickling. It was what I suspected about.

"Speaking of Brendan, is everything okay between you and him? It's none of my business, but I'm just curious, you know. . ."

"What do you mean?"

"Do you often go out together?

I saw in her the avidity to know the real score between Brendan and me or she'd turn darn crazy; when jealousy swells up in the heart, it damages the brain.

"We've never been together alone. Daly was always with us."

"That's awful. Three's a company, you know . . ."

"But Daly won't go out with him without a chaperone."

She chuckled. "So, it's Daly."

"Is it surprising?"

Bandy Moor laughed out loud.

"I thought it was you! Can we talk more about Daly and Brendan," Miss Moor said inviting me back inside. I propelled our conversation with questions.

"Is there something wrong? Is Brendan already married? Is . . .?"

"Brendan's a bachelor but he already had promised himself to somebody."

My curiosity blazed.

"Who's this somebody?"

Bandy Moor declared to my face without batting an eyelash: "Me".

"What . . .?" I jerked; I thought a mouse just crawled over my feet.

"Well, Jinee, please don't mention this to Brendan but would you believe that he proposed marriage to me recently?"

"Is that so . . .?" *Oh, Lord, have mercy; something's wrong with this poor soul.*

Bandy Moor nodded her head in an impulse; how I wanted to laugh out loud because I had known her to be a pathological liar.

"Yes, Jinee. You may not believe it, but it's true. Brendan proposed marriage to me. I thought he was just kidding, but . . ."

"You should have accepted it right away! Or did you?"

"I told him to give me time to think it over."

Was I stupid to believe this liar? Brendan Cameron isn't the kind who'd go after matrons, let alone ugly matrons with bumpy curves.

"And what had become of Joe Bower?"

"Joe's a friend, you know, with a shoulder to cry on."

"But how could Brendan be so unfair to you and Daly?"

"I don't know what's going on in his head, but I've learned to love the guy."

"I must tell Daly right away so that she'd stop seeing Brendan."

I went out of the room about to burst out with laughter. It was a perfect time to hurry home. Daly was off that day and Brendan must be paying her a visit that time.

Excited to see Brendan and break him the story, I kept my strides faster and I reached home panting. Yes, there was Brendan's car in the driveway! I was laughing hard as soon as Daly opened me the door.

"What's up? What happened?" Daly asked and laughed with me not knowing what I laughed about.

"Guess what . . . I talked to Brendan's fiancée today."

"Brendan's fiancée . . .?" Daly looked back at Brendan. "Did you hear that?"

"What? How could I have a fiancée if . . ." Brendan was a bit amused thinking I was kidding and forced himself to laugh.

"Well . . . that's what she told me!" I replied and gave Brendan a wink.

"Who told you?" Brendan asked; this time he looked blushed.

"Come on, buddy . . . you better admit it."

Somewhat wanting to laugh out, he asked me again. "Who's this woman?"

"Does the name Bandy Moor ring a bell?"

"What!" Brendan laughed so hard, freeing out this time his impeded emotions.

"You better tell the truth," Daly told Brendan with a stern expression in her face.

"That woman has the nerve to say; oh, she's having her fantasy again."

"Seriously, what's really the score between you and . . .?"

"Zero," Brendan replied hastily to Daly's question.

"Brendan Cameron beware of the wrath of a jilted lover," Daly said.

"What's this, an interrogation?"

"No, an interview," I replied.

"There's nothing really to talk about between me and Bandy Moor . . ."

"She won't have the nerve to say that if nothing is happening between . . ."

"Okay. I will tell you the entire story how I came to know that woman."

XXXVI

The Apple of Discord

With Bandy Moor openly showing her fondness
for Brendan Cameron, nobody anymore dared
to flirt with the cynosure of Moor's affection.

The focus of Bandy Moor's affection was an average-looking guy with a muscular build that made him look unlikely to work as Certified Nursing Assistant. He had finished high school when his parents separated, leaving him confused about what to do with his life. He came to Middletown upon the invitation of an uncle to work as merchandiser at Lowe's Foods his uncle managed, and studied Mechanical Engineering at NCSU, where he met Michael J. Young, a sports aficionado who was the school's popular hockey star. With all probabilities, Young made Cameron a star athlete.

Brendan Cameron was an army reservist when the Gulf War broke out in 1991. He would have been drafted to help run a prison in Kuwait was it not for a shoulder injury he suffered while playing ice hockey. He took the sport with a big dream of winning back the

Stanley Cup for the Carolina Hurricanes and hoped to end up playing with his favorite Ron Francis against the great Wayne Gretzky of Canada who captained the Edmonton Oilers when the team grabbed the Stanley Cup from the NY Islanders in 1988.

After finishing college, Brendan participated in an invitational hockey tournament where he was injured in a scrimmage. His mother wanted him home, but he had become stubborn to follow either his mother's or father's advice – an attitude that affected him with their separation. Brendan stayed in Middletown, submitted for chiropractic care and while recuperating, looked for a job that didn't require so much lifting.

One late night, Brendan took a pack of Heineken from the gas station that Joe Bower minded and went out of the store without checking out the liquor at the counter. Joe apprehended him. Brendan apologized for forgetfulness likely occurred on him due to the recent major surgery he underwent for a fractured shoulder. His deficiency with thiamine might have caused such an unlikely incident.

Not buying his explanations, Joe Bower tried calling a cop. Bandy Moor, who had witnessed the incident, interfered and told Joe that she could vouch to the guy's credibility as a good and honest person.

"It was amazing of her to save a total stranger. As if that wasn't enough, she offered me a job on knowing I was looking for one."

"And so, you were beholden to her," said Daly.

"It's like scratch my back and I'll scratch yours," I added with a jeer. "Miss Moor had a crush on Joe Bower, but the man she adored ignored her feelings. Then you came to the scene in your desperate situation. Miss Moor used it to wake up Joe's feelings and offered you a job to keep you always in touch. In the long run, you got her attention. Now, Bandy Moor's aware of your interest in Daly. To discourage Daly from going on with you, she exaggerated your relationship with her. Do I make sense?"

"She never hinted for something in return of her kindness . . ."

"She didn't, but she expected. What's behind that unbelievable kindness of a grass widow? If she had the nerve to tell me you're having special relationships with her, what's keeping her not to tell anybody?"

"That's ridiculous! I'd never been intimate with her. The attention I was giving her was a payback for the debt of gratitude I owed."

"She misconstrued it as insinuations," I told him.

"And I'm not totally dependent on her help. I have a degree to bank on."

"Precisely, Brendan," Daly commented.

"This is just a temporary job while I'm recuperating. What were those years of arduous work in college if I'd end up doing what a high school dropout would?"

"There you go," I said. "Find a job that compensates for what you'd been through in college. The longer you stay here, the more your life goes wasted."

Brendan had been evading Moor since then. He quit working for SJNC on the pretense he was preparing for the forthcoming board exams.

The working situation in the facility got worse. The old hag turned tougher to deal with. Her attitude towards me and Daly worsened. She was back to wearing the usual poker face I'd been familiar with and was finding ways again to make our job harder.

The tense between me and Moor had reached its boiling point. One day in early September of 1996, when Hurricane Fran was about to rough up the Tar Heel state, I had a confrontation with the evil woman.

"Brendan apprehended me before he left. How did he know?"

". . . Know what?"

". . . What I told you about."

"I didn't tell him anything but Daly," I denied.

"He mentioned your name."

She spoke with circumspection yet the anger in the tone of her voice was eminent, and it was brewing in her face; the glabella between her tattooed brows wrinkled while on the lookout of anybody approaching. She cast a sharp look at me once more before she slipped into her office and slammed the door before my face.

I didn't believe Brendan dropped my name. I knew the kind of person Brendan was as much as I knew Bandy Moor. They weren't of the same ilk, but if Brendan Cameron really did it, I was glad it made the evil Moor very upset.

XXXVII

The Collision

With winter season getting closer,
the atmosphere around was getting colder.
Between me and Bandy Moor, heat was brewing up.

As it had been at Christmastime, relatives back in my country were expecting presents from us abroad. The SJNC neither granted us a raise nor overtime. For extra income, I did a part-time job at the Laurels of Chatham some few miles away from Middletown. Daly had been working there for a year, which Moor was aware of and reprimanded Daly about it only after Brendan left the facility.

Daly, a submissive person, needed my help. I crashed into the administrator's office when I learned that the evil administrator was confronting her.

"I have a meeting here!" Bandy Moor barked at me.

"If this is about our part-time job, I'm a part of this meeting!"

"Very well, then! I demand that you quit your other job immediately. You must always be available to work on your off days when somebody couldn't."

"It's within our discretion on what to do with our day off . . . Right?"

"You better get out of here! You're not called to this meeting, bastard!"

"Look who's talking. Between the two of us, you are the bastard one for there wouldn't be bastard children if there are no bastard mothers."

Infuriated, Bandy Moor spread words that she was going to fire me. I barged again into her office one morning when she had a meeting with two nursing aides.

"It's you again! Where are your manners? Don't you know how to knock?" Bandy Moor screamed immediately as soon as I came in.

"You're asking for manners? Where are yours? Well, it's too late for you to embarrass me. Mrs. Hax already had my irrevocable resignation long before you bragged that you're firing me; everybody in this facility already knew about it."

"Very well, your resignation means peace and order will reign here once again!"

"It's your lack of moral integrity that brought chaos here! Don't be dumb about it!"

"Get out of here! Go back to where you came from," Bandy Moor yelled. "I hate the sight of you immigrants swarming all over America!"

"Immigrants are the backbones of America's economy. We help this country's industry move. Without us immigrants, this facility had long been doomed."

"Whatever! I hate to see you here a minute longer. Get out of my facility!"

"Your facility?" I said and followed it with mocking laughter. "It's Mrs. Hax who owns this, Big Head. You were just a nursing aide who was good at doing suck ups to get promoted. I don't need to do that. I graduated RN-BSN Summa Cum Laude. And you! What are your credentials? By the way, where in the world your ancestors came from?"

The woman screamed out curses and about to slap me, but I caught her hand, squeezed it hard and pushed her back. I was about to get out of the room when I saw her raging towards me. I met her with a sharp kick on her tummy that slammed her robust body down to the floor, her face crumbled in pain. The two nursing aides, who seemed amused by what I did, helped her stand up.

"You must pay for this! for what you did! I'll see you in court!"

"Then see you in court, Paper Tiger. Before the eyes of the jury, I'll shred you to pieces," I said and wriggled my middle finger close to her face.

I went out of her office feeling well accomplished for trampling down a mighty oak. The nursing aides spread words of what had happened. When I walked out of the facility later that day, my co-workers cheered for me: Bravo! Well done!

I received a subpoena from the County Courthouse, but the case was subsequently dismissed; the two lady witnesses, who resigned from their jobs, were willing to testify in my favor. What I did heightened more Bandy Moor's blood pressure. I got the sadistic trait of Aunt Merriam: enjoying one's misery.

The clash I had with the tigress was a blessing in disguise. I was released six-month short from my three-year contract. I got back my passport. The company lawyer told Bandy Moor that she had no right to keep it.

In a week after resigning, I got a letter from SJNC's newly hired lawyer ordering me to finish the six months short of my contract or face deportation that would bar me to reenter the country within ten years. That was the idea of the evil Moor. A vindictive woman as her name suggested, she wanted me to come back so she could carry her vengeance on me and hold it as warning to nurses who thought of leaving without finishing their contracts. I laughed off the lawyer's threat on the strength of the owner's acceptance of my resignation. Nothing happened with the threat and the more I urged my colleagues to find a job where they'd be treated with respect and dignity.

After I resigned from SJNC, Daly followed and both of us worked full time in the Laurels of Chatham to finish our contract of two years. My resignation turned precedent; the Indian nurses moved out. The census was reducing. Later that year, SJNC was ordered closed for the many deficiencies noted by the North Carolina Health Survey.

The closure order did not take effect, however. The St. Jude Nursing Care only changed its name to St. Jude of North Carolina – same dog with a new collar. On its reopening, it was advertised as under a 'new management', but Bandy Moor was still the administrator. Very well, she was the same ugly ogress who was forever arrogant, unfeeling, bossy and officious. I've heard she had been sent to attend seminar-training on human resources and business management, but I doubt if she were reformed. As the saying goes: It's easy to lead a horse to the water, but it's hard to make the horse drink.

XXXVIII

An Interlude

I was ready to return home.
It had been so many years
since I left my hometown.

Father James heaved a deep sigh
when I paused for seconds to have a quick gulp of water from the bottle
in my hand. He stood up and stretched. I thought he was tired and
bored listening to my story.

"Sorry, Father James . . . I'm afraid I wasted your time . . ."

"No, you did not, my dear. I'm enjoying it," the priest replied.
"Come with me to the office. Let's have a coffee break."

The lady office clerk was about to close the office when we came
in. On the priest's request, she prepared each of us a cup of hot regular
coffee before she took off.

"So, you resigned," said the priest after taking a sip from his cup.

"I did two weeks ago. Temporarily, I'm working with the Laurels
of Chatham to keep myself busy, but I applied in another facility in
Raleigh and got the job. I just have finished my orientation. I'll start
working regularly in two weeks as soon as I return."

"Return from where . . . You've got other plans?"

"I'm going to visit my country, Father James. It's been seven years."

"Then you must. Seven years is quite a long time . . ."

"My mother had been wishing I could come home as soon as possible. And my grandmother - she's very old now and sickly. Grandma needs me much more than the residents at the SJNC do."

"That's nice of you, Jinee. To spend some of your time with your family is your moral obligation. So, when are you leaving?"

"I'm scheduled to fly direct Philippines tomorrow morning."

"That's too soon. Are you coming back? Oh yes, you said you are."

"I already got my citizenship here and so I'm coming back for sure and this time with my mother and hopefully also with my grandmother. My promise to let them see America has been long overdue."

"Well, I can only wish you a happy trip. Take care of yourself."

"You, too. I appreciate talking with you."

"Come and see me again."

"Yes, of course."

"And I expect you'd tell me whatever happens in your vacation."

"It will be a long story again from me. I will write the details, Father James."

Time flies swiftly like a swallow. My vacation was over and the first person I was anxious to see again on my return was Father James O'Brian. I tried to see him in his parish the day following my arrival, but the good priest had gone to Ireland; his mother died. In a later month, I learned that the good priest was back to America but got a new assignment out of state. I thought I'd never see him again, but then I heard after five years that he was back in the parish of Saint Mary Magdalene.

Father James O'Brian looked back when I opened the door. He was kneeling on a pew close to the altar but must have done praying; it was way past three in the afternoon. He rested on a bench and watched me approaching.

Closer, his face beamed. The cascading black hair that gave an oval outline to my face, my eyes that are shaped like almonds, and this tiny black mole above the left corner of my mouth could have made him remember me so well.

"Jin?" the priest uttered my name in a surprise tone; he wasn't sure if it was me.

"Yes, Father James, it's me Jin Xeres Zaragoza!" I responded delightfully. The priest stood up and gave me a tight welcome hug.

"Welcome back! So, you're sporting the same name after all those years."

"Yes, I'm still using the same name, but I got married."

"You got married! Is that why you didn't care to see me anymore?"

"You were the first one I thought of seeing, but you were no longer around. Somebody told me that you went to your hometown for the death of your mother."

"She died of old age," said he priest as I took a seat on the bench next to his.

"I'm sorry to hear that. I know how it feels losing a loved one."

"Thanks, Jinee. It's time for her to rest, anyway. Well, this isn't a good time to talk about sad stories. Let's change the topic."

"I tried to see you as soon as I came back, but I heard you were no longer in this parish, that you were assigned out of state. I thought I won't be seeing you anymore."

"And I thought you were not coming back anymore. So, you got married."

"Yes, Father James, I was."

"To Vernon Vergel . . ."

"I lost my chance reconciling with Vernon. He had become a priest."

"Is that so? Then, who's the lucky guy?"

"I got married to an American I came to know in the facility where I worked on my return. He was the grandson of a resident there, but it wasn't for real; not a legal one per our agreement. Then during the attack of the World Trade Center, I lost him."

"You mean he died there . . ."

"No, I lost him to another woman."

"What really had happened?"

"It's another long story, Father James."

"I know, but I'm ready to listen for it."

XXXIX

A Sunset in Sacandaya

Some of its townsfolk may have come and gone forever,
but the town's fascinating sunset kept
on coming and going.

I came back to my homeland after seven years living in America. I should have done it earlier had Bandy Moor submitted our papers when the INS needed them; she did it only after we signed another three-year contract, and it was already late. The facility lawyer supported her demands. No one was there for us.

I didn't see any familiar face on my arrival at the NAIA. I heard screams of names, none was mine; shouts and screeches but not for me. *How could Mama forget my coming?*

Surprisingly, I saw Laura. I didn't expect to see her there. It had been a decade since we saw each other. We hugged and laughed out loud and didn't even care we were inviting other people's attention.

"I wouldn't have recognized you if it weren't of the mole in your face."

"It's been over a decade since then. Mama had told me in a letter that you're not going back to Saudi Arabia. Are you still interested to come to America?"

"Of course, my friend, I am. But, first, I must pass the CGFNS, right?"

"I'm sure you will make it. Are you married?"

Laura twitched her lips and whispered, "I don't even have a boyfriend!"

"From High School, circa '86, it seems we're the only ones left by the train."

"Marriage isn't a thing to rush into unless another world war is coming," Laura said with a chuckle. "By the way, about Vernon . . ."

I brushed aside what Laura was about to say.

"Are you here to meet somebody?"

"It's you that I'm here for," Laura said cheerfully. "Well, about Vernon . . ."

"But I didn't inform you of my coming. Is Mama with you?"

"She couldn't come. Your grandmother passed away last night."

Laura's answer was a heavy yoke that was suddenly dumped on my shoulders; my heart swelled; my knees wobbled. I was on the brink of falling when Laura helped me to a bench. She apologized for telling me about the grieving news without forewarning.

The last time Grandma and I had a talk, she hinted how badly she needed me because she was getting sickly, but I was serving instead American people of her age. My promise to bring her to America would never be fulfilled anymore.

We took a taxi to Sacandaya; arrived there by sunset. It was still the same beautiful sunset I used to watch back then. After dropping off Laura at their house, I proceeded to the town's outskirts. I was over excited to see again Villa Zaragoza but shuddered at the thought I wouldn't be seeing how my grandma would welcome me home.

Villa Zaragoza's landscape was no longer as beautiful as when Santiago was around. Gone were the roses that Grandma planted at the entrance to the villa in her belief that flowers blooming by the gateway would drive evil spirits away. The *kamunggay* trees that Grandpa planted in the backyard had all grown sturdy. Grandma used to tell me that this leafy vegetable, which is known as horse radish to Filipinos, is very nutritious. When I was spending a day at the villa, I always had for lunch a bowl of soup of fresh anchovies heavily spiced with crushed ginger, red tomato, and green onion, soured with green tamarind fruit and flavored with lemon grasses and of course, *kamunggay* leaves. Flora called it '*sinigang*'. I had to eat it to please my *abuela*. It amused her to see beads of sweat all over my face for the soup I was slurping was hot and very spicy.

Some trees were gone: the cacao trees, the star apples, sugar apples, and the *sereguellas* we threw stones at when its fruits had turned from green to burgundy. Storms felled all those fruit trees around the vicinity but the old tamarind tree which bore fruits that Flora used for her *sinigang*.

Like the trees, some people I knew were gone. Mr. Solano died of asthma. Miss Cruzes was found dead at her home. She was living alone and was suffering from sleep apnea. No one was there to help when her breathing temporarily stopped.

After Miss Via's demise, people talked about her being a comfort woman during the Japanese occupation. When Japan made reparations, many claimed to have been comfort women, but Miss Via was too embarrassed to come out even if many have known it already. In my time they had stopped talking about it, so it was strange to me for I never heard that before. People only talked about it again after her death. Flora said it was the reason why Via Cruzes never got married despite her good looks. Folks had said that she was meant to suffer in life because of her name.

I saw how happy my mother was seeing me home. Overwhelmed, she drew back to crying and so did I. How beautiful it was to cry the moment I felt her hand caressing my face, her knuckles rub my chin like how she did when I was little. I missed those times when she stroked my hair with her fingers; when she prepared a glass of milk for me and boned a fish in my plate; when she got mad because I refused to eat vegetables. She must have yearned to have me back to her side and wished I remained a child to cuddle forever, but I had grown older, and Fate had taken me away from her arms.

I saw in my mother the years that drifted away. The graying hair, the wrinkles and brown spots in her face and arms were visible. How was she without me? How was it when she rose from nightmares on some nights and realized I was no longer at her side?

"You're getting prettier," Flora shut off my reverie. I told her she'd have a wonderful present for the compliments. She appreciated it with a good laugh and gave me a peck on my cheek she never had done before.

Flora helped carry my luggage upstairs. The same energetic woman despite her age, she was a happy-go-lucky person except that time when Aunt Merriam slapped her in suspecting she connived with us in hiding the Persian lamp; she wept. It hurt me seeing her weep. I wondered if she ever thought of wishing for a life a little better than being a housemaid. Did she ever have at least one suitor in her lifetime? There must be one moment too many she spent dreaming of getting married and having a world of her own.

"Flora would never get married," my very superstitious grandmother once said when I asked her if the old housemaid had ever been married. In several times, Grandma said that if a woman sings before the stoves while cooking, no man will ever want to marry her. In many times, Grandma heard and saw Flora doing it. That was another superstitious belief that Grandma believed to be true.

XL

Forgiving is Sublime

I ended up yielding to my mother's wishes,
and realized that if vengeance is sweet,
forgiving is sweeter and sublime.

Villa Zaragoza was crowded with people paying their last respects to my grandmother. I recognized most of the older ones; a few from the younger generations. Some weren't so familiar to me, yet all looked surprised and happy seeing me after the many years I was away from their eyes.

The things in the living room were in the same arrangements that Aunt Thelma did: the seats, the piano, the closet which had Grandpa's wine collections, and the antique grandfather clock was still standing in the same corner endlessly chiming the time away. However, the Persian lamp was forever gone. I presumed my uncle still had it.

Grandma's beige casket was in the family room over a catafalque waist high from the floor and a foot apart from the wall that was draped with grandma's favorite burgundy blanket. I was about to view Grandma's remains when I recognized the person standing beside it - the person whose heart was as stolid as a stone. She looked so dolorous while viewing her mother's remains. I knew how this hyper-hypocrite could scream in her mother's face when she was still alive. What was she showing off when everybody in town knew what kind of a daughter she'd been?

I'll never forget how she yelled at our faces with all temerity that morning she drove us out of Villa Zaragoza notwithstanding my mother's plea. She was always unreasonably mad at my mother and at me for being my mother's daughter. I still could picture the anger in her eyes when she told me how her blood boils at the sight of my face. But I don't remember having done anything that upset her except perhaps when I had a fight with her daughter and when I tried to have a glass of Grandma's fresh milk for breakfast.

I abhorred seeing her face again. I turned around when I saw my mother gesturing to me to approach her sister.

For all I care.

I headed to Grandma's room with my mother following behind me.

"Listen!" Mama yelled immediately after she had closed the door.

"What's there to listen for?" I snarled back as I opened a window. A whiff of fresh air breezed in. It eased out a little the pain in my chest.

"For the sake of your grandmother's soul, let bygones be bygones."

Ignoring my mother's words, I was forced to divert my attention to the scenery outside, trying to find what difference the years made while I was away; nothing much. There was the belfry of the church my grandma's Spanish ancestors built a century ago. From there, I heard the angelus faintly. I should have said my prayer but hatred, infused with resentment, was overpowering me. I waited a long time for the day when I could carry out my retributions; now that I had the chance, I was baffled. A war was brewing between my mind and my heart: on toughness and softness; for retaliations or reconciliations.

I slid both sides of the window panels and flipped the awnings to give the land wind a wide passage. The air was soothing – fresh as an early sunless morning, sweet and soft as Grandma's smile, tender as the kisses of my mother, gentle as her words of kindness. I breathed it deep to loosen the tense gripping me.

"Even to God, no sin is ever unforgivable."

Mama was talking close behind me saying her words almost in a whisper, cool and gentle as the evening breeze that was puffing the tears off my face.

"Your aunt is paying for her mistakes," she continued talking when she didn't hear any response from me. "She regrets those wrongdoings. Your uncle Fidel left her for another woman. She's out of job, and her house is repossessed by the bank."

"Those weren't enough; she deserves to suffer more."

"It's evil to wish misfortunes to a person."

"It depends on the kind of person."

"How high and mighty you'd become!" Mama hollered but failed to perturb me. When I stayed silent, she shouted again: "Is that what you've learned living in America? Answer me! Is this what you've learned in America?"

"America's nothing to do with this. Your sister willed for this day to happen!"

I voiced out my words as softly as I could but was not able to hold my tears. Mama must have seen them. She fell silent for a moment. When she spoke again, her voice toned down. Softly, she gripped my arms.

"You forgot God's Beatitudes . . . the good thoughts that I had impressed on you."

"I have them reserved for people who are unlike your sister."

"She won't be asking for your help anymore . . ."

I turned around to face her.

"Then why are you telling me these things, Mama?" I had my voice raised.

"Because she needs your forgiveness; it helps unload her burden . . ."

"What about the burden she put on my shoulders? Did she ever care about it?"

"I got more than you had suffered," Mama said her words with softness. "But I managed to get off from my miseries. If you're generous in forgiving, you'd forget your pain. Your heart has lots of forgiveness to spare and to release one won't cost you anything. It wouldn't cost you anything."

I turned my back on her. "It cost much of my pride."

Her voice rose again. "How much is your pride?"

"Priceless, Mama, priceless."

"Everybody makes mistakes. Don't you ever ask God to forgive your sins?"

"Yes, I do. Every day, I ask God to forgive me of my debts. I forgive those who trespassed against me, but they must ask for it."

"Forgiveness doesn't need to be asked," Mama said gently and choppily as she did when I was little and could hardly understand what she was talking about.

"Without your sister's contrition, she isn't worth forgiving."

"It's because of your pride; that's a cardinal sin."

"It's not about pride but principles."

The world outside was turning dimmer. Little stars were blooming like white flowerets hanging loosely in the sky. They flashed upon me memoirs of my childhood – bitter and sweet – in a framed canvass hanging in the recess of my thoughts. I remembered those with fondness ended with tears leaving me with self-pity. Needing a salve, I invited the Holy Spirit to enlighten my mind and touch my heart with softness that would come easy for me to forgive. There's nobility in forgiving. My mother said it doesn't need to be asked. I wanted to be adamant to her persuasions, yet I was woven into her likeness – forbearing and forgiving. I was the same obsequious daughter that I'd been.

The breeze was cold. I inhaled it to sooth the anger raging within me. I told Mama of the miseries I had had that made me dauntless and daring. I felt her hands on my shoulders drawing me closer like wanting to cuddle me as she used to when I was in trouble. When I was little, oftentimes she'd say she saw in my eyes the light of her life.

"For many years I let myself believe that you're still here with me although a world apart. I wish I never had that dream for you, to keep you within my touch but I must go for it. I built that dream for you alone for mine is coming to end."

Mama's voice was breaking. I gripped her arm as I used to when she held me close to hear her sighs. Traces of her kisses on my forehead had remained imprinted there even if I was far away from home. Her words of guidance were part of my daily prayers. Mama had known me well for I came from her flesh; she had searched for my soul.

Stars were flickering; their faint lights burning brighter as darkness draped the sky - the same thing that Grandma watched with me on the eve of my departure for America. Nothing much was changed in Sacandaya as viewed from Villa Zaragoza except for the street lamps which yellowish radiance cast away a certain degree of darkness enveloping the town. It relieved me from something agonizing like how my mother warded off the anger that gripped my thoughts. Once I tried to find a way to free myself from these shackles of hatred, I failed. The desire for vengeance was just too strong to be resisted.

"After a long absence, aren't you delighted to see again your hometown?"

"Of course, I do, Mama. I missed watching these stars."

"Does America have the same stars as we have in our sky?"

She tried to amuse me with her childish question reminding me of the same kind of questions I asked when I was little. I turned around and gave her the smile which she described as engaging. She wrapped me in her arms. Close to her bosoms, I heard her heartbeat. What a lovely moment to cry.

"By the way, had your grandma told you why she named you Jin Xeres?"

"I don't think she had; I don't remember she had . . ."

Mama started her account with a brief glance at me then shifted her eyes outside.

"It was raining hard, the first after a year of drought, when you were baptized. Believing that it was the Roman goddess of Agriculture that brought in the rain, your grandmother suggested Ceres for your name with C changed to X to signify the tenth of June you were born. Jin is for June, and it means Golden Star in Chinese. Your Grandma said that for every child born on earth, a star in the sky was also born for him or her to wish for. Did I tell you which one is yours? Yes, I did. Now, point to me your star and I'll wish upon it for your safe return to America."

"I'm not returning to America, Mama. I must stay here to take care of you."

"You have your own life to lead. If you pursue something in the future, you must leave something in the past."

"You need me more than America does. If I go back, you must come with me."

"America is not in Manila; not in Mindanao," Mama forced herself to laugh. "It's a thousand dreams away from here. You know the drill in going there, the lengthy line at the embassy, the anguish of waiting for your call."

"I can wait again if I need to . . ."

"You must return to America. Whether you like it or not America owns you now."

"Nobody owns me, but you, Mama."

She gave me an eyeful and asked, "How about Vernon Vergel?"

I never thought she would mention the name at that moment. Finally, long after I had lost Vernon Vergel, I was able to tell my mother that I had a boyfriend while still in my college studies.

"Are you not mad?" I asked when she laughed carelessly.

"Why should I get mad? I'd been in that situation. If I didn't want you to get involved with boys, it was a precaution. You had to have something to be afraid about for you were at the age when falling in love was too exciting to resist."

"Mama! You're the 'bestest' mother in the whole wide world!" Mama laughed; amused at the childishness of my language which I used to say of her when I was little.

That instance, we heard the arrival of Uncle Ralph and Aunt Thelma. They were late again as they were when Grandpa died. Mama told me to stay while she got out to meet her younger siblings; she would surprise them with my presence, she said.

Alone in the room, I studied in details Grandma's touch in fixing her room. The curtains in cream were made of marquisette with floral spots in deep red and velvety as the bedspread that was covered with beige sheets of cotton hemmed with thick satin in burgundy. Her framed picture at the top of her dresser stood in situ. Her very elegant wedding dress, untouched by human hands for six decades except perhaps hers and mine, still looked exquisite although it had lost its radiant whiteness.

My sight blurred with tears thinking I didn't even get to say goodbye to the only person who would come to save me at times I was in trouble - a gesture Mama never showed for fear Aunt Merriam would rant accusing her of spoiling me.

I lay down in Grandma's bed and stretched - my soles reaching flat on the floor, my eyes roving on the ceiling while I recollected memories that grandma's mind had painted there. I'm fond of reminiscence. I got it from my grandmother.

I must have fallen asleep. I woke up to the voices gathering around me. What met my eyes was a congregation of the Zaragozas. Somehow, it gave me a brief nice feeling seeing them there all around. There was Uncle Benito, the least I expected, with his wife and his two boys who had grown taller than him. There was Madel; she had turned prettier than before. There was my mother and Uncle Ralph and Aunt Thelma and even Flora, but I didn't see Aunt Merriam. It was then I felt somebody's touch on my feet. Nimbly, I stood up and saw my mean aunt disgracefully kneeling on the floor before me.

Payback time had come. In many times I wished for that moment to come; have waited long for it, but I lost the guts to retaliate when my time came. I realized I could never do a bit of what she easily did to me in those years I was growing up.

Against my conscience, I helped her stand, but I responded awkwardly, rather superficially when she hugged me; that was the very first time I felt her warmth.

"Thelma told me you saved my house. Words of thanks, Jinee, aren't enough."

What Aunt Merriam said came out very surprising because it wasn't what I wanted to happen. For a long time, I had wanted to get back at my mean aunt, but Aunt Thelma mistook my words and that resulted in a different situation. I failed to get the chance and it only made me suffer more the pain of her atrocities for I found it hard to say harsh words towards her which she didn't hesitate to lash on my mother and me when we were briefly staying at the villa.

'Mama asked me to help you' was all I could say.

Aunt Merriam beckoned my mother to her arms; the very first time I saw them hugging. How joyful to see them getting along with each other, the same joy that beamed in Diep's face at the sight of the gift I gave; the kind of joy I felt on seeing Laura after a decade of not seeing her. What Grandma had been wishing to happen had come but ironically, it was her death that brought her children to reconciliation.

I identified myself with my cousins. They had become nice to me this time especially since I brought them chocolates they never had tried yet. In them, I saw how fast the years have flown. We had all grown mature and cultured; no more running or stumbling around, which gave Flora headaches; no more chanting of my being 'a bamboo offspring'. We recollected those days without remorse but laughter.

Life's a journey from birth to death which distance between is measured by years. Grandma reached her end at 80, about a score after Grandpa died. Her remains were interred Sunday morning conferred with the same rites my grandfather had.

In the evening, the Zaragoza siblings discussed the partition of their properties. Mama, who had plans of coming to America, entrusted her share to Aunt Merriam. Uncle Ralph, who was having a mission to Africa, did the same and so did Aunt Thelma. Uncle Benito didn't let Aunt Merriam get his share even if they were close siblings. He was greedy for money. I was little when I witnessed how this son of my grandmother, a physician at that, made his mother pay for the medical samples he got free from pharmaceutical companies. I told Uncle Ralph about it. He confronted his brother, who told him in return that I was inventing stories. Uncle Benito might have denied it, but what I had witnessed would stay forever in my mind.

My grandparents spent a fortune for Uncle Benito's medical studies but got no 'returns of investment'. There's an old saying that goes: 'he who never cares to look back where he came from will never reach his destination'. Uncle Benito had his karma. He wasn't doing well with his profession while his contemporaries had become medical specialists. He had become alcoholic, a chain-smoker and a heavy gambler. He lost his prestige and people lost their confidence in him. Not long after he opened his medical clinic, he was forced to close it.

When I was alone with my mother, she handed me my father's letter; she must have read it a thousand times already. When I was little, I was curious about what my father had written there, but Mama had told me not to read any letter that wasn't for me.

It was the first time I was privileged to touch a thing that bore my father's handprints. There wasn't a return address in the envelope. Per Brendan Cameron, letters from war shouldn't bear return address for security reasons. I decided not to open the letter and gave it back to my mother. It might have something not good for me to know.

Grandpa had promised to give the ancestral house to my mother, but Mama declined it thereafter. As agreed by everybody, Aunt Thelma, being the youngest in the family, had it in her name. Flora, who was stuck with the Zaragozas for lifetime and had no family of her own would be taking care of the villa for Aunt Thelma was about to enter the nunnery as a Dominican sister.

Grandma entrusted to Aunt Merriam the necklace she promised me. Aunt Merriam handed it to me in the morning I was going back to America. With regards to her house, I never thought of redeeming it for her. It was in auction, and I bought it with the help of Aunt Thelma, being a lawyer, but asked her to hold it confidential. She might have thought I did it to help her elder sister. What I planned was to banish Aunt Merriam from there to let her feel the angst of being ejected.

Pronto! Aunt Merriam yelled at my mother's face the day she took away from us the dignity to live. How delightful it was to shoo her out of her own home. It could have been her day of reckoning, but it didn't come out like that. My desire to get back at them who treated me unkindly failed; I failed to carry out my plans of getting back at my mother's mean siblings, ended up yielding to what my mother wished, and realizing that if vengeance is sweet, forgiving is sweeter and sublime.

XLI

To Have Loved and Lost

How I wanted to touch his face
to satisfy my longing for him that moment,
but showing how much I love him was already forbidden.

Laura was with me on my way
back to Manila. She was to take the CGFNS review at Becky Grajo's.
While up in the air, we talked about our days back in college. She
mentioned Vernon. *How is he now?* Brooding over how the man had
been gave me enthusiasm to see him again.

We were staying at the Pope Pious XII Center in Ermita. Enrolling
Laura at Becky Grajo's Review School packed our day.

At the cafeteria later in the evening, while Laura was ordering
our dinner at the counter, I walked to a table behind where a man in
black suit was sitting. He was busy reading, a bible perhaps, so didn't
notice me coming. At Laura's approach, he turned around. He caught
my breath: it was Vernon!

Excitement rose instantly within me but only for a moment; disillusion drained it down when I realized what had become of him. I froze like I was suddenly doused with a pail of ice water. I could only embrace myself to hide the chill that enwrapped me. I was the same demure person he'd known – uninfluenced by western culture and ideas.

"How have you been?" I hardly uttered my words; hardly heard my voice.

He stretched out his hand. I was a bit shaky when I reached for it while gazing at those eyes I had loved to stare at. I guess he was shaky too. The bobbling in his throat behind the stiff white band seemed to say there was something more he wanted to tell me. I thought of crying out my disappointments on Laura's shoulder, but she was gone, leaving me like a child groping for something to hold on in the dark. It was when I realized I wasn't yet ready to face Vernon Vergel. I wanted to laugh; wanted to cry. I wanted him to know what was going inside me that moment; I wished he felt it.

"I've known you as a 'Christ-ter' catholic; you go to church only on Christmas day and on Easter Sunday," I jested with a little chuckle to give him a jump-start, to show I wasn't really distressed, yet Vernon knew it. He handed me a tissue to wipe off my tears.

"God made me holy by receiving sacraments. Maybe, I was born to serve the church as you were to America. When you left, I was in quandary of what to do. I quit my job and had come here in Manila in search of whatever would make me forget you."

I could hardly believe what had become of him; could only imagine touching his face and kissing his eyes. Those were now forbidden. Following his other destination, the farther he drifted away from me and the more I turned desolate. What could have happened if I chose him over my dream of coming to America?

"Why settle to that vocation? God must have created somebody for you alone."

"If the Lord had someone for me, He wouldn't have told me to follow Him."

I rested my elbows on the table; my forehead on my hands shielding my eyes from his gaze that seemed melting me. I should have given up on his obsession. If only there was a more resentful word to say than saying sorry.

"God granted you good things that many had wished for, yet you wasted them . . ."

"I gave them back to God. Many of us were called but I was one of the few who were chosen. From being nominal, I turned devoted. Sacrifices gave me strong Faith which is now my greatest gift from Him. I bear no regrets."

"I regretted everything. I went to America and served its people, even failed to serve my own grandmother. I followed my dream and have lost you forever."

"You won't get anything for nothing. You've got to sacrifice to achieve a dream like you could never be a saint without suffering. We can't choose our destiny. The Lord writes the script for us to follow. If He made you a nurse to take care of the sickly, He made me an engineer to build up Faith in humanity."

"This shouldn't have happened had I given in to your wishes. You just didn't know how much I tried to find ways to find you after you left me in the park."

"I didn't leave you completely. I was there watching you from the dark. I saw you leaving when it started to rain, but I stayed there until past midnight."

"You stayed in the rain?"

"I scorned myself for not letting you follow your dreams."

"So, it wasn't for fear that being far apart would severe our relationships . . ."

"I was being selfish for wanting to confine you all the time within my reach."

"How I wished your face would be the last one I see before I leave for America."

"I was there at the airport. I was there to tell you I was ready to wait for your return whenever you could, but I didn't have the guts to show myself because of fear of so many things; didn't have the nerve to race with time even if I knew you were drifting with it."

"And it wasn't fair at all."

"I was afraid my presence would spoil your departure."

"Did you ever think how much I wanted to see you those moments?"

"I realized I should've shown myself, but it was your boarding time. I watched you walk up to the plane until it lifted off and drifted you away. And I was left there all alone, like a boy lost in the chaos, watching the plane until it got lost from my sight."

"You told me to stop thinking of you to make it easier for me to bear, but that wasn't easy at all. I would've thought that everything was fine if you only showed up."

"I was confused. After you left, I was lost for some time until I reached a crossroad. I asked the Holy Spirit of the path to take. I asked the Lord to give me strength to be faithful if He wanted me to serve in His vineyard. I realized then I'm destined to serve God in all my life. I wouldn't have achieved it if you've given up your dream of going to America."

"If you only answered my letters; if you didn't hang up when I called ..."

"If I got any of those, I'd never have ignored them. In fact, I've been waiting for your call, but none came until that day you were about to leave."

"If you only waited for my return ..."

"For more than a thousand days I did but you never came home until I found myself inside a church asking God if He were calling me. He was calling me I heard Him say."

"There are things we'd realize weren't the right things to do when we regret about it."

"We're destined to be what we are now. In the Lord's shadow, I found refuge."

His eyes were turning red and watery. At the first drops of his tears, I thought I had stopped breathing. I pressed my hands hard against my lips to prevent them from quivering. I didn't look at Vernon's eyes anymore. Seeing his tears only made me suffer more.

"I'll see you tomorrow," I heard him whisper. "We aren't ready for this moment, Jinee. This couldn't be a repetition of the last time we were with each other."

I closed my eyes for it hurt so much to watch him go, yet I heard his footsteps falling in the pavement, fading. In the next moments they were gone, completely gone. I prayed to hear his footfalls coming back in ten seconds, twenty seconds until a minute had passed. Vernon didn't come back anymore.

What's happening to me? I blamed it on my desire to get back at people who treated me unkindly but, being an obeisant daughter, I failed to carry out vengeance and ended up like my mother – forbearing and forgiving.

I prepared to leave early the following morning although my flight back to America was still in the late afternoon. Laura woke up to the little noises I made.

"Vernon called to see you at lunch," Laura told me while I was packing up.

"What for . . .?"

"I'm sorry for what transpired. I thought that by letting you see each other you'd find a chance to change your respective directions in life."

It is said that love is lovelier the second time around. While I was in America, I didn't let myself fall in love again with any other man hoping for reconciliation with Vernon. Then I found out there wasn't a second time anymore for us. I totally lost him, and I suffered more pain. I may not be afraid to love again - fall in love with another man. But how could Fate be uncertain? Life follows a certain pattern. What's happening at present has correlations with what had been in the past. Life has its own chain reaction. The cycle of life goes on and on like a Ferris wheel and people are but its riders; they come and go as years come and pass by.

At the airport, I kept thinking whether it was right for me to leave without waiting for Vernon. I thought of going back but then it would just make me appear stupid. I let the hours pass while my mind wandered - back to the last time I was with him. Have I done something wrong that drove us farther from each other? Did I make the right decision? Losing a dearest one was driving me to depression.

How had my life been?

I may not be one of the luckiest in the world, but not one of the unluckiest either. There are lots of unfortunate people all over the world. Some may give up life, but most are brave enough to face their miseries. Never did they give up.

Life is the most precious thing God had ever given to the living world. By the weed that rose through the crack in the pavement, Mama told me how precious life is. If the weed survived, so must I. There was my mother to live for. She had had many frustrations and depression yet never gave up for she had me to live for.

"Life is like the weather," my mother told me when I was still wondering why the grass is green and the cotton is white. "It varies in other places and changes with time. What we have today might not be what we had yesterday and may not be what we'll be having tomorrow. The sky isn't always blue. Clouds may appear but in different formations day after day. A storm may come and pass by, and sunshine would come again; the skies would be gloriously blue again. God is kind and merciful. He heals our pains. He'd never let us suffer more than we can endure."

XLII

When Luck Comes Along

We couldn't really tell when luck comes for us, but we feel it like an intuition when it's really coming our way.

Grandma had never known what had become of me after seven years of living in a far-away country – away from her side. She had closed her eyes to a dreamless sleep forever. As if that wasn't enough to pull me down, I lost my chance for a reconciliation with Vernon. Two of the people I have loved so much have gone forever - gone from my life.

Like a homing pigeon, I flew back to America, the country I now called my own. To her arms, I run for comfort; on her shoulders, I shed my tears. I rest my sorrows on her lap, my pain in her bosoms. She wipes off my worries; her touch heals my wounds.

I came back downhearted, but I mustn't give up. I'd rise and survive against all predicaments like a weed rising through the crack of a pavement. I'm a fighter from the start. I must survive! I have my mother to live for.

If my homecoming was grieving, Daly's was fulfilling. I was happy for her. It was heartfelt to learn that her parents were no longer against an American husband. Nice.

Life is like a book with episodes grouped into chapters. I hoped for good things to come in the next chapters of my life. I must overcome the odds waiting for me ahead.

I got a job at the Lakeside Assisted Residential Community in Raleigh. Daly was working also in Raleigh but in a different facility not too far from where I worked.

I'd be serving here another group of people, and I would fit myself in but what's coming here for me? Would I meet somebody like Bandy Moor? Would I find another Kitty Brown? Would I know another man like ...?

I met some residents in my orientation but couldn't remember which one was who. Some looked nice, a few appeared arrogant, but I hoped they'd turn nice to me for I'd dispense to them what circumstances deprived me to serve my mother's mother.

"Good morning . . ." greeted an elderly lady. "Miss Zaragoza? You're back! You were here a month ago, and suddenly disappeared but here you are!"

"Well, I'm back. I'm here to be of service to all of you."

"You'll be staying long with us? I thought you didn't like us here . . ."

"How can you say that?"

"We're dumped here like trash. Society doesn't care about us anymore."

"On the contrary, you deserve special attention."

"Oh thanks, honey for the kind words," the lady said and gave me a hug for my compliments. I smelled White Diamonds. It reminded me of her name.

"Am I glad to see you again, Miss Elizabeth Taylor Fuller?"

"Impressive! You remember my name fully well. I couldn't be wrong when I told my grandson I found a perfect wife for him. He came just when you left me that day."

Unknown to the lady, I almost bumped into her grandson that day. I intuited it was him for he asked if Mrs. Fuller was in her room.

"You don't look that old to have a grown-up grandson, Ms. Fuller."

"Crazy girl, but anyway, thanks for the compliment," the lady said with a light laugh. "Yes, I have a grown-up grandson. You should've met him if you weren't gone too soon."

"I was in a hurry to pack up for a long vacation."

"You went on vacation! Where did you go?"

"Back to my original country, the Philippines; my first homecoming in seven years."

"You're a Filipino! I thought you were Chinese or Japanese, a Thai, a . . ."

"I got a lot of that, Mrs. Fuller. It might interest you to know that most of us Filipinos have Spanish-sounding names that identify us from other Asians."

"I know; I was just kidding. Do Filipino women really make very good wives?"

"Do they?" I asked in return. "I'm not prideful, but I think it's true."

"I've heard a lot about that," she replied and whispered if I were single.

I responded awkwardly, "I haven't been married . . ."

"That's what I thought because you're not wearing a band in your finger."

The lady asked if I had a boyfriend. She apologized when I didn't respond.

"That's fine. I couldn't find yet a special someone," I said with a scoff.

"I told you he came here after you'd left; he's absolutely the right man for you."

Mrs. Fuller bragged about her grandson as if he were the greatest American alive. Hearsays won't interest me easily. I responded with 'Ohms' and 'Okays' and that made her think I wasn't interested in her grandson.

"I need to know him first in person before I'd say he's the right man for me."

"You'll meet him one day. He works in Manhattan, New York, the city that seems always in a hurry, and so is my grandson; always in a hurry whenever he calls me and I don't have time to sell you to his heart," said Mrs. Fuller, talking like she didn't want to get interrupted. "He's almost thirty; never been married – picky, you know. But he's the only one responsible to propagate his grandpa's name."

"A good-looking bachelor doing so well with his career sounds impossible if he doesn't have a fiancée at his age. You may not know it, my dear Mrs. Fuller."

"Well, he got a jilted one but not yet engaged. The first time I saw this woman, I could tell she was not the right one for my grandson.

You'd recognize her by the heart tattoo pierced with a dagger in her left breast. I don't like girls with tattoos. They look cheap and seemed not to be doing good things in their lifetime."

I freed out a careless laugh at the old lady's naivetes.

"That's today's fad, Madam. You may not believe this but there are some women of your age who also wear tattoos. They're everywhere . . ."

"Wherever and whatever, I can't accept that fad. Look, Richard and this woman with a tattoo had been on since high school. When my grandson was away for college studies, she ran with everybody around and without Richard's knowledge, was married to another guy, just like that and when her husband left her, she was with my grandson again, just like that. If she were a good woman, she won't be left behind by her husband."

"That's not always the case. Some husbands deserve to be jilted first."

"I've met that woman; felt her pulse and I knew she couldn't be a good wife."

"So just like that, by her pulse you knew what kind of person she is."

"That's where I got my ESP . . ."

"Can you feel mine?"

The lady held my hand and told me in a second: "Absolutely, you're a nice person – kind and loving - through and through."

"It's flattering but how did you know I could be a good wife?"

"My intuition is strong."

Mrs. Fuller was a steadfast person: she said what she believed and believed what she felt. She loved perfumes, especially Elizabeth Taylor's White Diamonds; adored sunsets and loved to listen to old popular songs. She was humming the song 'Too Young' one morning when I entered her room and belted it out to her surprise.

"It was quite popular in my grandmother's time," I replied.

"Thus, Filipinos also sing American songs?"

"Yes, we do. English is our second language; it's the medium of instruction used in our schools. We may not have the American accent, but we speak good English too."

"I was kidding," she said with a light laugh. "I know it; I wasn't born yesterday."

"Of course, you also know it that Filipinos love products made in America."

"I should have known better. Do you also love to have American husbands?"

"You should know," I chuckled. "You weren't born yesterday."

"Nope, but the day before that," she said and laughed, amused by her own gag. "Will you tell me more about the Philippines? My Richard told me it's a very beautiful country. In fact, many Americans have been there to see "

"Had he been there? Had Richard Fuller been to the Philippines?"

"That was before he went to Vietnam in 1964."

"You're confusing me, Mrs. Fuller. "

"I'm talking about what could have been your future father-in-law," she said and followed it with a loud laugh.

"Please, Mrs. Fuller, no more insinuations."

The lady was placing her medicines in her palm and said, "My son Richard was very concerned about my health. He would've been alive if he didn't marry that good-for- nothing woman."

"You know what . . . It amused me to know that Americans could easily fall in love with one another and even make love before getting to know each other well."

"It's the younger generation," she commented with a chuckle.

"So, it was not the practice during your time."

"Not that I knew of. Why are you drifting away from me?" Mrs. Fuller asked when she noticed I was moving gently towards the door. "I don't bite . . ."

"Mrs. Fuller, I'm still at work."

"It seems you're not enthusiastic to hear about my grandson."

"The truth is, I feel honored you chose me for him, but am I worthy of his attention? What if he's not interested in me after all?"

"Richard Joseph and I have the same likes and dislikes. The only thing he does which I don't like at all is his involvement with this woman who, I think, was sired by a Nazi father."

She started to bore me when she talked all over again what she had told me about his grandson's girlfriend named Helga Schwartz. I noticed the tiny tablet in her palm.

"Madame, your aspirin's melting."

"Sorry, my dear. Do I really have to take this tiny tablet every day?"

"For the sake of your health, my dear Madame . . . you should."

She placed the tablet in her tongue ang grabbed the glass which I filled with water. I hurriedly went out of her room before she could chance to say anything again.

XLIII

The Loves of Elizabeth

In my country, per restriction of social custom,
people way passed middle age must not
talk about being in love again.

I met Elizabeth Taylor Fuller
on the first morning of my orientation at the Lakeside Assisted
Residential Community. Even at her age, the lady looked winsome.
With a well-proportioned build to a height of 5'5", she could move
briskly one wouldn't think she was an octogenarian. Her nape-
length hair was grayish and gracefully curly. Her brows were neatly
trimmed. She wore fair eye shadows and had her face lightly made-up.
It amazed me to find out she did it herself. Her well- groomed looks
gave me the impression at first that she was a visitor there, but I saw
her again in the next two days of my orientation.

I had the chance to talk to this lady when I was in her room on
the last day of my orientation. An intellectual speaker, she was fond
of citing quotations and had an excellent decent sense of humor. A

thoroughly sophisticated lady, she addressed people sweetly as *'honey'* or *'sweetie'* or pleasantly, *'dahlin'* the way Talullah Bankhead did. She jested that the late Hollywood charmer was copying her style.

I couldn't help comparing Elizabeth Fuller to my late grandmother. They were of same age, had the same views; both thought that "Gone with the Wind" was the best book ever written and the best movie ever produced, idolized Clark Gable and held Vivien Leigh in esteem. Their husbands were of the same profession: Whereas Margarita Federica got married to a would-be lawyer named Aragon Zaragoza before the break of the Second World War, Elizabeth Taylor tied knots to Richard William Fuller, also a lawyer, when the war was over. The two women might have distinctive racial diversities because of culture differences yet both held the same degree of pleasantness to behold.

If Margarita Federica was a beauty queen in her youth, Elizabeth Taylor was mistaken for Miss Michigan during the 1939 Miss America pageant at the Steel Pier in Atlantic City. It was when she first met Richard William Fuller, then a young traveling writer of a newsmagazine, who asked her to pose for a magazine cover. Surprised, the demure young Elizabeth asked Richard why her of all interesting faces around to which he answered that his chief editor assigned him to interview Miss Michigan. Amused but embarrassed, she told him she wasn't the one.

"I treasured significantly that brief meeting especially that Patricia Donnelley, the beauty I was mistaken for won the title of Miss America of 1939."

They parted ways after knowing each other's name and it was all that, but as fate would have it, they stumbled at each other again in

New York when people were roaming on the streets in Manhattan merrily celebrating the end of the Second World War. She was walking down to a nearby café, and he was going across her way when their eyes met. Instantly, they remembered each other's faces although for a moment forgot each other's name. He offered to buy her a cup of coffee.

"I should've turned down his offer if not of . . ."

"If not of what?"

"You know what I mean."

"I don't know what you mean . . . what's that?"

She giggled. "I had a crush on that guy the first time we met at Steel Pier and after that I could only wish I would come across with him again."

"And it happened! Wasn't that cute? You were really meant for each other."

"After a long talk at the coffee shop, he invited me to his office across the street. Of course, I didn't want to miss the chance to know him better. He was then a budding criminal lawyer and was looking for an office clerk for his newly established Law Office. He offered me the job on learning I was looking for one. Was it not exciting?"

"That was extremely exciting!" I exclaimed after gasping.

"You may call it crazy, but how could I say no to a fine good-looking lawyer? You see, if good fortune is really meant for you, you don't have to look for it; somebody will come and offer it to you in a silver platter. That goes true with love and marriage."

The two fell in love and got married. Richard Matthew was born to them. He was 19 when he joined the Air Force where he met a

German nurse whom he married in '64 after he came home from Vietnam. In over a year, Richard Joseph was born.

Elizabeth Fuller didn't like her daughter-in-law from the start. Per her ESP, the woman wasn't right for her son. She gave him advice; he ignored her words. Elizabeth's intuition was right. In two years, her son's wife left him for another man. Richard Matthew turned alcoholic and died in a vehicular accident. In a battle of custody, the court entrusted Richard Joseph to the Fullers. The boy was barely two when his grandfather died.

"I don't mind telling you things like this because you'd also be a Fuller soon."

"Mrs. Fuller, your medicine . . ." I reminded her of the capsule in her palm intending to ignore her insinuations.

"When I was about your age, it never occurred to me that I would be dosing myself with so many medications when I get old. But not all medicines are safe."

I gave her an inquiring look. "What do you mean not safe?"

"Some medicines are recalled due to some hazardous side effects," she said and mimicked TV commercials: '*Did you suffer heart attack taking this medicine? Were you a victim of medical malpractice? Then you're entitled to damages. Call this Law Office.*"

"Lawyers can be tricky, Mrs. Fuller."

"One of them had tricked me to marry him," she responded and merrily laughed.

"My grandfather was also a lawyer and was a town mayor for many years."

"You must be from a well-off family; you didn't need to come here in that case."

"Some rich Filipinos also dream of coming to America. But I wasn't among the rich; my mother is just a schoolteacher."

"And your father . . .?"

"He was a soldier in Vietnam. He died there."

"Sorry to hear that. My son was declared Missing in Action for many days. Imagine the pain that tortured me thinking I had lost my only child. It turned out he was held captive by the commies. It wasn't a relief either. I feared he was heavily tortured and eventually killed. Had you ever experienced drowning your heart with joy?"

I didn't remember I ever had. She continued talking without my response.

"I had it when my son came back. Then he got married to that woman."

"So, your son got married to that German . . ."

"Her name's Bianca. Even if I didn't like her, I didn't care anymore. My son was alive and that mattered more. Two years after their marriage he found out his wife had an extra marital affair. Eventually, they got divorced and my son turned desperate. As he was destined to be lost from me, he died in an accident - slammed his car into a ditch, slid, and bumped into a tree."

"What had become of his wife?"

"Before my son died, Bianca had already remarried. My grandson was in my custody, but Bianca had the right to visit him. She was divorced again and got married for the third, no, the fourth time, and then stopped seeing her son."

"What made you move out from New York?"

"My husband died in '68 and so I was alone to raise my grandson. It was when revolutions raged in the streets of York: The Black Power Movement, the hippie counter- culture movement, the demos of gays against cops, and protests deployment of soldiers to 'Nam. I didn't want Dick to grow up amidst a troubled environment."

"Dick? . . . You mean Richard . . ."

"I used to call him Dick, you know, like Bill for William or Bob for Robert but my grandson doesn't want to be called with that nickname; he thinks it connotes obscenity. It wasn't in my time. I used to call his grandpa by that name."

"Changes evolve with time."

"Even human behaviors. What was immoral before is now accepted. A man can now be a woman and a woman can be a man. America is getting crazy!"

Her gestures amused me.

"It's also happening in my country."

"The world is really ending. We have one more year to go if the world really ends at the advent of the millennium. Look around and see more weird happenings like same-sex marriages. But everybody has the right to pursue his own happiness. What I couldn't accept was what I heard recently."

"What was that . . . ?"

"A lady schoolteacher sexually abused her student, a thirteen-year-old boy. I tell you, Jinee, time comes when you hear women raping men."

She had me astounded. Despite being old, she thought of unfeasible things.

"I'm sorry. Was I too open-minded?"

"Those are possibilities. We cannot prevent a weird vogue from coming."

She talked about her grandson again.

"Nobody took care of Dick but me. You're better off than him; you had parents."

"It was only my mother who raised me. My father died in Vietnam during the war before I was born. He had wanted to become a lawyer, but he came from a poor family."

"That profession isn't for the rich alone; anybody can be a lawyer. My husband worked his way through college, and he also had a student loan."

"You're right but in my country, student loans aren't available, and jobs are scarce that even college graduates are working abroad as domestic helpers. In the case of my father . . . oh, it's a long story, Mrs. Fuller."

"We better change the topic. How did you know the song 'Too Young'?"

"My grandmother used to play that song on the piano. During Grandma's time, lovers used to hold a song to remember each other by. That song of Nathalie Cole was my grandparents' theme song."

"What a coincidence! It's also our theme song!"

I stopped making her bed.

"Our theme song? Who are you referring to?"

"Warren Bates . . .!" Mrs. Fuller responded with delight; her excitement was quite amusing because I didn't expect she'd react like that.

"Sounds like a movie actor's name," I said.

"You're thinkin' of Warren Beatty, dah'lin. My boyfriend isn't in movies."

Her words tingled in my ears. In my country, women her age won't talk about boyfriends anymore. It's embarrassing for them and might be scoffed at if they do.

"Does this Warren Bates visit you often?"

"Oh," she giggled again like a love-struck teenage girl watching her crush pass by. "He's in Hall 400. Haven't you noticed that older version of Keanu Reeves?"

"Oh, that hot hunk!" I exclaimed, showing her my delight even if I didn't know who she was referring to.

"Yes!" the old woman nodded proudly and gave me 'high five'.

"Uh…" That was all I could say. So, they were the two old people I heard about acting like love birds in the western patio of the facility from where they used to watch sunsets on weekends. Some people were sardonic of it. I never thought they were referring to Elizabeth Fuller and her Warren Bates.

"You look disgusted. Is it odd for two senior citizens to fall in love?"

"Oh no, I'd never think of that, Mrs. Fuller."

"Thank you. So not everybody around thinks the same."

"Think what?"

"That we no longer have the right to fall in love. They laugh at us."

"They were wrong . . . of course they were wrong!"

"But I couldn't care less. I have the right to pursue my own happiness."

"Right. . .! Ignore them, Mrs. Fuller and they'd get tired of it."

"By the way, can you just call me by my first name?"

"That's too disrespectful of me considering your age and stature."

"I may look very antiquated but my heart's still as young as yours."

"Okay, Beth . . . Anyway, age is just a number."

Mrs. Fuller laughed heartily. "Hey, Jinee . . . We could get along with each other."

She raised her hand again for another 'high five'.

"We got the same sense of humor," I said and laughed with her.

"Exactly. Hey, how about coming here this Saturday and meet my Warren Bates?"

"It's my pleasure."

She opened her arms to me. "I'm not mistaken choosing you for my grandson."

She noticed the blush on my face. I stepped back. She changed the topic.

"Did you say, 'Too Young' was a record of Nathalie Cole?"

"Yes," I answered briefly.

"Wrong. It was Nat 'King' Cole's."

I didn't argue and headed to the door.

"Come back soon. We'll talk more about Richard and Warren Bates."

I responded faintly; she might have thought I didn't like the idea.

"More on Warren Bates," she said before I could close the door behind me.

XLIV

It Happened One Summer

I didn't mind anymore if darkness had fallen.
If the world had shut off its eyes on us;
if daylight had bidden us goodbye.

My new job was rewarding me with better pay and benefits, and a fat bonus if I could work for two consecutive years, which I intended to do. Unlike in SJNC where I did a job demeaning to my profession, in my new job, I was well-respected; treated with dignity. The residents, as well as the administrative staff, were all nice and friendly. Most of the residents were past their sixties but some didn't like to be referred to as *'old'* but *'seniors'*.

Two octogenarians, who were referred to as the 'lovey-dovey' couple, were frequenting the patio in the afternoon on weekends. They weren't seeing each other on weekdays 'to make one's heart grow fonder' but were texting sweet nothings to each other's cellphones. To me, that was tickly, but loving is not only for the young; it comes from the heart of every normal person like a breath one needs to live. Yet, both were very much aware that their lives were getting dimmer; that one would vanish forever from the other's eyes sooner or later.

I met Warren Bates the Saturday Mrs. Fuller invited me to come and made me a part of their rendezvous watching the reddish coppery sun sinking behind the Appalachian Mountains that looked gray at a distance across the Yellow Lagoon. That sunset they shared may not have looked like the sunset I used to watch back home in Sacandaya but it left the same message: it pains to say goodbye.

I have never seen a sunset in America as captivating as we had in Sacandaya. Once upon a summer, I shared that sunset with Vernon. It was one of the rare moments when Vernon and I could hold close to each other.

So, we were there, Vernon and I, sitting on a sandbar - legs stretched down to where wavelets could lap on our heels. They rippled up to our calves and in receding, simmered through the grains as they flowed back to the sea.

Vernon's thoughts were on the sun that was shimmering down behind the horizon.

"Why do sunsets look fascinating?" Vernon casually raised a question that didn't need an answer. I tried to perceive what was on his mind by gazing into his eyes which he turned conscious of. I loved the way he looked at that very moment. If I could only freeze the sun, hang it suspended to stretch my moments with him, inbreathe his presence like there was a wonderful essence exuding from his being, I would have loved to breathe all I could as if that was all I needed to live.

I thanked Vernon for coming into my life; said it with profound sincerity. He squeezed my hand; his gesture of appreciation for loving him in return. He kissed my forehead then shifted his eyes back to the ocean. In that fleeting moment, I saw the reasons why many-a-women fell for him, and it wasn't only for his manly pretty face, his athletic physique, his skills and talents, or his involvement with campus activities, but more for his sense of humor and eloquence in speaking. He was a lady's heartthrob and I wondered how many had been involved with him before me. I accept I was one of those who desired to be loved by him; didn't care what he had been.

I gripped his muscled arm and smooched his splendid shoulder. He gazed deep into my eyes – letting him seduce me. His face smoldered red with the glow of the sinking sun. His jaw firmed; a smile deliciously dangled in his lips turning himself too seductive to be resisted that I kissed him more passionately than I ever did; it could have made him laugh up his sleeve.

"Do you promise to love me until the sunset of our lives?"

As melodious as the breeze that swept in soft and cool from the sea, Vernon asked. The timbre of his voice became enthralling; it gripped the whole of me. Even without his asking, I loved to love him until forever ceases to become forever; he'd be the first and the last man I would have adored in all my life. None would ever come between us. I made that promise in silence. It's better to leave a commitment unspoken. He didn't insist on an answer but gave me a brief gentle smooch on my lips that left me wanting for more - wanted them passionate.

I looked around for Laura; didn't see her.

A flock of geese forming a letter "V" flew across the sky over us - heading to nowhere – a sign it was getting late. The sound of tiny waves reaching our ankles was faintly heard; the tide was ebbing away. Patches of mossy stones were surfacing in shallow waters. Except for some glints of light emanating from somewhere not too distant, darkness had come. The golden sparkles that flooded the sea surface had vanished from sight and so were the children playing nearby; their voices were gone. Farther, figures of people silhouetted by the purple-amber light from the western skies were shadows in a dream; their voices muffled with the murmur of the wind. Offshore, a group of small fishing boats were circling around a certain spot. Their lamplights converged. Not too far from them over yonder there were well-lit bigger fishing boats as fish would gather around a bright light on moonless nights. That scenery I saw around us that evening seemed to be a once- in-a-lifetime dream I'd never wish to end.

I looked around again but didn't see anybody nearby. Laura may have gone home without my knowing, leaving all those lovely moments to me and Vernon. It seemed as if everybody had left the world all alone for us to share.

"Laura could just be around," Vernon said when he thought I was seeking safety with Laura's company. "Don't be afraid, I won't harm you, would I?"

I told Vernon I wouldn't be afraid of anything if I were with him, yet I was – the fear that my mother would find out I was seeing a boyfriend that summer. I was turning twenty-one but still afraid to disclose to my mother that I was in love with a man and old enough to be responsible for myself; I didn't want to hurt her.

Vernon ran his fingers on my lips. I caught one with my teeth, bit it hard to squeeze out of him a grunt of pain but instead he freed out his boyish laughter that rhymed with the sound of the waves rushing in and lapping on the shore.

I drew myself closer to him, leaned my head on his shoulder and when I felt his touch on my face, I closed my eyes gently, thrilled with his next moves and I heard myself breathing so hard with so much excitement. Here was the object of many-a-female heartthrob, so close and real I didn't need to daydream. The sensation was so fervent that I didn't resist his moves - the fear of losing him if I refused pervaded. Never did I show a gesture of resisting for those were the moments I long have waited to happen. I realized then that I could get rid of my inhibitions and give up on his advances. It was one of those rarest moments when the existence of temptation was greeted with appreciation.

I quivered when he cuddled me in his arms and placed me in a bed of sand like he was putting a sleeping infant on a crib. While his eyes were digging deep into mine, he combed my hair with his fingers like what my mother did when I was little. This time the strokes were sending an amorous kind of feeling. I closed my eyes, but I could still imagine his face drawing closer. I breathed in his breaths. They were as sweet as the newly bloomed blossoms of *kamuning*, warm against the sea breeze that was growing colder. Or it was just what I thought. A summer night in Sacandaya wasn't cold at all.

He pressed his lips on my forehead. The warmth of his body and the tenderness in his touch on my face made me yearn for more passion from him. I saw that fervency in a flash of his face. When I closed my eyes again, I held my breath. He kissed my eyelids – one after the other - lending warmth all over my face; I was levitating. Gently, he slipped his lips down to my nose, fluttered them to the corners of my mouth sending a joyous irresistible temptation that I couldn't care about anymore if there were eyes watching us.

I gasped for breath, inhaled it deeply but held it to conceal a sound and when I exhaled, I heard myself gasping again like I was running out of breath. I released more sighs – choppy that they rhymed with the sound of the rippling wavelets on the shore.

My whole body heaved with excitement when he climbed over me. I turned listless to resist when I felt his weight. I held my breath again, completely enthralled by Vernon's advances, totally surrendering to his next moves.

I hugged him fervently as if I was afraid Vernon would release himself off my hold. I slipped my fingers up to his nape, felt his hair and fondly played the edges of the strands with my fingers. With his hands caressing my skin, his touch stimulated my flesh, and I couldn't help but ask him to possess me: body and soul.

When I opened my eyes, he pressed his lips again softly on mine. Even if I knew he was to do it again, I was dying to have it when he left me hanging suspended. He gazed at me zealously. How I loved that lustrous look in his eyes; those enthralling lips that made me close my eyes giving him a hint that I didn't mind at all if he'd conquer the whole of me those moments; I didn't mind at all.

He turned more passionate, exuding a kind of warmth wrapping all over me and the more he roused up my sensuality. I responded to his advances and moaned I couldn't care less if he wondered where had all my reticence gone.

Captivated by Vernon's caresses that were aborted the first time he tried to do it; I didn't mind anymore if darkness had completely fallen; if the world had shut its eyes on us, if the last glow of daylight had bidden us goodbye. With my inhibitions and my naivety vanished with daylight, I felt a kind of gladness I never ever had. How beautiful it was to love and be loved. How lucky I was to find a perfect guy to love at a youthful age. I wished I were 21 forever.

XLV

Tomorrow When I'm Gone

Think of things and ways to cheer.
Close your eyes; think of me.
I'd be with you forever.

Warren Bates snapped his fingers before me; it woke me up from reminiscing. Warren was having fun, but Mrs. Fuller reproached his boyish naughtiness. Warren apologized.

To divert my attention, I moved to a bench under an old maple tree but within hearing distance from where the old lovers were seated, and I couldn't help stealing glances at them from time to time. They were gazing into each other's eyes behind thick spectacles. It tickled me watching them, but then I realized that Love knows no barriers; it doesn't grow old; always smells pleasant and fresh like the exotic *dama de noche* not forbidden to spread its sweetness even at twilight.

"As if it was only yesterday," I heard the old man addressing to his lady. She freed a girlish giggle. They were clasping each other's hand while gazing at the western skies with those winsome smiles on their faces as they began collecting memories.

"It seems it was only yesterday the first time we met at the park," the woman finished what the man was about to say.

"How fast the time could fly. You were young and naive,"

"And you were already a lad. A stupid young lad," Elizabeth chuckled.

"My shyness made me look stupid. I didn't have the guts to tell you what I felt about you. I waited for a good chance but then came up the war; it was my time to go."

"We met once more before your combat training but all you could tell me was . . ."

Without finishing her words, she drew herself closer, so close that I thought she was inviting him to kiss her on the lips. I waited for that romantic interlude, but Warren only gave the woman a quick peck on her wrinkled cheek.

". . . Remember me," the old man quipped. He dropped his arm over her right shoulder, and she slumped for comfort to his side. Squirming, I shifted my eyes at the sun sinking behind the Appalachian Mountains. How mean fate can be. The couple were in the twilight of their years; they'd be losing each other forever sooner than they could be expecting. I was sorry for them; tears were clinging in my eyes.

"We made promises to meet again after the war." It was Mrs. Fuller's voice I heard. I squinted at them; the mirth in their faces had turned to frown.

"I went to the park right after coming home hoping to see you there, but there never was you," Warren said. He was still gazing at the western hemisphere when he spoke. "I did that for three successive days always hoping you'd come. How it tormented me on realizing that my hopes to see you again were drifting with time. And I realized I was facing loneliness. How hard it was to be alone and lonely."

"I had the same pain, Warren; I had it when you failed to return after the war. You were in my thoughts for a thousand days, hoping against hope that you were still alive and that you were holding me in your thoughts. Then came the time when my family had to move out of the state. If you only knew how much I wanted to stay in the park and wait for your coming be it throughout the day or throughout the night, but I didn't have a choice. I was drifting afar and the hope of seeing you again was draining with every sunset that passed by. I kept hoping for your coming until I met the man who helped me forget you."

"In the battlefield, I wept for my fallen comrades. If I knew I was losing you, it could've been better if I had died there with them. It rained hard that night I was waiting for you in the park. I let the rain battered my body wishing those raindrops were bullets piercing my flesh."

"You were in the battle and all I had from you was your promise to return. It could've been better if you didn't promise anything at all."

Mrs. Fuller's words were the same words I heard from Vernon when he found out I was chasing an American dream. *It's better not to promise anything at all.* How sincere is a promise? It's but a group of empty words – dull and listless unless fulfilled.

"It was better than nothing to wait for."

"We may have lost thousands of days, but we still have some to keep for ourselves now that we found each other," the lady quipped with a smile.

Warren looked at her; gazed deep into her eyes. They were simply recollecting memories. I thought they were just a couple of strangers who secretly fell in love with each other, separated by war bound only with shackles of words to meet again.

What I witnessed brought Vernon to my thoughts. Unlike Elizabeth and Warren, Vernon and I had lost the chance for reconciliation. We could never tell what was coming for us. He was committed to his new vocation while I was fettered to my American dream. Forever, I lost the first man in my life. *But am I losing him forever?*

Warren beckoned me to come nearer and asked me to read the poem he wrote for his lady love. I could see excitement in the face of Mrs. Fuller.

With One More Breath to Breathe

Let me hear no songs of sorrow.
Wipe away the pain in your heart.
Swear to me that by tomorrow
You wouldn't cry when I depart.

Give me one more breath to breathe.
Fill it with joy and laughter.
I weave music in the wind.
You'd hear me sing in whisper.

Spare me a moment to live.
Let me dream for a while.
If ever I leave you now,
I'm leaving with a smile.

Save the color of my smile.
Paint it over your rainbow.
Today may be too misty,
Your rainbow comes tomorrow.

And tomorrow when I'm gone.
Think of things and ways to cheer.
Close your eyes and think of me,
I'd be with you forever.

An impassioned emotion glowed in the face of Mrs. Fuller while I was reading the poem; read it with exquisiteness. Tears shimmered in her eyes. I, too, was about to cry with her. She responded to Warren's kiss on her lips with passion. I was watching close-up their smooching for about a minute. I felt embarrassed; I wasn't used to watching old people interlocking their lips that long. Yet, I felt sadness for them; their twilight was coming. I shied my eyes and tried to focus my attention on the cloudscape burning over the banks.

Moving back to the old maple tree, I let my thoughts wander aimlessly across a landscape of trees and mountains like a fleeting butterfly feasting in a variety of flowers.

The last gleam of the day was dwindling fast. In the western horizon, the red clouds had turned dull and gray. Over my head was a tiny star, faintly shining, perhaps the first to shine that night, hanging a million dreams away. Silently, I wished upon it to grant Warren and Elizabeth a million moments more to enjoy each other's company:

> *Starlight, star bright . . .*
> *The first star I see tonight . . .*
> *I wish I may, wish I might . . .*
> *Have this wish I wish tonight.*

Looking back at the lovey-dovey duo, I reminded Mrs. Fuller of the time. It was rude of me to interrupt their romantic interludes, but the night was getting chiller, and it seemed the old lovers didn't care about it. As they were carried by their emotions, they never cared about it at all.

"You're right, honey. Thanks for your concern. Come here for a second."

Elizabeth Fuller invited me to sit beside her, which I quickly did. She put her arm over my shoulder like what my grandmother always did.

"By the way, Warren, had I told you that this pretty angel here is going to be my granddaughter-in-law?"

Warren winked an eye at me.

"That's wonderful! Your grandson is a lucky guy."

"Indeed, my grandson is . . ."

"Mr. Warren, I haven't even met her grandson yet."

"Well, prepare for that grand meeting, young lady," Mrs. Fuller concluded. "It would come sooner than you think."

XLVI

A Day with the Fullers

We spent a little time making pleasantries,
exchanging ideas and thoughts, but most of the time
they were asking about me and the country where I came from.

I was working for a co-worker one Sunday and had mentioned it to Mrs. Fuller. That morning of the said Sunday, when I came to her room to administer her medicine, the woman surprised me with the presence of her grandson who extended his hand to me right when I slipped into the room. Offhanded, I found myself gripping his hand. I noticed it was soft and smooth –could be the kind that only holds pens and spoons unlike Vernon's – they were as rough as a handyman's.

True to his grandmother's words, Richard Joseph Fuller looked bonny. His well- groomed hair was auburn as his brows were; eyes looked expressive; cheerful is a better word to describe. His well-formed nose made him looked to me like the god of love in Greek mythology. He had reddish full lips and high cheek bones that gave prominence to his manly lower jaw. Suave and spruce in a light gray coat over a white sweatshirt that matched his dark gray wool pants and a pair of black shoes, Richard Joseph Fuller looked so sleek and quite comely like a brand new white and gray Ferrari. From how he moved and spoke, I gleamed he had on him a host of great positive attributes which I would so admire. I would expect a wide difference of personalities if I were to compare Vernon to him – them, of different race and upbringing.

"Pleased to meet you, Mr. Fuller," I said coyly with utmost respect. Feeling inferior to his aristocratic personality, I deemed I wasn't the kind of girl the man could be attracted to. Courteously, I withdrew my hand from his hold.

"Uhhh . . . Do I look too old to be addressed with such formality?"

"I'm sorry. That's how I address people I just met."

"Grandma's right! Not only you're pretty . . . you're charming as well."

His words didn't flatter me. *Why are some men cheeky and daring?*

"Thank you, sir but compliments blush me."

He apologized; might not be that fresh at all but nice to flatter an ego. Gentlemanliness augured well for a special lasting friendship, but with Richard Fuller's classy stature, I shouldn't expect more than plain acquaintanceship.

"Have we met before?"

A déjà vu, Richard raised the same question that Vernon did when I was in college and met him again after many years of not seeing each other.

"Yes, we did . . ."

"I know it! We almost bumped into each other one day. It was here . . . in the corridor . . . right? I had the feeling it was you my granny told me about - that mole in your face and that smile, those eyes, that . . ."

"Well, you need more time to know each other better," Mrs. Fuller interfered.

"Mrs. Fuller, I can't stay any longer; I'm at work."

"Okay, but you must come with us later. Richard invited me to lunch outside."

"Did I?" Richard impulsively asked. "Yes, I did. Why am I so forgetful?"

"Mesmerism," Elizabeth said and rolled her eyes then told me to come with them.

"I'm not sure if I should," politely, I begged off.

She was insistent. "Richard might find it boring to go with two oldies."

"What two oldies?" Richard seemed surprised.

"You turn forgetful in front of a pretty lady. Did you forget Warren Bates?"

"Uh, you mean your Rhett Butler," Richard said. "Grandma's daydreaming."

"Daydreaming enlivens senses; an aroma that sweetens bland moments."

"Okay, he's your Rhett Butler," Richard said admonishing the old lady with a peck. "Now, where's this Rhett? I'd like to meet him."

"You'd like Warren as you would've loved your grandfather if he were alive."

Mrs. Fuller reminded me of the lunch date when I was going out of her room. I told her I couldn't go dating with someone I just met; it was a disgrace in Filipino culture.

"What are you talking about, silly girl; this is a foursome."

"I know, but... but..."

"Shut off that *but* and send it back to the Philippines. You're now in America. When you're in Rome . . . well, you know how that saying goes."

The Midori is a contemporary Asian bistro serving mostly Japanese food at the Waverly Place Shopping Center in Cary. Richard drove us there in his white Lexus SUV, an expensive car that indicates financial stability. My grandmother wanted me to marry a man of my own level, if possible, a Filipino and not a rich American for fear he would just dump me if I could never come up to his expectations. I thought I was about to shrug off what Grandma had cautioned me.

Highlighted by potted plants, paper lanterns, and shades of bamboo, I found the restaurant warm and cozy and classy. *Lunch could be expensive here,* I thought.

A Japanese lady who introduced herself to me as Meiko, led us to one of the tables which Richard termed as *shokutaku*. I was moving meekly in my fear I might accidentally break any of those expensive ornaments.

"*Konnichiwa, minna-san,*" Meiko said after giving us each a menu book in Hiragana. She addressed Richard in a manner that she had known him fully well and asked me something in her language which made me look stupid not knowing what it was."*Nanni ga nomitai desu ka?*"Meiko asked again.

"*Gomennasai*," Richard came to my rescue. "The lady is not a Nipponese."

"*Gomennasai*," the waitress repeated the word and vowed, her hand on her chest. I presumed it was an apology. I responded with a smile and nodded in acknowledgement.

"She thought you were Yoshiko Yamasaki," Richard told me.

It wasn't the first time I was mistaken for Japanese. In SJNC, an old male resident vehemently despised me thinking I was Japanese. He was in the Philippines during the war and suffered the Japanese soldiers' atrocities in the infamous Bataan Death March. I couldn't blame him for being rude to me at first as I couldn't blame my grandfather for his immense hatred against a Japanese nationality. His version of how cruel the Japanese soldiers were during the war was confirmed many times over with the other stories I've read or heard. That was the situation half-a-century ago which I could hardly believe because all the Japanese that I've got acquainted with were adorable: humble and meek.

"Meiko's waiting for your order," Richard whispered.

"That's fine. Take your time," the waitress told me in English and smiled naively.

Meiko had a totally different accent but thicker than mine. She attracted my attention with her face and neck completely shaded in white that reminded me of Solvera's *Chin- Chin*. Her lips were fully painted in strawberry red, and heavy black lines were drawn around her eyes making them appear wide. Her hair was a big peach split from the forehead, plunged with something that looked like a pair of black chopsticks. Her attire made me wonder how a geisha looks like.

"This is my first time here. I really don't know what drink to order."

"How about *shimatta?*" Richard suggested.

"I don't even know what that is -" I whispered without hesitation even if I suspected that Richard would silently comment about my ignorance.

"Well, it's a cocktail of *stoli* orange infused with fresh pineapple served with martini style. It's good," Richard explained. I ordered a glass of *shimatta* and Richard ordered *mai tai* for his Granny and another glass for Mr. Warren.

The waitress excused herself and came back immediately with earthenware of Japanese green tea with four teacups on a tray she held with both hands. She placed a cup before each of us and cautiously poured over the liquid from the tiny jug.

Lunch was served.

Richard intuited I wasn't comfortable using chopsticks. He asked Meiko for a spoon and fork. She responded with a light *"oh"*, tapping her lips with her fingers. I could perceive she wondered why anyone who couldn't use chopsticks would come to this place. That made me feel awkward especially since I was in my working clothes while my companions were dressed for the occasion. Why did I come then? Mrs. Fuller was persuasive. She wanted my company, so she'd have the reason to tag along with her beau.

We finished our lunch.

I took a sip of *shimatta* but hardly touched my food. Mrs. Fuller asked if I was watching my diet, to which I shyly nodded. I hardly spoke. I could be a good conversationalist, but my heavy accent held me back. They might not get what I was saying. I felt embarrassed to hear them say: "Will you say that again?"

We spent a little time making pleasantries and exchanging thoughts about storms and the tornadoes that ravaged the city of Oklahoma on the third of May that year. It was 1999 and it had been eight years since the first time I came to America. If I was aware that snowstorms are natural occurrences in the upper states during winter and fall, it was only then I learned that tornadoes are prevalent during spring and summer. I boasted about my country's excellent weather and exotic scenery. Richard expressed his desire of visiting the Philippines in the future and I feared I might have exaggerated my descriptions of how beautiful my country is. It was because I was too proud of the country I came from.

Meiko acknowledged the generous tip Richard left on the table. She apologized again for mistaking me for the Japanese warbler who, she said, would be singing at a soon-to- open nightclub off Crabtree Valley. *Yuki No Hana* would be a plain restaurant by day and would come up with live music after six, Meiko said. The Japanese lady would be working there during evenings on weekends. She let me promise to be there on its grand opening night which was a month away.

XLVII

Strange Encounters

Meeting someone unexpectedly oftentimes happens to me.
Strangely, I met Richard Fuller again one evening.
And this time, he was with Helga Schwartz.

Daly and I were working in different facilities in Raleigh about three miles apart but kept our residency in Middletown. We were working the first shift, commuting in one car - be hers or mine - leaving at six in the morning to beat heavy traffic.

One Friday afternoon, we hurried home for Brendan's promise to treat us to dinner at TGI Friday. It was Daly's birthday and I thought Brendan was too proud to show us how much bonus he got that year. Sky is the limit, he told us.

As soon as we got inside our house in Middletown, the phone rang. It was Brendan. He told Daly that he was coming down to US 1 from Capital Boulevard at 70 mph. I was listening to Daly telling Brendan that he was over speeding when a loud knock on the door cut her off. Daly and I stared at each other and asked the same question at the same time.

"Is it Brendan?"

"It couldn't be," I said in a loud whisper. "He's still an hour away?"

"He might already be around when he called. Brendan's fond of playing pranks."

The Carolina Knights crossed my mind. It was a paramilitary group suspected as metastasis of the dreaded Ku Klux Klan that was organized with the help of some soldiers from Fort Bragg. These knights of white supremacy were dwelling in the hinterlands and aiming to eliminate immigrants and minorities.

Again, there was the loud banging on the door. Daly moved to the foyer.

"Don't open," I whispered aloud. "Brendan won't bang the door that hard."

Daly peeped through the tiny hole in the lid then she looked at me, looking scared.

Impulsively, I yelled addressing the stranger outside: "Who's there?!"

A male voice, not Brendan's, shouted back: "I want to talk to Cathy!"

He could be the man Cathy was living with.

"Cathy who? . . ."

"I don't have time to play with your 'knock-knock' game!"

"There's no Cathy here!"

"Liar! I know who you are . . ." The man's voice was intimidating.

"I couldn't give a damn! Go back to hell or I will call a cop! Try me!"

No response. Daly peeped through the hole again and reached for the knob.

"No! Don't open yet! He's just waiting for us to come out. It's Cathy's boyfriend! Obviously, the two had a fight."

"Oh, Lord . . . Where could be the girl by now?" Daly said. "I'll call 911."

"Old fool. If you call 911, fire trucks come, the EMS, police cars with their sirens blown in full and you must pay them hundreds of bucks for running across red lights with their sirens screaming. Neighbors will swarm. Don't panic; the intruder couldn't come in."

I got the phone from Daly, placed it back on the receiver when it rang. I responded.

"Jinee? Did you call?" Brendan asked from the other end.

"Where are you by now?"

"I've just crossed Buck Jones. Please tell Daly I'm okay."

"She isn't worried about you; just excited for this dinner."

"Shut up, you fool!" Daly blasted, upset with my joke. I handed her the phone.

"Brendan . . .? Hello?" She turned off the phone. "He's gone."

We heard noise from outside - the squirrels squeaking as they ran up and down the old oak tree in the front yard. Nervousness bothered Daly badly so that in the span of half an hour, she relieved herself twice. Then we heard footfalls approaching the door. We looked at each other with fear. The doorbell blared. Jolted, we screamed together.

"Don't open!" I told Daly when she dashed to the door.

"That's Brendan," she said. "I know the sound of his footfalls."

T.G.I Friday was full. We couldn't find a parking space near to the restaurant but the one close to Wall Mart – too far to walk for Daly and me who were in heels. On my suggestion, we thought of going to the Vietnamese restaurant down Tryon Road.

The "Green Papaya" wasn't crowded that Friday evening; few cars were parking nearby. I noticed a familiar white SUV. *There must be somebody I know inside.*

A lady wearing a green traditional Vietnamese female dress over black pants greeted us. As indicated in the plastic nameplate on her breast, her name was Kim Cuc.

"Does your name imply something," I asked the Vietnamese lady while she was leading us to the table nearer to the door.

"Yes, it does. Golden Chrysanthemum," she replied shyly with a smile.

After we were seated, the Vietnamese waitress handed us menu books to browse. I noticed the dots and dashes over some words in the menu book. That reminded me of the word that was written at the escutcheon of the boat used by the refugees that was washed up in my hometown many years ago. *Old Tam Nguyen could be dead by now and Diep. . .? Could she be the person I'm facing right now? . . . It could be possible!*

"Jinee," Brendan caught my attention. "Kim's waiting for your order."

Kim Cuc smiled at me. She reminded me of Tam Nguyen who was forever smiling while recollecting the miseries his company of refugees encountered during their flight across the seas.

"I'm sorry. I was thinking of somebody."

"She remembers her old flame who'd been dead years ago," Daly concluded.

"Vernon isn't dead . . ."

"Don't waste your time," Daly said. "A woman mustn't stay a spinster past thirty. That's the danger line. There are lots of fishes in the ocean." Daly looked around. "Now's your chance," she said squinting at one corner to her right.

At the table that Daly meant sat the owner of the white SUV parked outside. But he wasn't alone; I noticed there was another set of dishes.

"I know him . . ."

"Your intuition to find him here was right." Daly cut in.

"I didn't know. I didn't expect him to be here this time."

"He's with a lady companion. I think it's their third time here," the waitress meddled in. "Are you Asians?"

"Uh-huh," Daly and I chanted simultaneously in the same manner Americans do.

"I'm also Asian . . . from Vietnam," the waitress said without waiting to be asked.

"We're from the Philippines," said Daly.

"The Philippines! That was where we landed after fleeing Saigon," Kim Cuc said.

"Oh . . .! You'd been there?" Daly looked delighted.

"We were camped in Bataan for some months before we were transported to America. It was a hard life back there but far better than in our troubled country."

Drawn by empathy, Daly gave Kim Cuc a hug. I was about to do the same when my attention was diverted to a sexy red-haired lady who came out of women's room and flaunted herself across the tables.

She looked provocative in a flashy blouse with a plunging neckline that exposed the heart tattoo pierced with a dagger over her left boob - the woman Mrs. Fuller told me about.

"That's Helga Schwartz, the German shepherd . . . I mean German girlfriend." We laughed at Kim Cuc's humor. Helga must have heard us; she turned her eyes at us before proceeding to her seat. "They've been here before twice or thrice. The guy is nice, but the woman is somewhat . . . you know what I mean."

"Well, … are we here to eat or talk about strangers?" Brendan interrupted.

Daly had a serving of *Pho Dac Biet.* I ordered a dish called *Com Suon Trung.*

"You'd love it . . . very *co vi,*" Kim Cuc said of my order and left.

"Miss Zaragoza?"

The voice sounded familiar.

"Mr. Fuller!" I exclaimed on pretense it surprised me to see him there.

"How've you been, Jinee?"

"Pretty good!" I responded by shaking his hand at the same time. ". . . And you?"

"I'm fine. I never thought I'd see you here."

"Same here but the world is small to some people."

After I introduced him to Brendan and Daly, Richard Fuller excused himself to get something from his car passing by the woman he was with who was standing by the door with crossed arms; eyes plastered at me while twisting her mouth with a chewing gum. She forwarded ostentatiously. I stood up in acknowledgement of her presence, but she displayed arrogance by displaying a menacing look.

"I'm Richard Fuller's fiancée."

"They know it already," Kim interrupted.

"I'm not talking to you, Miss Saigon," said the German woman with candor snapping her fingers at the waitress who immediately walked away.

"Glad to meet you," I greeted her with sincerity despite her arrogance.

"Well, I'm not," she snapped.

I was about to set back when the arrogant woman took out the wad from her mouth, pasted it on our table and left - leaving us dumbfounded with her incivility.

Richard came back with a paperback book for his grandmother. Helga reentered and positioned herself at the same place as if she were the door guard.

"If you can do me a favor, please give this to Mrs. Fuller," Richard said.

"Aren't you going there sometime later?"

"I was there this morning, but I'm afraid I don't have time to be there again."

In all those moments, Richard Fuller's fiancée was showing petulance in her face with her nostrils flaring; mouth pouting; eyes glaring and brows scowling. I shied away from her stare. It reminded me of the bloodshot eyes of Bandy Moor.

XLVIII

The Prodigal Returned

Lord, remember her as one of your sheep
that had gone astray - misled and misguided.
My Lord, please welcome her back to your folds.

Brendan downed a few bottles of Heineken; didn't appear groggy but wasn't as sober as a judge. I heard him say he'd be driving back to New Jersey later that evening, which wasn't safe for him. Cops on late nights, especially on weekends, were as vigilant as beasts searching for prey. Besides, it was drizzling and the road to New Jersey might be slippery. I insisted he should spend the night with us; Daly was the one driving Brendan's car back to Middletown.

We had a little chat in the living room while Brendan had his hot coffee when the doorbell blared. I thought of the man who banged the door earlier. This time he rang the doorbell successively.

"Jinee!"

It was a woman's voice. Cathy's!

Cathy impetuously went inside as soon as I opened the door. A white man in black leather jacket leaped at behind her. Hurriedly, I pulled Cathy in and locked the door.

"Open it!" It was the same antagonizing voice I heard earlier that evening. He banged and kicked the lid too hard it occurred to me he was drunk and as mad as hell.

"Leave me alone, Kevin!" Cathy yelled. "Get away from here!"

"Come out or your friends will suffer my wrath!"

"I will talk to him," the intoxicated Brendan intervened.

"You're not with this, Brendan," I reacted. "I'll talk to him."

"Don't open the door," Cathy warned. "He has a gun."

"Mister," I yelled at the man outside, "you better leave right now, or I will . . .!"

"Don't scare me with your blusters, asshole! Send Cathy out! Send her out right now or you will suffer my wrath!"

Defied, I decided to open the door.

Cathy held me when I was about to reach for the knob, but I was confident I could handle the situation well. I turned the knob. The intruder kicked the lid open and would have banged on my face were I not quick to move back. The man flung in and snatched Cathy's wrist. In an impulse, I chopped the man's forearm that freed Cathy from his hold. The intruder cast upon me his fiercest look like a beast about to devour his prey. That made me more cautious for his next moves. He threw a punch; quickly, I dodged. Stepping aside to my left, I grabbed his wrist and shoulder and swept his right leg with my left foot. He fell to the floor. I stomped on his belly putting all my weight onto my foot. I noticed him pulling a handgun. I kicked it off but missed. I lost my balance in time when the assailant squeezed the trigger. The bullet almost got me in the face had I not fallen to the floor. The bullet must have whizzed out through the open door.

The man aimed his gun at me when he got up to his knees. Brendan rushed in behind him and kicked his hand tossing the pistol away. The weapon dropped to the floor not far from the intruder. He slithered on the floor to where the gun was. I got up in a wink, jumped at the gun and grabbed its handle; he got the muzzle. We grappled – squeezing the handgun from each other's grip. Losing to his strength, I applied what I learned in fighting with bare hands. I tried a wallop against the left side of his face. That made him tougher. The pistol was slipping out of my control. The man's finger could have touched the trigger; the gun blew up. We rolled again and when he was on top of me, Brendan hit his head with something that toppled him down. Then I heard a siren stopping by; Daly had called 911.

Two cops came up. One handcuffed the intruder and led him out while reading his rights. The other cop got the intruder's firearm.

"We'll book him for assault and attempted murder. We need somebody's statement at the precinct."

"I'll follow, Officer," I told the cop. "Give me a minute to dress up."

"Take your time," said the cop. "Is everybody okay?"

That was when we noticed Cathy on the floor, bleeding. Brendan alerted the paramedics outside. Two men in dark blue uniform with a stretcher came in followed by a woman with a stethoscope hanging on her neck. She asked, "Was she hit?"

"I think she was!" Daly replied. Cathy was cupping her belly, groaning in pain.

"There's no bullet wound but she's bleeding," the lady said after examining Cathy. "She was probably kicked on the abdomen!"

Daly's eyes met mine and at the same time we screamed: "Miscarriage!"

Brendan followed the ambulance; the incident had made him sober. Daly and I went with a police officer to give our statements. Kevin was arraigned for assault and attempted murder. He was kept in jail that night.

The following morning, Brendan went back to Jersey while Daly and I went to the police precinct to formally indict Kevin. Afterwards, we went to Rex Hospital to see how Cathy was doing. We learned that a male fetus fell off from her womb. Silently, I prayed: *Dear Lord, she's one of your sheep gone misled. She wants to come back to your fold, please open your arms for her.*

At the hospital's receiving area, Kim Cuc's presence surprised us. She was visiting her mother who was admitted a day before, she said. We went to see her mother.

Kim introduced us to Minh Le. In an hour-long conversation Minh Le mentioned about how they survived the Vietnam War and how they lost their other daughter in Saigon when they fled from their own country during the fall of the city.

Cathy was released from the hospital and stayed with us in Middletown while recuperating. She said she lost her fiancée back home when she got involved with Kevin. It could be the same reason why Vernon was against my coming to America.

On her third try, Cathy passed the state board for nurses and obtained her American citizenship. It was late for her to realize she didn't need Kevin's help to acquire citizenship; worse was that Kevin had a penchant for sadism. She should have left him right away after she found it out and shouldn't have become a battered wife; wasn't even a legal one. She turned out a concubine and got pregnant which Kevin, who was a married man, didn't want to happen. When he suggested abortion, Cathy ran away to save her baby's life, yet the fetus fell off. It might be God's way to save Cathy from a stormy life.

I also had a stormy life, a factor that strengthened my desire to reach America. My fate brought me to a dormant town to encounter another adversary like Bandy Moor. It was Daly's fate to wind up in Middletown and meet Brendan Cameron. It was Cathy's fate to get involved with a man she didn't know from what corner of the world he came from. We never know what's coming for us so we must brave these uncertainties with our survival instincts. We grasp for breath when we're drowning or when we're hanging on a precipice, we cling to whatever we can to save ourselves.

The will to live is instinctive, but there are beings too weak to resist the grip of death. They give up life without showing a good fight. They must have nobody to live for.

Cathy got a job at Windsor Point in Fuquay-Varina with a free quarter within the compound. The Johnsons, the kind-hearted couple who owned the facility, gave her the option to stay as long as she wanted, but Cathy had plans to move out of state after a year for fear Kevin might bother her again after his release from incarceration.

Daly told me that Brendan suggested a marriage plan before the year's end, and I must find somebody in her place if she would have to move out. Daly expressed her concern over me living alone. Being alone wasn't new to me. I'd been there before.

"It's not what I mean, Jinee. Do you want to stay a spinster throughout your life?"

I gave Daly's words a thought. I didn't want to end up living like Flora or like Miss Via Cruzes. There might be the old lady Fuller to keep me company, but not the kind of company I needed in life. Daly told me that I must find a man to love and live for. Anyway, Mrs. Fuller hadn't stopped courting me for her grandson. She had learned that Richard's relationship with Helga Schwartz was crumbling down.

At one time, Helga called and accused me of stealing Richard from her. She left a threat. I didn't come to America to wage a war against Helga Schwartz but if she'd really make good of her threats, I was ready for it. What's the use of being in the second degree of advanced proficiency in Tae Kwon Do if I can't physically defend myself?

Antagonists are good elements to energize the essence of a story. When it comes to food, they are condiments to enhance piquancy. My life in America would have been a little uninteresting if I didn't meet the likes of Bandy Moor and Cathy's Kevin. Then there was this Schwartz. She should know how I smashed Bandy Moor's nose but this unfortunate being seemed to be too aggressive to collide with me.

Well, Helga Schwartz would surely get what she wanted.

Loving is Learning

Love is learned when two individuals
have reciprocal attachments
towards each other.

          I believe that love doesn't come as instantaneous as a crush, but it's learned if two individuals have reciprocal attachments. To say I wasn't attracted to Richard is hypocritical. The man had an inevitably appealing physique, a replica of what the ancient noble Romans called "*patrician*". But physicality isn't at all that matters. Learning to love requires thorough soul-searching, so to speak.

Richard and I were learning some few good things mutually at each other at times we discussed about his grandmother's health. We were in the process of knowing each other more than plain acquaintances could share.

Richard Joseph Fuller was already a successful Certified Public Accountant when his grandmother prompted him to take up Law. He finished his Bachelor of Laws at Duke University where his grandfather graduated with excellent distinction. He was the only inheritor of what God bestowed on the grand old Fuller if physical or mental endowments are must inheritance. He could've been a prestigious lawyer if he took the bar, but not his cup of tea to the great frustration of his old lady. Richard saw how a sophistic lawyer manipulated things whatever it takes to win – saving the guilty or framing the innocent – which a counselor must do, not solely to save a client but for professional reputation - a distinction that matters to achieve fame and fortune. From him, I had learned of how a lady lawyer from Arkansas, who shared political limelight with her hubby in the nineties, saved her client even if she was fully aware her client, who was accused of raping a 12-year-old girl in 1975, was guilty as such.

Richard J. Fuller wasn't of the same ilk. How he hated to sashay in convincing the jury that he was right and truthful when he was wrong and lying. A man of few words but eloquent as much a glibber as Vernon Vergel, he spoke with perfect syntax that won't leave his listeners bedazzled. A book and street smart, he could be a good writer in the likes of the author Grisham; could be a great criminal lawyer as his grandfather was, but the guy was entangled with his accountancy job in a busy district in Manhattan.

Richard had stopped visiting his mother living in Morrisville with her third husband whom Richard couldn't get along with, yet once or twice a month, he would visit his grandmother at the LARC and would always bring her a dozen yellow roses. Only recently did he start seeing her every weekend and whenever he did, he was bringing not only a bundle of yellow roses but also another bouquet, the red ones.

How elated I was on finding out that those were for me. In Filipino culture, a man giving red roses to a woman unrelated to him is up for something. Whatever Americans regard about it, I believed Richard Joseph Fuller was only showing his appreciation of my concern over his grandmother's health. Elizabeth Taylor Fuller thought differently; I heard her say: "Somebody is learning to love somebody."

"It's me who's jealous of your Rhett Butler," Richard responded to her jest.

I shut my ears from their conversation. When Richard handed me the flowers, Elizabeth threw me a naughty glance, excused herself and slipped out of her room.

"I appreciate this gesture, but don't you think your fiancée won't get jealous of this?"

". . . My fiancée! Where did you learn that?"

"She, herself, told me at the restaurant . . . that you're getting married with her."

"And you believe that nonsense?"

"I may not believe it, but it was an indication that I must avoid you."

"I never had proposed anything to her."

"You haven't but . . .?"

"I'm not thinking about that either."

"But even though . . ."

"Why are you making this a problem?"

"I don't want to be the cause of your breakup."

"If I'm learning to love you, no one can prevent me from doing so."

Richard's audacity was stunning, like a rush of a whirlwind that suddenly wrapped around me; I only could think impulsively of getting out of it right away.

"If you excuse me, Mr. Fuller, I'm still at work."

"No, you're not. You're off at three; it's way past the hour."

"In that case, I know it now why Mrs. Fuller asked me to come here when I get off."

"I asked Grandma to do it for me."

"Does Helga know you're here?"

"I thought we should not be talking about her."

"That's why I want to leave now."

"Can we talk again sometime?"

"Sorry, but we've got nothing to talk about."

"Or does your boyfriend forbid?"

"I don't have a boyfriend."

What I said, I realized later, sounded like an insinuation.

"That spells loneliness. Did you ever have one before?"

"I had but we broke up because of my decision to come to America."

"And you haven't found yet any replacement, have you?"

"I don't intend to," I said shying away from his eyes. "I'd been there once."

"Once is not enough."

I left Richard right there without saying goodbye. He must have known that unlike Helga Schwartz, I felt awkward discussing intimate thoughts. I was born and raised in a third-world country; had a different upbringing and wrapped up in a different culture. I may have been living in America for almost a decade, yet I was still to adapt myself to the way American ladies deal love and courtship.

L

In the Realm of Decency

Human behaviors are changing with time,
what was considered indecent before
may be acceptable now to society.

I must have offended Richard when I left him abruptly. I had a slight apprehension he'd be despising me.

Or maybe not . . .

The next morning when I came to visit Mrs. Fuller, I found a note pasted on her headboard written in the form of a poem and obviously meant for me.

> To the lady named Jin X:
> *"The love you've lost stays in your heart.*
> *Love doesn't leave 'though lovers part.*
> *You live to love; you love to live.*
> *There's always love your heart can give."*

Richard's note had given me inspiring thoughts. *He wasn't hurt after all,* I consoled myself although I felt a little bit embarrassed of the bad conduct I showed. He was right. Why should I deprive myself of love for somebody?

Nobody should forbid anybody to love somebody for it's everybody's rights, an inherent emotion which God granted to humanity. Elizabeth and Warren were showing it openly notwithstanding their ages.

But in a month that Richard didn't visit his grandmother, I was apprehensive again.

"I'm sorry, Mrs. Fuller. The last time Richard and I had a talk, I left him abruptly."

"Why? Did he do something wrong?"

"No, he did not. Your grandson is ever nice and gentle. It was just . . ."

"You found yourself falling for him, and you're afraid to love again," bluntly, the old lady said. "Don't deny because I sense it. I wasn't born yesterday."

"Was he offended when I left him?"

"Tell me honestly . . . are you falling in love with my grandson?"

Avoiding her question, I moved to the window and peeped outside.

"It's a beautiful day outside, Mrs. Fuller!"

"You haven't answered me. I will rephrase my question: Do you like my grandson?"

I laughed at her insistence.

"I like him but that doesn't mean that I . . ."

"I know you do. Stop pretending, honey and make the first move."

"Mrs. Fuller!"

"You may think it indecent but it's happening nowadays all over America."

"Mrs. Fuller, how disgusting could that be!"

"Listen . . . I was born in the 20's and had thought that today's generation is disgusting but time's changing, honey. Women are now coming up front."

"They can do very well what men can. Is that what you mean, Mrs. Fuller?"

"Look, they're now in politics. They go to war. They can . . ."

"I know your point. If men can court women, why can't women woo men?"

"Exactly . . . the word itself signifies that a woman can woo a man."

God created the world and created a man out of His image to rule the world. Then, realizing that the Man was alone and lonely, He created a Woman to give him a company.

That was the beginning of humanity. Since then, list of the world's greatest warriors and rulers is men-dominated and that made women referred to as the weaker gender. The bible itself speaks of man's prowess than of woman's adroitness as discoveries and inventions had been by the stronger gender. The fact that a family should bear the husband's surname evidenced men's superiority.

"Mrs. Fuller, what I said didn't mean I love him. Loving isn't as instant as liking; it's more felt than thought of - not a plaything to be discarded when it has turned boring. I believe loving is learned.

I'd learn to love a man without inhibition. If I were to marry him, I must know him undoubtedly well for as his wife, I'm bound to devote myself to him for marriage to me is an eternal communion with God."

"You must know him fully well before you'd love him. Is that what you mean?"

"I can't love a man I haven't known fully well . . ."

"Was I wrong in marrying Richard's grandfather?"

"Why should I say that . . .?"

"Well, I married him without knowing him so well?"

"We're of different beliefs and cultures; of different generations."

"I'm not intruding my grandson's privacy, but I don't want his marriage to suffer. I see in you the most ideal things for a wife. Marry my grandson, Jinee."

Mrs. Fuller said her words very ordinarily as if marriage was a very simple thing to happen. For us Filipinos, marriage follows detailed lists of 'must do'.

"We're not even on yet," I said with a dry laughter; forcing myself to laugh.

"I told you, make the first move . . ."

I burst out laughing tinged with discourteousness in my disapproval of Mrs. Fuller's idea. Her advice was more shocking than stunning. She was born scores ago, and I could hardly believe she could tell me those advocacies of hers openly. Here was me with conformed decency that could be hypocritical in some outlook and classified as totally outlandish; wrapped with old morals handed down from older generations with pride and dignity. Gone were the years when women were regarded the weaker sex, but even if it was a Sadie Hawkins Day, I never would do what the old lady suggested.

"Oh, Mrs. Fuller, what you suggested is very impossible to happen."

"I got something to tell you. Sit down and listen . . ."

Like a child that I was - listening to my own grandmother's tale, I sat on the footstool in front of her. The old Lady Fuller gazed into my eyes like wanting to measure how intellectual I was to absorb what she was going to tell. Gazing back, I could picture how she looked when she was mistaken for Patricia Donnelly, the Miss America of 1939.

Mrs. Fuller began her anecdote with her eyes cast outside in retrospection; a smile formed faintly on her lips. It made me so curious to know what she was going to tell me.

"There was once a young girl so naïve and diffident. And there was this young lad, so timid, so reticent," the old lady started her story. Another exquisite pleasure surfaced in her lips which heightened the curiosity in me to listen further. "By chance they had seen each other a few times in the park, felt an instantaneous mutual fondness but no one of them dared to confide what the other felt."

Mrs. Fuller paused. Her eyes glinted - probably amused by what she had to tell me which could be fragments of her memory; I sensed it well.

"Then came a war which both the boy and the girl feared could draw them apart. Following each other's intuition, they met at the park once more but all they did in that meeting was introduce themselves to each other, exchange tokens and promise to see each other again after the war was over. True to her promise, when the war was over, the girl came to the park with high hopes she would see him there as he promised. She left the park only when sunset came. For almost a month, the girl kept coming to that place in the park, but the boy never came there anymore."

Mrs. Fuller fell silent again. I was staring closely at her eyes which seemed nailed at quite a distance. I could see tears starting to shimmer there. When she shifted her eyes at me, her tears fell. Quickly, she wiped those tears with her fingers. Then she continued to talk. This time she had her eyes on me.

"Countless years had passed. The girl was married to another man and had totally forgotten about the boy. Then one day, at the twilight of their lives, they met again."

I was anxious to hear what she was going to say next, but she must have ended her story already. She took off the necklace she was wearing and opened the silver locket before my eyes. It revealed a sepia-colored photo of a young woman. I didn't see the resemblance right away, but I had the feeling it was her.

"This was you! And the boy you were talking about, who was he?"

"He was Warren Bates," Mrs. Fuller said with bitter sadness in her face.

I heard them unfolding their story. They were young then – young and foolish for letting chances pass by. War separated them and after over six decades, they met again there at the place where both were supposed to be waiting for the twilight of their years. It would have been better if they hadn't met anymore.

"Why are you telling me this?"

"To let you realize that moments we lost are crucial in changing our future."

I gave Mrs. Fuller an appreciating smile for the wisdom she imparted. She could be right, but we can't make use of every moment that passes by. I couldn't just hurry Richard to court and marry me to avoid losing some moments. The lady was right about her grandson, but it wasn't worth debasing decency and dignity of my womanhood. I could never make the first move as Mrs. Fuller suggested.

"You're always telling me to uphold the dignity of the Filipino womanhood," Daly told me when I asked her opinion. Of course, she was against Mrs. Fuller's idea. "Don't tell me to be an American because I'm in America," Daly quipped and walked away.

Daly was right as my old folks could be. Everybody was right but Mrs. Fuller! Her open-mindedness was sometimes shocking. She had discussed this before, and I wasn't sure if I admired her candidness or thought of it as bizarre.

At one instance, Mrs. Fuller asked me what to do if I desired to eat the red delicious- looking apple hanging high up in its tree. Would I wait till the fruit drops to my mouth? I told her I would find a way, of course, to pluck it out. Mrs. Fuller wasn't always right in doing things her way for loving a man and picking some fruit from its tree are quite irrelevant to each other. In this area, she was different from my grandmother, but she claimed that seldom did she make wrong decisions because she was open to possibilities, which in her thoughts might not have been existent. She said there was no harm about being candid; I just wasn't used to it.

It is said that the Almighty God wrote the fate of every human born on Earth, yet I believe that we're responsible of the fate we got because we let things happen. To achieve what's best for us depends on our dreams, on our guts and on our instincts.

Making advances to catch the man that makes a perfect husband is another story. I'm not tailored for that; even abhor flirting. I don't care if I'm fated to follow the likes of Flora and Miss Via and my own Aunt Thelma. If the Lord wants me to end up a spinster, that's fine. This time I won't mind anymore what fate my Lord has written for me.

LI

To Love Again

Through the years
I deprived myself to love again.
Now, I wish I had someone to care for.

I was off from work at three one
Saturday, but Daly informed me earlier that she'd be working late and would call when she was ready. I've got to wait; I had her car.

While waiting for Daly's call, I drove to Barnes & Noble to buy a copy of Arthur Golden's *'Memoirs of a Geisha'*. The lady Fuller mentioned the book to me when she talked about her grandson having been to Japan and experienced meeting a geisha. I had the wrong impression of a geisha. It almost cost me a good relationship with Vernon.

At the bookstore's coffee stand, while sipping café noir, I browsed pages of *'Cold Mountains'* by Charles Frazier, a Carolinian from the Blue Ridge Mountains. Mrs. Fuller had a penchant for southern authors and had been reading this book at the patio while waiting for her 'Rhett Butler'.

That reminded me of Warren being rushed to the hospital the previous night for some complications that need constant monitoring. I had to tell Elizabeth about it in person so that if she needed somebody for comfort, I was around.

The lady had her afternoon catnap.

I remembered it was the weekend that Richard was going to visit his grandmother. Not wanting to meet him, I must get out of the room immediately. I signed the book I bought for Mrs. Fuller then hurried back outside in the nick of time - Richard was walking down the hall with two bouquets of red and yellow roses. I hid behind a pillar and after he passed by, briskly walked away until I reached the back of the building that housed the 400 Hall. It was the same old place where the old lovey-dovey had their weekend rendezvous - a vantage point to watch the sun setting down behind the Appalachian Mountains.

I stood there for a moment watching the sunset while recollecting memories. As a child, it intrigued me no end what place was there where the sun had gone. I thought it was America. I only realized it when I came of age that there wasn't any place beneath the western skies. The firmament has limitless expanse; boundless as one's imaginations; endless as the cycle of life.

I had that idea one late summer afternoon when Vernon came to Sacandaya and watched the sunset with me. How pleasurable it was to recollect those moments but sad to know it would never be realized again. Vernon had become a soldier of God.

Was he really destined to serve God that way? What if I caved into his persuasions? Ahhh . . . no one had ever declared going against Fate and came out triumphant.

"Jinee . . ."

"Yes, Vernon . . ."

"It's me . . . Richard." The voice came from behind.

"Oh, I'm sorry," I said. Somewhat embarrassed, I didn't turn around to face him.

"You'd never forget him. Is Vernon his name?"

"Yes, it is," I said coyly, nodding at the same time but didn't turn around.

"You'd never get away from his memories unless you find someone to help you forget him. You need somebody to love and care for you. You deserve another chance, Jinee and I'm here for that."

He said those words daringly fast and fresh; he turned me stiff.

I heard nothing more after a while; I thought everything was but a figment of my hallucination. A few seconds had passed when I turned around, but lo and behold! Richard was standing there, close behind me, so that when I avoided bumping into him, I tripped. He caught me in his arms - held my shoulders and when I didn't attempt to free myself, he moved his hands gently down to my waist. His gestures petrified me but at the same time, thrilled me. I felt melting in his warm hands that even if I wanted to resist, I hadn't.

Through the years, I deprived myself to fall in love again. In that inescapable situation, when I could almost hear his heartbeats, when his breath was blowing wondrous warmth in my face, I turned unsure of what I believed in – not to fall in love with a man who already had commitments to somebody. Richard intruded into my loneliness, and I let him seduce me although I knew where that situation would lead to. I was wrapped up in irresistibility - surrendering to his advances.

Tenderly, I felt the touch of his lips on mine. He did it lightly, but it brought sensation that turned me unresisting – sizzling my whole being. I gasped and was about to give out an ardent response when I realized that we were at a vantage point for people who might be watching us at that moment. Deeply abashed, I pushed him back.

Richard apologized for intruding in my solitude, but I was so embarrassed that I couldn't even throw a glance at him; couldn't say a word about it.

Seconds of silence passed by when I heard him excusing himself to get the roses he brought for me from his grandmother's room. When he was out of sight, I hurriedly walked away. I was already inside the car when I realized what I did was unethical. Either to go back or to go on wasn't any better than the other but I chose the latter decision.

Daly was behind the wheel searching for the US1 Highway while asking senseless things I hardly responded; all I had in mind was Richard. How was it when he returned to the patio and found I was no longer around? *That wasn't funny!*

"Are you okay?"

I didn't want to respond; Daly was upsetting me, but I knew her: the more she became irritating if she found me upset.

"Hoy, are you okay?"

"Yes, I am."

"No, I don't think you are."

"I'm fine, okay?"

Daly insisted something was disturbing me. I confessed.

"What? Richard made a pass to you. What did he do?"

"He kissed me on my lips."

"He did? Without precaution? Without permission? Was it good? Did you respond? Hoy, did you kiss back?"

She laughed out loud when I said I didn't.

"Liar! I know you liked it. You let him kiss you because you missed Vernon's kisses."

Daly's reaction turned me so upset but I stayed silent; she was right.

Daly freed an upsetting laughter again as she entered the highway, speeding up at ten more than the maximum. She wasn't cautious of her speed anymore.

"Watch out!" I cautioned. "You're over the speed limit."

"I know," she snapped. "But I've to be home by six. Brendan would be calling."

"It's not a reason to race with death."

"This time, it's you who's scared."

"Because you're not an expert driver . . ."

"Well, watch me."

The red needle on the speedometer had reached 80 in the 65-mph zone. The car screeched as she followed a sharp curve to the right.

"Slow down!"

"You're scared. Watch me . . ."

"I should be watching for a police car instead. Gosh! Here's one coming!"

She slowed down abruptly. The car's speedometer moved fast back to 65.

"You fooled me."

"And why are you such in a hurry?"

"Brendan must be calling me at home by now. We're coming late."

"Why doesn't he call on your cell phone?"

"He knows I don't want to chat on the phone while driving."

"He doesn't know you're driving by this time."

"That's why he calls the home phone to be sure. I'll tell Brendan about this."

"About your reckless driving . . .?"

"About Richard's progress . . ."

"What's it to him?"

"When Brendan proposed marriage, I told him I'd let you get married first."

"Are you sure of Brendan? You know, it had happened to Cathy . . ."

"I couldn't ask for a better one . . ."

"In that case, then marry him. Grandma told me about this song that goes: Once you have found him never let him go."

"I don't want to leave you all alone . . ."

"Don't worry about me. Cathy's here."

"But Cathy has plans to move to California. You know that."

"My mother is coming, anyway."

"That's not what I mean, Jinee. Do you intend to stay a spinster all your life? Of course, no! Now here comes Richard. Should you let him go out of your life?"

"I'm worried about it. I don't want to love somebody and lost him again."

"Who says you're going to lose him?"

"You could be right . . . But I might have changed Richard's perception on me; I left him abruptly today without excusing myself."

"You did? Where are your manners?"

"When I realized that was rude, I was already in the car, and it would be stupid of me to come back and apologize. I drove away."

"You did it to him twice already and that's very embarrassing," Daly said as if she knew better how things are rightly done. "Now, you have to call him and apologize."

I dialed the number in Mrs. Fuller's room. It was Richard who answered. My first reaction was to hang up but wanting to talk to him was the reason why I called.

"Richard? I thought you're on the way back to New York."

"Grandma asked me to stay."

"Then, when are you going back?"

"Probably, tomorrow. . . ."

"Richard, about earlier today . . ."

"I know; I scared you."

"It was my fault," I said, and Richard was mumbling the same thing simultaneously.

"I shouldn't have approached you that way," he said apologetically.

"And I shouldn't have left you that way   "

"I think we should see each other again to make amends in person," he proposed.

"That's what I thought."

"See, we really are meant for each other, Jinee; we have the same thinking. So, is it possible to see you tomorrow?"

"How about making it the next time you come to visit your grandmother? It's a Sunday tomorrow and you need to drive back to New York, aren't you?"

"No, not until we see each other again. Can it be tomorrow?"

"Okay . . . tomorrow's fine with me."

"Where can I meet you? Would you like me to come down there?"

"You don't know where I live."

"Well, it's not a problem. What's my GPS for?"

"Anyway, I must go to the facility for something. Will you meet me at the patio?"

"Okay then . . . at the patio. I can't hardly wait   "

"Richard, did you say it's a date?"

"I guess it is," Richard quipped and laughed. "You aren't scared, are you?"

"No, Mr. Fuller. Unless you have plans to rape me . . ."

We both laughed heartily.

"Jinee, you haven't been to Yuki No Hana at night . . ."

"I haven't. I think of going there someday; I promised Meiko."

"Perfect! We'll go there tomorrow; I haven't been there for quite a time now."

"Is grandma, I mean your grandma, coming with us?"

"No, Jinee. It will only be you and me. This time, Yuki No Hana belongs to us."

LII

An Enchanted Evening

He held my hand, squeezed it.
I heard him say what he felt about me.
I gripped his hand but shied away from his stare.

Yuki No Hana glittered like Tokyo by night, according to Richard; he'd been to that exotic city of Japan for business convention the previous summer. Jesting, I asked him if he'd spent some nights with a geisha and he responded with a grin like how Vernon reacted when I asked him the same question enough to tell me he did. It occurred to me that a machismo setting afoot in the Land of the Rising Sun for the first time, sleeping with a geisha is his baptism of fire. *Men are men*, the thought flashed in my mind.

Despite of the heavy facial make-up she had and the décor she wore in her head, I easily recognized the waitress from Midori's. Her enthused reaction told me how delighted she was seeing me there. Meiko led us to the table where I could have a close look at the chanteuse whose eyes, she said, were like mine.

The food was delightful. I could've finished the whole serving if Richard hadn't kept an eye on me while raising questions about Vernon Vergel. I avoided talking about it as he hinted to me not to talk about Helga Schwartz.

By eight, the house was packed out. A middle-aged man in black coat tinkled the keys of the piano. The appearance of Yoshiko silhouetted against a kaleidoscope of dancing colors was met with ovation. In a short while, a shaft of light revealed her in a splendid white kimono with a red obi around her waist which dangled down to her ankle; her hair coiffed bun-like was loaded with fancy goods. In measured steps, she drifted gracefully to the front edge of the platform. There, she stood still until the applause subsided. As the spotlight roved around, she greeted the diners even mentioning names of regular habitués. She mentioned Richard's name when the beam was on us and to my surprise, announced my presence. I stood up and nodded in appreciation for her acknowledgement.

"How did she know me?"

"Don't you remember Kim Cuc, the Vietnamese waitress?" Richard grinned.

My jaw dropped. Who could ever think of that waitress as a nightclub crooner.

"Is she the person that Meiko mistook me for?"

"Yes, she is.

"Do I really look like her?"

"I noticed the resemblance in your eyes."

The pianist opened the show with the intro of *Yuki No Hana*, the nightclub's theme song. Yoshiko's voice blended with it softly like the gentle flowing of a stream with its rustles rhyming beneath a full moon in an early dawn. In appreciation, the customers greeted it with loud applause.

I could hardly believe that the Kim Cuc I met at the Vietnamese restaurant had a singing voice that was velvety sweet and soothing and as dreamy as that starry evening. Richard faintly laughed at my reaction. He squeezed my hand; I let him do it.

At one moment, I pressed his hand in reflex. That compelled him to whisper what he felt about me. It was something joyous and it gave me lovely feelings like there were butterflies fluttering inside me. I didn't say anything in response, but gripped his hand enough to let him sense I had a special feeling for him, too. When he inclined to kiss me, I evaded. I had this intuition that someone's eyes were piercing my back that moment.

Yoshiko Yamasaki belted out Japanese ditties before she came up with English songs. Then before taking her break, she announced the name of the man on the piano. Hiroshi Yamasaki immediately stood up to acknowledge the applause. I saw only the right side of the pianist, but I could tell very well he bore that distinct distinction of a native Asian.

Back to his bench, the pianist played a classic nostalgia of the sixties when songs were imbued with sentimentalism and worded with fervent emotions. The music of Hiroshi Yamasaki would have brought my mother to tears if she were there.

I stood up as Richard did when Yoshiko approached us. All the while, I was staring at her face intently. I didn't realize the resemblance of our eyes even at a closer look – hers were heavily shaded in purple

- but somehow, it flattered me to know I have some similarities with this celebrity who wore different names in separate places and in different races with separate personalities. That was Kim Cuc, the waitperson I met once at a Vietnamese bistro.

"I was baptized as Kim Cuc. When I got older my father changed my name to Yoshiko as a reminder of my heritage, but my mom, a Montagnard, keeps calling me by my Vietnamese name."

"Is the pianist your father?" I asked even if I knew it already; Richard told me. "He did great with his renditions of the old favorites."

"I told my father of your presence, and he said he'd play the song he learned from a Filipino friend he got acquainted with in Vietnam if you have a little time to linger . . ."

"What a surprise!" I exclaimed. "I feel honored . . ."

Yoshiko excused herself and approached her father. Then Hiroshi started to prelude the song he wanted to play for me. I could tell it was the lullaby that Mama used to send me to sleep, the favorite song of my father. I stood up and clapped my hands to acknowledge it.

I was about to settle back to my seat when somebody slugged me in the face so hard. I lost my balance and was thrown down to the floor. I looked up and saw Helga Schwartz standing proud and mighty over me.

Richard got me up and I was about to strike back at Helga, but Richard stood between us keeping me behind him. The termagant would have suffered my wrath. Two security men led her out of the club.

There could've been a big brawl that evening and had us landing in jail while our faces were gracing the front page of The News & Observer the following morning.

LIII

The Unexpected Guest

I didn't want to cross paths with Richard's mother.
Mrs. Fuller had told me to avoid meeting Bianca
in the dark, but suddenly, there she appeared.

What happened in Yuki No Hana was nothing compared to the physical combats I'd been through when back in college, I joined intense student street demonstrations. I often found myself with other student demonstrators clashing against men in uniform who were armed with truncheons and pistols. I wasn't ever afraid of those cops. In my teens, I got a lot of courage.

Helga caught me unaware. It never came to my mind that she'd be spying on us that time in Yuki No Hana although I got the feeling someone was eyeing my back. Helga Schwartz, the latest addition to my list of adversaries should know who she was bullyragging. She should have seen what I did to Bandy Moor.

Richard drove me back to LARC to get my car. Before I traced my way back home, I paid Mrs. Fuller a courtesy call. I thought that would take me only a few minutes, but the lady noticed the bruise in my face. I was thinking of a good alibi when Richard told her what transpired. Mrs. Fuller persuaded me to file damages, but I didn't intend to. That would have placed Richard between me and Helga if summoned as a principal witness together with Yoshiko Yamasaki. Richard was a very busy person; had more important things to do in his accounting office in Manhattan and I knew Yoshiko had a sickly mother to attend to and was apprehensive in facing investigations.

My list of adversaries wouldn't end with Helga's name. There was Bianca Stan, Mrs. Fuller's former daughter-in-law whom the old lady loathed. She said I wouldn't like to meet Richard's mother in the dark. I didn't get her dictum but deemed it a warning.

I avoided crossing path with Bianca but a day after Richard had gone back to New York she intruded into Elizabeth Fuller's room, walked in through the door like an evil specter, even ignoring the presence of her former mother-in-law who was in her bed right in front of the door. I wouldn't have thought Bianca was trespassing had I not seen Mrs. Fuller's face fuming in anger.

"I never invited you to come here," she told Bianca straight to her face.

"You never did but aren't you glad I'm paying you a visit?"

"You're not welcome here, Mrs. Satan!"

"It's Stan, Mrs. Fuller!"

"Whatever! Why are you here? What do you want from me?"

"Excuse me, Mrs. Fuller. The truth is I didn't come here to see you, but this girl."

Bianca glanced at me maliciously. I should have left the room immediately, but it wasn't a clever idea to leave Mrs. Fuller alone with an evil specter.

"You don't have any business with her."

"Yes, I have; my son's dating her and I got information that she comes here often."

Helga must have told her of the incident.

I nailed my eyes on Bianca – preparing myself for the situation – when she forwarded towards me.

"What's that contusion in your face, young lady?" Bianca asked when she already knew it. Helga Schwartz must have told her what had happened the past Sunday evening.

"Why are you asking?" Mrs. Fuller interrupted. "I'd like you to know, Jinee, how this once a Fuller became a Satan."

"It's Stan!"

"Satan befits you better, false accuser! You accused my son of having extra marital affair when it was you who had it."

Bianca ignored what she heard – intentionally maybe; her attention was on me. I took my eyes off her and pretended to be doing something relative to my work. The evil woman kept staring at me from head to toe; I could see it from the corner of my eyes.

"You can go back to the nurse's station, Jinee. Leave me alone with this devil. I know how to handle her."

"You haven't answered me yet, young lady," Bianca blurted.

"You don't have to answer her, Jinee," Mrs. Fuller intervened.

"Ahhh . . . her name's Jinee; I didn't get it right away."

"What's it to you, Bianca?"

". . . and where the hell she's from?"

"You're out of line. That's Richard's concern."

"— and mine, too. You forgot that Richard Joseph is my son!"

"Not anymore! You gave him up on me in favor of your second marriage. Now you have the audacity to tell me that Richard's life is your personal concern! That's baloney!"

"I gave him life!" Bianca yelled.

"You gave him trouble!" Mrs. Fuller snapped back. "Where were you in those years when he needed your attention? You were nowhere enjoying the company of your husbands. I brought him to what he's now and I'd never trade those years with this day when you come to claim that his life is your concern. You better get out of here! Get out!"

Bianca cast a sharp stare at her former mother-in-law. When she tried to speak again, outright Elizabeth pressed the buzzer. A male nurse aide immediately rushed in. Bianca buzzed off. Elizabeth grabbed the phone and dialed a number. I had a hunch she was calling her grandson. I hurried out instantly leaving Mrs. Fuller alone in her room.

LIV

The Unholy Trinity

The unholy three were all against me.
I gave them what they wanted
and that made my day.

Richard must have ironed out the creases between his folks. Mrs. Fuller didn't object when Richard told her that he'd take me to Bianca's house to introduce me formally to his mother, to which I also concurred; it might wipe off Bianca's antipathies towards me.

Autumn was at its peak but that Sunday morning in November, although colder than the few past days, promised a wonderful day. We almost missed the Sunday Holy Mass had I not remembered America was back to Standard Time.

We proceeded to Stan's in Morrisville afterwards. Richard hadn't been there for some time due to his stepfather's indifference. Bianca assured him that Mr. Stan was out of state that weekend.

I was looking forward to a very pleasant day with Richard's mother, but then what I saw in Stan's driveway foreboded a displeasing event: There was Helga's flashy red sedan and aside from Bianca's black car, there was another black sedan unfamiliar to Richard. At first, I was hesitant to go on but on second thought, I realized I had been looking forward to the day I could get back at Helga. A payback from her was what I was waiting for.

As if I knew what was coming, I had prepared myself for that event; I didn't wear my usual Sunday habiliments but denims, shirt and sneakers; my hair hung loose.

"Sorry, Jin. I didn't expect Helga would be here. We can go back if you want to. This time, the decision is yours."

"Let's go on." I said, forwarding a step.

"Are you ready for another face off?" Richard asked when he raced past me.

"This could be the moment I was waiting for: to meet her again for a showdown."

The truth is I wanted Helga to see me again with Richard – jealousy can kill. Challenges measure my prowess to overcome obstacles. Richard didn't know I could be a fiery fox if the situation was needed. If I let myself cower, then I shouldn't have come to try my life in a foreign land.

Helga laid her eyes on me the moment I entered the house. By her glances I could anticipate bad situations coming our way. Bianca introduced her to me inducing a malicious meaning. Richard barged into his mother's impropriety.

"The three of us had already agreed to lunch together today," Bianca reasoned out.

"What three of us, Mom?" Richard retorted.

Bianca pouted her lips towards the bar. There sat the haughty creature I never thought I'd meet again.

"You still remember Miss Moor, don't you?"

"You didn't tell me this would be the situation . . ." Richard said brusquely.

"Is it necessary to inform you about it?" Bianca retorted.

Richard's mother was fond of surprising people; that was her nature. Recently, she surprised Mrs. Fuller at the facility with her presence. Then she did it to me. *This could be what Mrs. Fuller warned me about: Never to meet Bianca Stan in the dark.*

Bandy Moor looked unbothered. She was as if in deep concentration on what was painted in the porcelain jar that was on the ledge of the bar. She took out a cigarette stick, placed it between her lips. She lit the cigarette stick with her hand quivering, and I could tell the aggressiveness whirring in her by the way she puffed the cigarette. It smoldered fast leaving half-an-inch long of ashes. She inhaled the smoke and exhaled it through her nostrils. Before she stubbed the ashes on the tray, she puffed it once more, took a deep breath and belched out a large volume of smoke before she squelched the fire. After adding more wine to her glass, she took a little sip and stood up. She squinted at me showing a mirthless grin without saying a word. I noticed she had replaced her missing front teeth with dentures, but with the same shaggy hair not to mention her usual bumpy curves, she still looked like a troll.

"Do you know each other?" I heard Bianca throwing her question in a casual manner, but neither Bandy Moor nor I gave her a response.

"Stop those pretenses, Mom. When you learned that Jinee had worked with the SJNC, you got in touch with Miss Moor, a CNA then when you were the nursing director.

"So, what is it to you?" Bianca asked impetuously.

"If you have plans to ruin our presence here, forget about it; we can leave right now," Richard told his mother; the anger in his face surfaced in his voice.

Bianca forwarded some steps closer to her son, "And what made you think of that?"

"Grandma told me that you'd been to the facility looking for Jinee."

"What more did that old bitch tell you?"

"Mom, please give a little respect to my father's mother. Grandma would never put me at her beck and call for she knows how steadfast I am - the reason why I can't get along with your manipulative husband because I won't ever bow down to his wishes."

"We better get out of here," I told Richard and pulled him towards the door.

"I still have an unfinished business with you!" Bandy Moor butted in screaming. "I won't let this chance pass by

"And so, do I," Helga Schwartz bragged in.

"And do you think I just watch here without doing anything?" Richard yelled.

"Leave this to me, Richard. I can handle this."

That was my time to get even with Helga; the time I long have waited for.

This German Shepperd dog would get what she wants. And Bandy Moor. . . this old troll needs one more knock-out punch to make her realize she isn't a good match to me.

Stealthily like a slithering snake, the tigress forwarded with her smoldering eyes plastered on mine. In them, I saw repercussions of the bad incident between us back in Middletown. In her right hand was a glass half-full of ice cubes saturated with wine. Slivers rattled as she was shaking the glass slightly.

Knowing her tricks and theatrics, I prepared for her faintest move. Thinking I let my guard down, she whisked the wine in my face right when she was close in front of me. I slipped aside more quickly in time Bianca was passing behind and the ice pebbles rained like hail over her head, drenching her made-up face. Bandy's eyes jutted out and so were Helga's; their jaws dropped awfully as they watched Richard's mother gasp for breath.

I almost burst into laughter. My reaction heightened Bandy Moor's anger. She was about to throw at me the glass she was holding, but Richard was quick to hold her and squeezed the glass from her hand. The troll became more aggressive. Knowing her stunt, I was able to evade when she jumped at me, budged her back with my elbow and followed it with my foot snapping her buttocks that banged her against the wall; she dropped down yelping like a dog in pain. She had to realize that not her kind could scare me.

Before I could turn to Schwartz, she had clenched at my back, her fingernails slicing my skin. I turned around in fast motion banging her against the wall. She was thrown off my back and smashed head-on against the troll. Both slumped to the floor, their faces twitched miserably which looked funny to me and I could have freed a good laugh when they groaned simultaneously.

That didn't calm them down; they posed to gang up again.

Helga dashed in but missed. I kicked her butt, bumping her hard against the couch. A whack on Moor's face made her turn around in 360 degrees and with a good force hit her thigh with my right foot slumping her again against the wall. She fell flat on her back, squirming. I grabbed the porcelain jar from the bar, and with her head between my knees, I raised the jar high with both hands to smash it on Moor's face.

"My jar . . . my antique jar . . .!" Bianca screamed out. "Richard, do something!"

Richard took the jar from my hands and placed it back on the counter and aided Moor to her feet. Helga was also struggling to stand up. Bianca grunted like an angry wild sow; she had witnessed how I crushed her two German shepherds with my bare hands.

Richard raised my right arm, jeering like he did when he watched how the Duke Blue Devils smashed the UNC Tar Heels by one point.

"Jinee is open for rematch. Just call," he taunted.

Richard freed out boisterous laughter as we stepped out of the door. That would've left Hitler's advocates angrier. We walked out without goodbyes passing by Bianca Stan who stood petrified at the doorway. "Well, mother, don't ever unleash your German Shepherd's again; they'll end up dead."

To me, revenge is immeasurable, and retaliation is never satisfying. True satisfaction according to my mother is achieved by forgiving; it's sweeter than taking revenge. I was into it, but it depends on the situation. Those dogs were up against me, and it was just right for me to defend myself; they got what they were looking for.

As if what happened that day wasn't enough to make it a remarkable one, the following Monday, it was in The News and Observer that the administrator of the SJNC was arrested for driving erratically back to Middletown. Failing the Breathalyzer test, she was charged with DUI, was placed on 36-month probation and ordered to attend alcohol education classes for a month.

That happened at high noon, but it was as if the whole day was already over; it had become very satisfying!

LV

Warren's
Whereabouts

Warren Bates had been gone.
Nobody told Elizabeth Fuller about it.
The consensus was: better for her not to know.

It was noontime when we got out
of Stan's, but it looked like twilight had come. The skies were covered
with rain clouds. That Sunday in November was much colder than
the past days; autumn was at its peak.

Inside the car, I noticed a bruise in my face and scratching
marks on my shoulders. Anyway, my adversaries had paid what
they owed me. They must realize I wasn't the kind they could
easily mess with. I had exacted my vengeance against Helga –
hitting her face twice and harder than how she did to me in Yuki
No Hana. Bandy Moor suffered the same pain. Had I smashed her
face with Bianca's jar, she would have turned uglier than ever. At
the height of anger, I didn't think how precious that Chinese jar
of Satan's was.

"Mom was worried more about her antique jar than Moor's antique face," Richard scoffed. He said something funnier when his phone chirped. He looked at the caller ID.

"If it's your mother, give her a chance to explain her side."

He tossed the phone to the back seat.

"Let her suffer."

"Calm down; you're driving."

"I'm okay . . . I could even drive back to New York later."

"You're not in a good mood. It's going to rain; the road to New York is slippery."

"Thanks, Jin for your concern," he said and freed out a light laugh. "After the old bruise healed, you got another in the same spot. Sorry, girl; I didn't expect it would turn out like that."

I fingered the bruise in my face. "Nobody's to be blamed but circumstances."

"Hey, you're good in Martial Arts."

"I learned it in college when I was a student militant. Learning martial arts was a must and an advantage for we often clashed with cops whenever we held rallies.

"That was when you met Vernon."

Pretending not to have heard him, I called his attention to a burger stand. We stopped and grabbed sandwiches for lunch. Then Richard talked of Vernon again.

"I just want to know more about him. Do I have what he had?"

"Do you have what he had . . . Of course, you have!"

"Don't give it another meaning."

"You're implying it . . ."

"Why did you love him?"

"Tell me first why you loved Helga Schwartz?"

"Helga was a hell of mistakes."

"Vernon was not; he was the first man I ever have loved."

"Then, why did you break up with him?"

"Coming to America was my mother's dream for me. I had that dream too, but Vernon was against it, so we parted ways. Now, it's my turn to ask."

"Shoot," Richard replied right away like he was ready to answer any inquiry.

"Why did you break up with Helga?"

"I hate her jealousy tantrums. She was always upset and suspecting."

"You must have given her reasons to act like that."

"She's just too possessive – doesn't like me talk with other women or say nice things about them and it became worse lately: she didn't want me to look at any woman's eyes anymore. It had become suffocating."

"Did she tell you what she did at the Vietnamese restaurant?"

"Yes, she did, and we had a serious quarrel when we drove away from there."

"In Yuki No Hana, how come she knew we're there that evening?"

"I mentioned it to my mother," Richard confessed. "You wouldn't have crossed path with Helga were it not of me."

"Give her a break; little misunderstandings are easy to patch up."

"Are you telling me to kiss up with her?"

"I'm afraid you're making me her substitute – another hell of mistakes."

"Definitely not; in fact, I'm ready to marry you right now."

"What! What are you talking about?"

"I'm proposing marriage . . ."

"You're talking as if marriage is a board game that can be played whenever you want to. It's not something that you could easily run into . . ."

"That's where we're going later. First, I will ask your friend's permission."

"Daly's at work."

"Not Daly, but your other friend, Elizabeth Fuller."

We came to the facility after we had our lunch. We found Mrs. Fuller on the patio, alone on a bench, looking like she was badly in need of somebody to talk to. I told Richard to stay out of sight before I walked towards his grandmother.

"Mrs. Fuller . . ." She looked at me when I sat beside her and held her hand. "Mrs. Fuller, you must go to your room. It's not good to stay outside; a heavy rain is coming."

The faint smile dangling on her lips failed to conceal the anguish she tried to hide from me. There was something she wanted to tell me; was just hesitating.

I studied her face while waiting for her to muster some guts to say what's bothering her. I saw in her my own grandmother's face: her sullen eyes, her creased lips, and the wrinkles in her forehead and cheeks: they signified the span of years she had lived. Grandma said that each passing day is a step forward towards death. I often drew precise parallelism between them; this time, they ran contrary to each other. If my grandmother was afraid of dying, Richard's grandmother was dying for it.

"I had lived life to the fullest. It's been four scores and I had become useless - an overstaying tenant of the world. I should deserve a good rest."

Tears streamed down her cheeks. She wiped them with the tissue in her hand.

I wrapped her in my arms as I had wished my mother did whenever Aunt Merriam laid her hand on me. Mrs. Fuller let her chin rest on my shoulder. I felt her tears on my skin - cold as the wind that passed by. She said that Warren left her again without saying goodbye. I gazed into her eyes with the pretense I knew nothing of what had happened. I asked the lady where Warren went.

"The first time he left was when he went to war. He never came back anymore. But miracles still happen nowadays. It was in this patio when we met again. I didn't have a clue about him until he approached me and introduced himself like it was for the first time he did. That swept us back to the day in the park the first time we saw each other."

Mrs. Fuller stopped her monologue. She looked deep into my eyes as if asking if I got what she felt. I gave her a nod. She threw back her gaze at the western hemisphere.

"How joyous it was when he promised never to leave me again; he made me laugh and cry at the same time. But a person's mind changes fast like the weather. Like the wonderful day the sky promised this morning, suddenly it's gone. Warren left me again and this time, I believe he won't be coming back anymore."

"Where did he go?"

". . . Back to Georgia . . ."

"I thought his wife had long been dead."

"I mean the state. Someone said Warren had gone back to his home state."

"And he didn't even call to say goodbye. . ."

"He never said goodbye," Mrs. Fuller said desperately. "He just disappeared."

"Whoever told you that could be wrong."

"I tried to call Warren in his room many times, but he never answered anymore."

I called Richard to watch his grandmother before I went to the Nurses' Station to inquire about the old man. I learned from there that Warren succumbed to cardiopulmonary arrest. Elizabeth Fuller wasn't informed. The consensus was: better for her not to know.

When I came back to the patio, the old lady was surprisingly in high spirits.

"Richard told me the good news that the two of you are getting married soon."

I wanted to deny it but seeing the utmost joy in Mrs. Fuller's face, I admitted what her grandson told her about.

"It's the best thing I could think of at this time," Richard later explained. "Grandma's end is nearing and just for now that she's depressed, I want her to be happy and that's one thing that will surely make her happy. Nothing will happen between us, I promise. You can keep your maiden name except perhaps in the presence of my grandmother if that's to give strength to what she believes in. When Grandma's gone, I'll stay away from you if that's what you want. Until then I want to cheer her up."

Good bachelors were in short supply, and rarely do they marry a woman who's at the border of spinsterhood; they just pass by. With Richard, I felt it was my chance.

I informed my mother about that latest happening in my life. Mama told me to get married when I had the chance even without her presence. She didn't know my marriage to Richard wasn't for real. In fact, nobody knew the marriage arrangement that Richard and I planned. I agreed with his idea without weighing over whether it was right or wrong.

Brendan and Daly had learned about our plans but didn't know that it wasn't for real. Immediately, they arranged theirs and coincidentally on the same date as ours but on separate occasions. Theirs was for real; it was officiated in the church in the morning with only a few attending while we had ours at the civil court in the late afternoon. I didn't have any knowledge of how Richard arranged a fake marriage with the proper authorities. I didn't ask him about it.

Richard took a leave from his work for a week. He told his business partner that he got married suddenly and was on honeymoon. Brendan did the same.

The Cycle of Life

God created Eve for Adam's company,
be the mother of his children
to propagate humanity.

From the Scriptures, we learned that God is the Creator of all the living things on earth. He created Man out of dust in His image not in His physicality for He's always the Almighty One, couldn't be outsmarted, not to be overpowered. Yet God gifted mankind a wisdom that had evolved to exceptional geniuses and made man defiant of His powers.

But why did God create man? And what for is the woman?

I learned the answers from my grandmother. She didn't dig deeper at first, believing I was still a child mentally and emotionally. In the later years, her discussions with me about womanhood were more spectacular than appalling that I found it inoffensive however vital. I had passed adolescence and Grandma discussed with me facts on adulthood with subtlety. It wasn't offensive in believing that a woman is blessed with the inherent gift of motherhood to give birth to the man's offspring although on most instances, conception wasn't thought of in the consummation of lust.

Eve yielded to the devil's lure. After all, she was created mainly to propagate humanity and populate God's Kingdom which hugeness could accommodate a multitude of multifarious living things that come as continuous as the incessant spinning of the globe on its axis. Birth replaces death occurring by millions in a spin of the globe that every human follows the same pattern of life: from cradle to casket; from womb to tomb.

Our first nights as "married couple" were spent in Middletown; considered honeymoon passé. And what was it for when our marriage wasn't for real?

Brendan and Daly were in the same house but knew nothing about our marriage arrangement. Of course, they'd wonder if they found Richard sleeping on the couch on our first night. On Richard's persuasion, I let him sleep inside my room but on the floor.

I couldn't sleep right away due to Brendan's giggling and groaning from the adjacent room. I let the lamp stay open so that when I looked down at the floor, I saw Richard also wide awake. Our eyes locked at each other while listening to Brendan's Oh's and ohm's.

"Richard," Brendan called from the other room. "Round one is over!"

Daly shushed him. In a minute, he called again.

"Richard? Don't sleep on it, dude."

Brendan made my blood curdle. I turned around. Richard misconstrued it as an invitation to lie beside me. When I turned back, he locked me in his arms.

Daly didn't come out for breakfast. Inside her room, I found her crying. I hunched it was about last night – the first time he slept with Brendan.

"There's nothing to be ashamed of. That was supposed to happen."

"I'm afraid of pregnancy. My biological mother died giving me birth."

"Then, what for that you went steady with somebody?"

"Brendan had always been nice to me. He was too special to be turned down."

". . . And if you didn't want to get married, why did you accept his proposal?"

"You were getting married, and I was afraid I had nobody anymore to turn to. When Brendan proposed again to marry me, I accepted it without a second thought. My other regret is that I didn't inform my parents about it."

"There's no use crying over it. The best thing to do is to let them know."

"What if I get pregnant?"

"What's the big deal? You're married."

"What if I die giving birth to my first-born? That was what happened to my mother; she died giving me life."

"What are you talking about? Cross the bridge when you've come to it. What happened to your mother doesn't mean would also happen to you."

I couldn't figure out what Daly was complaining about, and I got fed up with her. I was the only one she could confide to with her problems, but I didn't give her a chance and after she moved out with Brendan, I felt guilty about it.

It hurt me seeing Daly leave for good. My mother said I would be having more of it - being left behind - throughout my life. I thought I had prepared myself for this situation; still I found it painful. Richard's presence wasn't a good replacement for Daly's absence. The things that Daly and I used to talk about would be different from what Richard would be interested in.

With Daly gone, I moved nearer to my workplace. Richard won't let me stay alone in Middletown. He was home only twice a month and was afraid of the rumors that the metastasis of Ku Klux Klan organized by the soldiers from Fort Bragg was believed to be dwelling nearby.

The next time we went to Yuki No Hana, Yoshiko introduced me as Jenny Fuller to her father. I noticed that Mr. Yamasaki couldn't look straight at me like he was hiding the scar in his face right below his left eye from a wound that almost killed him during an encounter with the Viet Congs. I learned from Yoshiko that her father was a half-bloodied Japanese and was a resident of South Vietnam until they left Saigon.

It was from Tam Nguyen that I learned why people ran away from their own country. The hope of seeing him and Diep in America was as vague as a stormy night. I could recollect the structure of the old man's face, but probably couldn't tell how he looked after a score. Diep must have grown into a beautiful woman: tall, willowy, and fair skinned. We might stumble into each other again in some unexpected places.

That night, Mr. Yamasaki played on the piano the Filipino song he promised to play for me that was hindered by Helga's assault.

Mama used to sing it to me as a lullaby. She said it was my father's favorite song. Yoshiko said that her father learned the song from a Filipino comrade during the Vietnam War. My interest rose in knowing more about Yoshiko's father. She invited me to come and spend some time in their house to let me know her father so well. I planned to come with Richard whenever possible.

Yoshiko was taking care of her sickly mother. She doubted if she'd find a husband willing to live with his in-laws. It's an Asian culture that westerners find hard to adapt.

By the way: Richard was able to make a home run in bed not on our first night but after Daly and Brendan left, when we had the entire world for us. Whatever prearrangements we had agreed upon, I had it all put behind us.

LVII

Afterthoughts

In the first summer of the new millennium,
in less than a month after losing Warren Bates,
Elizabeth Fuller fell into a deep slumber, forever.

No one knew that my marriage to
Richard was fake. I was on pretense even had my last name changed to
Fuller on Richard's persuasions. How he made it possible, I had no clue.

I agreed to have a fake marriage to Richard if only to please Mrs.
Fuller, but I had regrets as Cathy had in marrying Kevin for the
purpose of acquiring her citizenship.

Cathy was physically abused. She had already passed the board
for nurses and acquired permanent residency yet didn't get the guts
to leave Kevin until she was conceiving. Kevin wanted an abortion.
Cathy ran away to save her child's life and that saved her as well from
a life laden with miseries. God's will: the fetus fell; that would have
been her surging guilt if the fetus survived.

If Daly turned infirm, Cathy turned intrepid. She resigned from
Windsor Point to work with me at the LARC and moved to my

apartment. We both needed a friend to confide in our problems and worries. From her, I learned that she broke up with her fiancé back home. She had plans to move to California to avoid seeing Kevin again in case he got freed from prison.

Mrs. Fuller was no longer the same cheerful woman that went around with agility, not anymore mingling with other residents to celebrate special occasions. She had stopped looking forward to the coming of the weekend. I missed her distinct laughter.

I noticed the gradual deterioration of Mrs. Fuller's health as I gradually accepted Richard as a husband for real. I cherished those weekends he spent with me as his grandma did when she watched sunsets with Warren Bates. Then she lost him. Her depression affected me; I shared her pains when I had enough to weigh me down.

I saw ardor in the old woman's eyes when Richard told her of our coming marriage. I saw it again when I told her one Sunday afternoon that Christmastime was coming while we watched the sunset on the patio. It was the second time I saw her in a happy mood since the disappearance of Warren Bates from her life.

"Is Richard coming on Christmas?" asked Mrs. Fuller.

"Yes, he is and would be staying with us longer this time."

"By the way, there's one thing I want to tell you when your husband comes."

"There's something I also want to tell you, Grandma Fuller."

"What is it, honey?"

"About Warren Bates . . ."

"I know it now where he went," Mrs. Fuller responded casually.

I felt afraid for her; I held her hands. "Where did he go?"

She squinted at me then shifted her eyes to the Westside where the sun had gone.

"One late Saturday afternoon, after the sun had gone, Warren came. I didn't expect him to come that moment for I thought he'd be staying forevermore in Georgia, so it surprised me to see him. The more it surprised me when he seemed so close to me yet he was out of my reach. Everything seemed very unbelievable; it was like a dream, but it was not. He spoke yet his voice seemed to come from afar, like an echo. Fear struck my head when he said he'd gone to the other world that to touch him was already forbidden. I closed my eyes when I felt his touch on my hair, felt it like a whiff of the wind – fresh and fragrant caressing my face – passing by. Suddenly, I felt weary as if something was driving me to sleep but only for seconds. I woke up and saw Warren turning into somewhat like a smoke drifting away and I could only cry after he disappeared."

The hair in my nape and arms stood on end.

"That was how you knew what happened to Warren . . ."

"I realized what had become of him, but I stayed calm. I remembered the poem he wrote for me: *And tomorrow when I'm gone, think of things and ways to cheer.*"

Mrs. Fuller was recently diagnosed with dementia. She thought of some things that weren't happening. I was half-believing what she narrated but her words strangely carried me away and in dilemma I couldn't tell whether to believe her or not.

"How much do you love my grandson, Jinee? . . . Jinee, you're not listening."

"Oh . . . do I love Richard? Yes, I do as much as you love Warren . . ."

She smiled enthusiastically; the trace of bitterness in her face was gone.

"Love is the most beautiful emotion God gifted to humanity. When Warren was around, twilight glowed with glory; resplendent as daybreak gleaming with hope. Now, my twilight glooms in despair. Life is bright and wonderful when you're having someone to love; it turns dull and listless when nobody loves you anymore."

I had her pain; I know how it is to be alone and lonely. I wiped the tears that were swelling in my eyes before Mrs. Fuller could notice them. She took off her necklace.

"Take diligent care of this for me."

The lady opened the locket. Inside it, I saw not her picture anymore, but Richard's.

"As you wish, Grandma Fuller. Mementos are quite valuable to me."

She gripped my hand and gazed into my eyes as if asking me to stay by her side longer. She had told me that there was something she wanted to tell me, but her lips hardly moved this time. She just stared at me without saying anything. In a little while, I realized her stare went blank; life was gone from her eyes. Her eyelids drooped and her grip on my hand loosened. I felt her pulse, tried to revive her in any way I could, but to no avail. Twilight had come when Mrs. Fuller was gone that mournful day of the new millennium.

I was all alone that moment when I needed somebody's hug to ease out the grief that was weighing me down. I haven't turned invulnerable even after the many losses I'd gone through. I mourned over the loss of a woman who'd been dearly attached to me like she was my own grandmother. Again, I felt the pain of being left behind.

I was already aware I'd feel the same pain so many times before my time to leave would come.

Elizabeth Fuller passed away peacefully; it left me with an impression that the journey to heaven is something to be rejoiced. Miss Via said that Death shouldn't be feared of unless we had sinned excessively that no contrition was good enough to rescue us from damnation; then dying would be an eternal punishment in Hell. The godly are spared from agony; to them, Death is a welcoming journey.

LVIII

That Tragic Tuesday

*At 8:45 in the morning, I opened the TV set
and saw a plane ram across one of the
towers of the World Trade Center.*

Daly and Brendan called to convey condolences; they had read the obituary in a newspaper. Daly mentioned having met Kitty Brown and that Kitty would be getting in touch with me. The Lord was about to bring me another dear person as He took one away.

Richard and I got married in conformity with what Mrs. Fuller wished. In a short span of time, I learned to love him truly so that when he proposed marriage for real after the death of his grandmother, I accepted it in a heartbeat even I had doubts of his sincerity - that it might only be in return of the services I did to his grandmother. I was into believing I wasn't really the kind of a woman he wanted for a wife. Compared to Helga Schwartz, I paled. Anyway, I accepted his proposal to marry him in the church but in the presence of my mother; she promised to come in spring of next year.

Springtime had come but not my mother. She had to come again to the embassy in Manila for her second interview. My mother passed the interview on the second time but had to defer her trip because autumn had started; she couldn't stand a chilly temperature. For that matter, Richard and I kept postponing our church wedding.

Everything was going fine between Richard and me while waiting for my mother until came the day when we had a heated argument that was but a very ordinary fracas between husbands and wives. The trouble started when Helga told me over the phone that Richard had plans to leave me for good as soon as the Fuller properties are in his name. As proof, she sent me a copy of Mrs. Fuller's will which stated, among other things, that Richard could only inherit her wealth if he had me for his wife. Was that the thing that Mrs. Fuller had wanted to tell me about before she breathed her last?

I couldn't help but confront Richard when he came home that weekend. He denied it saying that Helga had a motive and the document she had was fraud. Richard might be right yet, that confrontation gave way to a heated discussion.

Richard and I parted with heavy hearts and hadn't talked to each other since then. I might be wrong in confronting him. I tried to call him to apologize, but he didn't respond. That made me suspect Richard was looking for a justifiable alibi to leave me for good. My grandmother was right in telling me not to marry an American, but a Filipino for an American husband would leave me if I couldn't come up to his expectations. Days passed with Richard completely gone from my life.

Then came that tragic Tuesday morning. I was watching TV newsbreaks when a commercial jetliner flying over the New York skyline caught my eye. It was too low, giving me fear it might ram into a building down in lower Manhattan. And it did!

The plane rammed against one tower of the World Trade Center so suddenly that I screamed out loud it made Cathy dash in. About thirty minutes after another passenger plane came flying at the same altitude, speeding towards the other tower. I saw people jumping out of the windows when one of the towers started to crumble.

I tried to call Richard's accounting office knowing it was within the area. A lady answered informing me that Richard was in the office briefly to get some documents and left in a hurry to meet a client at the World Trade Center that very morning. I shuddered at the thought that Richard was inside any of the two buildings when the first plane attacked. My chest tightened; my heart was beating fast and hard. I was out of breath.

Another thirty minutes had passed when the north tower gave in. Giant clouds of dust and debris bellowed. From there, people with dust-covered faces emerged and scattered themselves to safer places. The deafening sound of a siren followed. I closed my eyes when my surroundings were spinning around me. I passed out.

I hadn't heard anything about Richard after that day. I feared he might have been one of those buried beneath the ruins of the twin towers. His office was closed since then.

Mama's fear had come true – the fear that I might really have the same fate she had.

Talks about that tragic Tuesday echoed away. Christmas passed by – the dullest Christmas ever for me. The year 2001 was over without any sign of Richard's return.

Springtime of the following year was again in the offing. At that time my mother had secured her visa and informed me she was finally coming.

Cathy accompanied me to the airport. At terminal C of the RDU, I was extra careful watching women passengers coming out of gate 10 lest I miss my mother. I presumed she hadn't changed a lot on her since the last time I saw her.

My speculation turned out wrong. My mother had completely changed her looks - far different from what I thought of. I hardly recognized her with a face fully made-up. She was wearing high-heeled shoes that made her look very uncomfortable and awkward.

"Do you like it?" Mama asked when she caught me staring at her from head to toe.

"You look so nice with it," Cathy interrupted.

"By the way, Mama . . . this is the Cathy I mentioned in my letters."

"Hey . . . I'm glad to see you, Cathy."

Mama had a lot of news stories from home. She said that the recent presidential election in my country was heavily smeared with fraud; that the Philippines had run out of honorable people to lead by example. The greed for power and money among elected officials was infecting the military. The wives of some generals were spending wantonly the taxpayers' money with their yearly gallivanting around the world.

The news about Santiago was exhilarating. He went to Mindanao and worked in a logging company. Although at the middle age, he studied and finished accounting, passed accountancy board and eventually became the company's chief accountant. His life was in highlight when he married a well-off spinster. If Santiago had stayed in our town throughout his life, nothing better would have come of him.

Laura passed the CGFNS exams but won't be coming to America anymore. She married a British engineer she met in Manila while taking the board exams. She'd be joining her husband in London before the end of the year.

I didn't tell Mama that Laura had written to me about this. In Laura's letter, she mentioned about Vernon being back to Cebu as an associate pastor of Saint Augustine Church. From Laura, Vernon got my address.

Unbeknown to my mother, before she came to America, Vernon had written to me about his wishes and hopes to see me again. I fell in quandary whether I would communicate with him even if I know that he already had become a soldier of God. The many sleepless nights I spent thinking about him made me realize I still have special feelings for Vernon Vergel. I couldn't deny myself. I replied to him expressing the same desire he had.

Mama and I spent the next day going around the big malls in Raleigh. Mama commented that none of those could match the grandeur of the Mall of Asia in the Philippines that was always full of shoppers. That was surprising for I thought Filipinos couldn't afford wanton extravagance.

Back home, Cathy said Kitty Brown called and left her number. I called Kitty when I got a chance.

"Is this Jinee? Praise the Lord you called!"

"I just got the message from Cathy. How are you, Mother Brown?"

"Pretty good. . . Are you still the same Jin Xeres Zaragoza I knew?"

"Yes, of course, but I have changed my name . . ."

"You got married?"

"Yes, I did. His name was Richard, but he had been gone."

"Gone to where . . . what do you mean?"

"He had left me already."

"He left you for another woman. Jinee, I don't like that kind of joke . . ."

"I'm not sure, Mother Brown. I'm not sure where he could be now. He's believed to have died during the attack of the twin towers, but before that happened, we had a heated argument. He left for New York where he had his accounting office and didn't come home anymore until nine-one-one happened. By the way, how did you get my number?"

"Incidentally, I met Daly Pascual in the subway. She told me she already got married but she didn't tell me you also had."

"She didn't tell you because she knows that Richard already left me for good."

"If you're not sure that your husband really died during 9/11, then it's possible he's still alive. Did you look for him? Did you call his office?"

"I did. His office was in lower Manhattan, and it's now closed."

"In Manhattan; that's where my shop is, Jinee."

"Your shop . . .? You've got a business!"

"It's called Kitty's Knitwear. Its grand opening will be in September yet. You've got to be here that day. If not of you, I won't ever reach this point in my life."

"It's an honor, Miss Kitty Brown, I'll keep in touch. My mother's coming with me."

"Then, I'm doubly excited. Come and let's talk more about your disappearing husband. Visit us this Monday; it's a holiday anyway."

"Yes, it is, but I've promised to let Mama see Washington DC on Memorial Day. Anyway, I'm sure of coming there in September."

Kitty's life bounced back after a tsunami drained down all her hopes. That was when her only daughter had trashed her in a facility and never came back to see her again. She was struggling to live; my presence had given back her hopes. Oftentimes, she confined to me her desperations and I told her of the weed that creeps out through the crack in a concrete pavement in its desire to live.

"Hang on, Miss Kitty, God won't let you suffer more than you can endure."

Like a dying plant that she was, I nourished her back to life. Then one day her daughter came back. The return of her daughter rescued her from complete hopelessness.

Indeed, Life is uncertain. We could never tell what God has for us in the future.

LIX

The Reunion

It was a grand reunion
for Daly and Cathy and me and
it had been a while since Richard left me.

We drove to Washington DC for the celebration of Memorial Day. Seeing those places which she discussed with her students for years greatly enthused my mother. At the national cemetery in Arlington, we passed by rows of small, elongated tombstones that mark burials of unknown soldiers.

My father's remains weren't buried there; his body wasn't found. His remains withered through the years were now windblown to nowhere.

We joined the people that were crowding at the Vietnam's Veterans Memorial Wall where names of those who either died or were missing during the Vietnam War were inscribed. I noticed the roses some visitors were bringing - red for those who died and yellow for the missing ones.

We looked over those names on the wall for my father's but didn't find it regardless of how diligent we were. I might have overlooked it. Or it could be that my poor father wasn't officially registered as a PhilCAG volunteer so that he spent miserable years on a foreign battlefield for nothing.

Mama looked exhausted. I could feel she was giving up searching for my father's name among those inscribed on the wall. She may still be hoping my father was alive and was only missing. In my mind, my father had been dead before I was born.

In July of 2002, Daly and Brendan Cameron came to visit and to celebrate with us the arrival of their first son. To us, Asians, if the first born is a boy, it means good luck to the family. Filipinos got that belief from the Chinese.

The celebration was held in Yuki No Hana. I told my mother that the pianist was the crooner's father and he knew by heart the Filipino song my father loved so well. Yoshiko informed her dad of our presence. During Yoshiko's break the pianist played the same song he promised to play for me the night Helga smacked my face. It was the same song Mama used to lull me to sleep when I was little; it surely reminded her of my father, but contrary to what I thought, I noticed my mother wasn't pleased with it. It wasn't chilly that evening, but my mother was trembling and was looking pale; something was bothering her that I drove her home immediately. We left Yuki No Hana that evening ahead of everybody.

At home, without asking for it, Mama handed me the only letter she got from my father. The letter was typewritten. It mentioned how my father survived the ambush. It gave details on how a swishing bullet could have struck him dead. The specification of events gave me a hint that my father didn't die there in Quang Nam.

The scar in Mr. Hiroshi's face crossed my mind. Yoshiko had told me that her father almost lost his left eye but survived the ambush that happened in Quang Nam sometime in May of 1969. It concurred with what my father wrote. What if Hiroshi Yamasaki was the one my mother had been searching for? But there was no Japanese person mentioned in my father's letter. An influx of fear and anxiety was draining out my strength.

That very night I called Yoshiko at Yuki No Hana. It was her breaktime. I asked her to arrange a time when I could talk to her father privately. She must have wondered about it but, without asking anything, she promised to call me the following morning.

Daly and Brendan left for New Jersey the next day while I was waiting for Yoshiko's call; I got it by noon. Yoshiko said that her mother prepared a special Vietnamese lunch and even suggested to bring the whole group with me and that included my mother. I told Yoshiko I wanted a private talk and that nobody should be with me on that occasion. Yoshiko then asked what it was about.

"I promise to tell you afterwards," I said and hung up.

Leaving my mother in Cathy's care, I went out that very noon and headed to the house of Mr. Yamasaki. I chanced to talk to him while Yoshiko and Minh Le were preparing the table for lunch. The whole time while I was with him, I tried to feel any symbiosis between us; didn't find any. I could've read his feelings through his eyes if he weren't wearing dark glasses that partly covered the big scar below his left eye. The things that might have bothered my mother every time she gazed at that eastern hemisphere back home were coming in and out of my mind. Was this the father I had been waiting for? Could this be the man in Da Nang that Nguyen Tam was talking about?

"Sorry, I don't remember meeting that person," Mr. Hiroshi said referring to Nguyen Tam. "How did you know him?"

"I met him many years ago when a boat of people from Vietnam was washed ashore in our town. I haven't met nor heard about any of them anymore since they left our town."

Mr. Yamasaki didn't respond. His attention was directed outside through an open window. Many things could have been bothering his thoughts.

"By the way, you said that a Filipino soldier was felled by the swishing bullet that grazed your face. Do you remember his name?"

He didn't say a word, but I could see in his face trouble in recollecting the past. Yoshiko had told me before that her father was still suffering the Post Traumatic Stress Disorder even after the many years that passed since the Vietnam War ended.

I wanted to know what really happened to my father during the ambush in Quang Nam. While I waited for Mr. Hiroshi to mention a name, fear gripped me again – very intense this time that I suddenly left him before he could say a name. I left the special lunch Yoshiko and her mother prepared for me; left them without parting words; they must be wondering what had happened.

Mama didn't know where I was going to; didn't ask anything when I came home, but I told Cathy that I was about to find my father. Cathy promised to keep it between us.

LX

The Grace of Life

Good graces were coming to Kitty Brown.
Her life was coming back bouncing
after her hopes were all gone

The heinous attack on the World Trade Center in New York was perhaps the worst in the history of America. Fatalities were more than three thousand and I feared Richard could be one of those. My search for him yielded nothing. I had had my most depressing moments, but I couldn't reprimand the Lord for all the miseries I'd been through considering there were people who suffered more than I did, not to count the blessings I received without my asking.

It was almost September again; about a year had passed since the attack on the World Trade Center. The place was now known as Ground Zero. We planned to see the place when we come to attend the inauguration of Kitty's Knitwear. My mother was excited about it, but I could see apprehension in her face.

"I think it's cold there by this time . . ."

"No, Mama, it's still warm there by this time."

"Do you think I can stand the weather?"

"Yes, you can. It's just like December in the Philippines."

I wasn't sure of the weather in the upper states. In North Carolina, chilly days were possible even at the waning of summer. New York could be worse.

We left Raleigh early Saturday morn. Cathy went with us; she wouldn't be moving to LA until she'd find favorable results of her reciprocity test.

On the way, I thought of Richard. I wanted to see him again if he were still alive. I realized I still needed him in my life.

We had a brief stopover on Atlantic City's boardwalk.

I let my mother and Cathy go shop-hopping in the little shops along the beach, I preferred to stay outside; the breeze from the Atlantic Ocean was refreshing. I took a stroll and enjoyed myself studying the faces of the people I came across with, trying to guess what country they were from.

Out of the blue, unbelievable as it should be, I saw Richard at a distance, waving at me. It had been quite a time that I hadn't seen him and suddenly, he was there.

Overwhelmed with excitement, I ran towards Richard and before the eyes of the many strollers, I hugged and kissed him passionately, casting aside my inhibitions.

"Jinee, what are you doing?"

It was my mother I heard, shocked of what I did. That was enough to awaken me. Terribly disgraced, I fell to my knees, wrapped with shame and I found myself crying. I must have stunned Richard, but when I looked up at him, the more I was doused with embarrassments; the man wasn't Richard Joseph Fuller but a stranger. Instead of me apologizing, the stranger did and walked away.

I'd been into hallucinations - had imagined too much of Richard returning home that sometimes I mistook some men I passed by to be him. The craziness that affected most of the residents in my job could have infected me; I was into believing that Alzheimer's disease was contagious.

We arrived in Bayonne earlier than I expected and spent the day with the Camerons. As we had time to linger, we strolled on Jersey Beach with Daly and Brendan. There was New York on the opposite side. Viewed from the beach of New Jersey, the Manhattan skyline looked fascinating as ever even with the absence of the twin towers. Did Richard really die there on the spot where the towers were? What if I were made to believe he was dead but living freely with Helga Schwartz?

I shut off my mind about Richard. Anyway, I was already accustomed to living without him. But I couldn't deny to myself that there were times when he came into my mind and it was strange that sometimes it seemed I saw him in the crowd, in some unexpected places like what happened when I was beach-strolling in Atlantic City.

I prayed for peace of mind. I prayed that if Richard were alive, let him come to me even just for a moment. It was enough for me to know that he was doing well through all the days I hadn't seen him; that was all I wanted. I won't care if he despised me like what my father did to my mother.

It may have taken my mother a very long time to believe that my father wouldn't be coming back anymore, but at least, she had survived without him. I will survive too without Richard. I already had accepted my mother and I had the same fate.

We left Bayonne Sunday morning with Cathy on the wheel heading to Kitty's. She said she was familiar with the area where Kitty's shop was located.

Kitty Brown burst into tears as she did when her long lost daughter returned. This time, it was me she referred to as her lost daughter. She said how lucky my mother was for having a daughter like me and how lucky was the man who took me for a wife. I showed her and Tabitha the medallion of Mrs. Fuller which had Richard's picture on it.

The Other Wife

I was in quandary whether or not
to tell her that I was the wife of the
man she referred to as her husband.

Cathy had moved to California so Mama was stuck with me through the comings and goings of the seasons; she couldn't just let me spend Christmas all alone. On Christmas Eve, the first we had together after many years, she experienced the chilliest night in her life.

Winter was over and Spring of the following year quickly passed by. My mother was still with me. She was able to secure her American citizenship.

In summer, we drove back to New Jersey for the baptism of the Cameron's first born. Proceeding to Kitty's shop, we passed by Ground Zero. It had been a long while since the tragedy happened, but the question if Richard really perished there was still bothering me.

"Thinking of the devil . . ." Kitty Brown screamed delightedly on seeing me.

"You may not know it, Mother Brown, but these past days kept me busy."

"Busy on searching for your lost husband?" Kitty asked when we got inside.

"No. There's no way I'd find him after those years. I need to close that chapter of my life and must have to move on."

"What if I told you we found him. The revenant was here last week."

"Are you sure he was the same Richard Joseph Fuller?"

"He was the same guy in the picture you showed us," Tabitha confirmed. "He even introduced himself with the same name. Incidentally, he's coming back today to get the shirts he ordered for his son."

My strength drained out. I felt afraid thinking how Richard would react seeing me after a long time. I held on to my mother; she comforted me in return.

It didn't take long when a man came in. Yes, it was Richard! But there was a young woman – pretty and expectant – who came with him.

So, he got a new family. Where had he been during the past six hundred days?

I was chilling when Tabitha introduced me to him. Richard acknowledged me like I was a total stranger. Except for the faint scar from the burnt wound in his forehead, he still looked practically the same guy I had learned to love. He introduced the lady with him as his wife, Samantha; I felt betrayed. I felt my mother's hand pressing my waist.

Kitty Brown told them I was also a customer who was getting an order. She got the pink shawl I hung loose covering my back and exposed to their faces the 'JXZ' initials embroidered on it. Kitty did it on purpose.

A fragment of his past must have flashed in Richard's mind; his brows wrinkled. I clasped my hands against my lips as I always did when I was in fear.

"Have we met before?" Richard asked the same question the very first time we met. .

I fell in quandary whether to tell him who was me to him. I lost the nerve; in my chest, the pain was congesting. Tabitha must have noticed the tears shimmering in my eyes. She pulled me away from the group, led me to a fitting room where she embraced me tightly to give me comfort; I cried on her shoulder.

"Calm down," Tabitha whispered while tapping my back. "You've got to find out first what really happened to him."

"I can tell what happened."

It was the lady Richard introduced to us as his wife. She caught us by surprise.

"Pardon my intrusion, but I owe you an explanation. The name of the person I'm with is Richard Joseph Fuller and he's the father of this child I'm expecting but he isn't my husband. He proposed marriage to me, but I refused."

Dumbfounded, Tabitha and I could only look at each other. Nobody between us said a word for a moment.

"How did it happen?" Tabitha raised the question.

"I refused to marry him for he doesn't know who he is. When he asked if he had met you before, I had a hunch you're the one I'd been looking for."

"My husband, Richard, was meeting a client in the World Trade Center that Tuesday morning," I forced myself to say something between sobs.

"On that same day, I drove my fiancé to work," Samantha cut me in. "He was getting late that morning and, in a hurry, left in the car the document he had to work on. Knowing the importance of that document to my fiancée, I brought it to him on the fifth floor of the north tower. I used the staircase on my way down and was reaching the ground floor when a plane suddenly rammed into the building like there was an earthquake. I looked up. In the next moment came the throng of people rushing down the stairs racing behind me. I was already on the ground floor when I saw my fiancé among those descending the last flight of stairs just in time when a piece of iron hit him on the forehead. I saw him fall to the ground floor. Instantly, I pulled him away to avoid the stampede. He was bleeding. I wiped the blood from his face and found out he wasn't my fiancé after all. He was alive and semi-conscious, and I just couldn't leave him there to help himself. The stranger was half-conscious. Instinctively, I squeezed him out through the thick crowd. Outside, a cop lifted him to an ambulance parked nearby and I only found myself riding with the stranger forgetting all about my fiancé. He lost consciousness on the way to the hospital. I looked for any identification of him in his pockets, but I couldn't find any, not even his wallet, except for a brief note in his shirt pocket where a name was written. I presumed that was his name and so I registered him there as Richard Joseph Fuller. He was wearing a gold ring – perhaps a wedding band. I took off the ring from his finger and hid it. In the emergency room of the Bellevue

Hospital Center, somebody asked me if I was the patient's spouse. In an impulse I said: Yes, I am."

"And your fiancé, what happened to him?" Tabitha asked.

"I learned later that my fiancé perished in the fire. The stranger I saved gained consciousness after three days but in total amnesia. I remembered scrutinizing his ring and I found only initials. It was "JXZ". Richard was released after weeks of recuperating but until that day, nobody came to claim him. I made him believe I was his spouse. I paid his bills and brought him home. I tried to look for the real wife, but I gave up after months of searching. I've learned to love him and that scared me all the while. What if he found out I was a fraud? The fear was tormenting that one day his real wife might surface to claim him. When Mrs. Brown showed us the shawl where "JXZ" was embroidered, that reminded me of the ring I was keeping from him. The ring in your finger looked the same as the ring I'm hiding. I wasn't at peace living with the stolen husband –taking advantage of his mental condition and I thought of an incoming pain. I'm pregnant with your husband's child but I'm returning him to you, Mrs. Fuller. I can only be sorry for the days I was keeping him from you. I'll vanish myself from here and I promise you won't ever see me again."

"But you're having his child . . ."

"I'm ready to face the consequences. I will tell my son what had happened when he's old enough to understand this situation."

I had sympathy for Samantha in the situation she was in. She did what should have been my duties at those times Richard needed help. I took off the necklace that Mrs. Fuller had given me and handed it to Samantha.

"Don't deprive your son of his father. Go on pretending you're his wife. I had survived without him. When your son's ready to learn what happened, give him this necklace. Inside the locker is the picture of his father. That's the time when you can tell Richard the truth."

I gave Samantha a hug as if that was enough to tell her that was my final decision.

"Thank you, Jinee. Time will come when I'll be ready to tell my son of how Fate had drawn us together. You'd be a part of my family."

We went out of the fitting room in time for me to take a last glimpse of Richard Joseph Fuller. I noticed he was looking around and it could be me he was looking for, but I concealed myself from his eyes. I saw them slipping out of the store, followed them with my eyes until they were gone. I didn't meet Richard and Samantha anymore nor heard about them since then.

The fullness of autumn was days away, but the countryside had already turned into a landscape of various colors. Mama watched it with nostalgia on our way home. With her quick glances at me I sensed there was something she wanted to know about it but said nothing. I did the same when I was a child and didn't understand why grasses were green and flowers had assorted colors. I wanted to ask her the whys and wherefores but speculating she wasn't in the mood to answer, I kept my questions within me leaving me wondering of things and events happening in the world beyond my understanding.

While driving back to North Carolina, I thought of the bickering that Helga caused between Richard and me. That trivial matter resulted in consequential separation. Richard left leaving the trouble unsettled and didn't return anymore; he didn't care to call. I tried to contact him be in his cell phone or in his office, but I failed until the attack of the twin towers happened.

Then came that day.

Richard's reaction on seeing the pink shawl gave me thoughts that fragments of the past flashed in his mind; there was a wide possibility he remembered me wearing it. If he had recovered, would he choose me over Samantha who had his child in her womb? I didn't think he would. I hope I did right. Giving up Richard wasn't a mistake unlike what I did to Vernon in favor of my American dream.

LXII

He Called Himself Hiroshi

Hiroshi Yamasaki got his name after Hiroshima,
the city in Japan that America bombed
on the day my father was born.

Home by midnight, I slept late pondering if I was right to give up Richard to Samantha. Richard's other woman won me over with her honesty and humility. She bore Richard's son and I didn't want the boy to grow up fatherless and suffer the same tribulations I had had.

Mama had no comments of my decision in giving up Richard to the other woman; Kitty Brown praised my nobility, but Tabitha didn't like what I did. She didn't know I wasn't legally married to Richard. In fact, nobody knew it, not even my closest friends and neither my mother nor the late Mrs. Fuller.

Richard Fuller didn't suffer the same fate my father had: my father was believed to have died in Vietnam but the only letter he sent to my mother evidenced he didn't die during that ambush that happened in Quang Nam. What Yoshiko had told me crossed my mind: the incident, the place, and the date it happened coincided with what was said in the obituary my mother received. I asked Yoshiko if I could talk once again to her father. She invited me to come to their rehearsals at Yuki No Hana the next morning.

The rehearsals were over when I came, but Mr. Yamasaki bid me his time. He was waiting for me alone at a table while the lady at the bar was preparing coffee for us.

"I lost my father in the Vietnam War," I opened our conversation after the lady had served us coffee. The Japanese seemed not bothered with my opening statement; didn't even look up at me. He still had his dark glasses covering his eyes, but I sensed he was staring at his coffee blankly.

"I was a volunteer of the LRRP," the Japanese started his account without looking at me. "We were on a recon mission in the hinterlands of Quang Nam province. By midnight, we had a brief stand-down in a place we thought was safe. I had laid down my weapons, about to take off my backpack when I heard movements. Then suddenly, a bullet swished across me, leaving a cut in my face and killed the soldier beside me."

"That soldier was my father, but he didn't die there instantly," I butted in at that instance but realized that was uncalled for. Seemed awakened of what I said, the Japanese pianist looked at me in surprise.

"How did you know?" Mr. Yamasaki asked in a muffled voice.

"A week after I was born, my mother received a letter from my father telling her of the ambush in Quang Nam. That made me believe the man hit by the bullet that wounded your face was my father . . .but he didn't die right there."

"I thought it hit him dead. I panicked and ran aimlessly after seeing all my comrades fall. An enemy chased me. He was getting closer when he fired his gun, hitting me on my left leg. I stumbled to the ground right at the doorstep of a small house. The enemy kept on getting closer when a man suddenly came out of the house and immediately fired a shot and killed the oncoming gook. Without wasting a moment, he pulled me into his house.

My savior's name was a Montagnard named Minh Ken. Inside the house, his daughter immediately took care of the wound in my face. After a few minutes, while his daughter was swathing the wound in my leg, we heard the rushing in of footfalls. Thinking they were companions of the man he had shot, Minh Ken pushed me out through the back door, telling me to run away. Even though I felt a severe pain in my left leg, I dashed towards the woods and was able to run quite a distance when I realized that the lives of my saviors were in jeopardy. I went back, getting near the house when gunshots erupted, then a commotion. I was petrified knowing I was facing a clear danger.

The sight of the Viet Congs running away from the house alerted me. I rushed in and found the Montagnard man lying dead on the bamboo floor. His daughter was alive but sexually assaulted."

All the while, Mr. Yamasaki avoided looking at my eyes as he told me of what he remembered about the ambush in Quang Nam. I tried to find any gestures of his that would tell me his real identity; I found none except for the faint scar below his left eye.

"What had become of his daughter since then?"

"You've met Minh Le . . ."

"You mean Yoshiko's mother?"

"She had no other choice but to come with me. After we buried the body of her father, she followed me across a thick forest and a wild lagoon until we reached the city of Hue, where we found an abandoned small house which we made our home. We stayed there for a couple of years. In that house, Minh Le gave birth to our first daughter."

"It was Yoshiko . . ."

"No, it was the elder one. Yoshiko was born a year after."

"So, Yoshiko isn't your only daughter. What happened to the other one?"

"The day the commies invaded Saigon, I thought of seeking refuge at the US embassy with my family, but there was this great mayhem all over the vicinity. It was when I lost my first daughter. Our search for her was futile. The commies were coming close driving us farther from there. I had to save myself, my wife and my other daughter."

A myriad of thoughts was flashing in my mind like there was the Vietnamese waitress of The Green Papaya, the Japanese warbler of Yuki No Hana, and here was this man who called himself Hiroshi. He could have peppered his accounts with lies. I knew it, I felt it. That urged me to leave, and so I left him there and then all of a sudden.

Mama was hanging up the phone when I came home. On seeing me, she asked indignantly: "Did you talk to him? Is there something that I need to know?"

Ignoring her questions, I went straight to her room to get my father's letter. I knew well where she was keeping it.

"What something, Mama?" I asked when I came out.

"You know what, Jinee . . . He told me about it."

"About what . . .? That I found out he's using a false name?"

"He still uses the same name only that he carries the title of Reverend Father."

"Who are you referring to?"

"Father Vernon Vergel . . ."

I sighed in relief. "What about him?"

"I know it now why you decided to give up Richard to Samantha."

"It's not what you think. I told you my reasons."

"And one of those which you kept to yourself is your plan to marry that priest."

I ignored Mama's inquisition. To see Mr. Yamasaki again occupied my mind.

LXIII

Sins of My Grandfather

I found my father, learned his miseries,
and at the same instance, I uncovered
the kind of person my grandpa was.

"Why are we stopping here?" Mama asked when I drove my car to a parking space in Yuki No Hana on our way back home after buying groceries the following morning.

"You need to talk to him, Mama. He was with the group that was ambushed in Quang Nam. This is your opportune time to know what really happened to my father."

"I'd given up my search; I'm through with it. I'm now fully convinced that your father had been dead before you were born," Mama told me in her hesitance to see the Japanese pianist of Yuki No Hana. She lost interest in finding my father now that I had found a lead.

I got out of the car and proceeded to see Mr. Yamasaki and although I didn't persuade my mother to come with me, she followed anyway.

Minh Le invited us to come inside and went out of the room as we came in. Hiroshi Yamasaki was sitting in his swivel chair facing the mirror from where he saw us entering. This time he wasn't covering his eyes with dark glasses so that I was able to study his reaction in his eyes. He looked unbothered. I greeted him; heard no response. After throwing a brief glance at my mother, Mr. Yamasaki invited her to a seat. By this time, I didn't hear any words from my mother. I was eager to hear what she and the Japanese would be discussing, but I thought it was proper to give them privacy.

I went out of Hiroshi's dressing quarter.

Outside, I sat at the table which Richard and I occupied the first time I went with him to Yuki No Hana. It surprised me to know that the club's crooner was the same person who served us at the Green Papaya. From Richard, I learned that the man on the piano, Hiroshi Yamasaki, was the chanteuse's father.

That night, on knowing I came from the Philippines, Mr. Yamasaki offered to play for me a song that was distinctly Filipino. Surprisingly, it was the same song Mama used to lull me to sleep when I was a child. As if those weren't enough to surprise me that night, there was Helga Schwartz, who surprised me with a smack on my face.

The sight of my mother leaving the Japanese pianist's dressing room in a fast-paced motion interrupted my thoughts. I had the instinct to follow her, but instead I went to see Mr. Yamasaki in my curiosity to know what transpired in their conversation. I entered unheralded into the pianist's room which my mother had left unlocked.

"Is there something you forgot?" Mr. Yamasaki asked, probably thinking my mother had come back. He was still sitting in his swivel chair with his back facing the front door. He turned around his chair when he heard no response.

"Yes, there is," I replied after a few seconds while taking out from my pocket the letter from my father which my mother kept with her for years. I opened it before his eyes.

"My father sent this letter to my mother about thirty years ago."

He stared at it only for a couple of seconds then shifted his gaze to somewhere.

"What am I to do with that?" Mr. Yamasaki asked. With his eyes still cast outside, he turned his back on me.

"This is the only thing my mother received from my father ever since he left for the Vietnam War. It details what really happened in Quang Nam sometime in May of 1969. Two Vietnamese soldiers and three Green Berets were with him that night. What you told me is the same thing that's written here except that there's no Japanese soldier mentioned in this letter."

I heard no response.

"Was it you who sent this to my mother?"

Still, I heard no response. I reached for his swivel chair and once more turned it around to have him facing me again. With his eyes meeting mine, we could only stare at each other for a moment.

"Did you write this letter, Mr. Yamasaki?"

I put more force in my voice, but he stayed silent; this time he was trying to avoid my eyes. It made my suspicion stronger that he was the person my mother was looking for.

"Did you send this letter to my mother?" I repeated the question like demanding for an answer, sounding like I was losing my temper. When Mr. Yamasaki stayed mum, I screamed at him: "Answer me!"

Still, there was no answer. Yet I waited for him to say something, but after a minute that he didn't say a word, I decided to give up what I wanted to know. *No use persuading: he'd never admit it.*

Slowly, I turned around, opened the door, and was about to take a step outside when I heard him say in a toned-down voice that I almost failed to hear it.

"You must know why I didn't come home anymore."

His words astounded me. Immediately, I turned back. With my eyes plastered at him, I moved closer, quivering, while staring at him intensely. He must have noticed the intensity in my eyes, must have felt the anger boiling within me. He dropped his stare on the floor and only spoke again when tears started to swell in his eyes. I realized then that Yoshiko had his eyes. That reminded me of my mother's reply when I asked her what I got from my father.

"It was at the height of the Vietnam War," Mr. Yamasaki started to talk with eyes now staring blankly at the wall. "America requested for more Filipino soldier-volunteers. Mr. Zaragoza summoned me to his office. He demanded that I must join the PhilCAG which was scheduled to be deployed to Vietnam. He heard me refusing his demands. With a high- raised voice, he offered a bribe saying it was enough to help me finish my law studies in college, but I mustn't set foot in Sacandaya anymore. All that I desired in life at that time was to have a family of my own and be a dignified lawyer which my family could be proud of. It came to my thoughts that it was impossible for me to attain both."

What Mr. Yamasaki said was a hard pound on my head; it almost knocked me out. Was he lying to justify his reason why he didn't come home anymore?

"People in Sacandaya might have thought I was too brave to go to a foreign war. The truth is I was a coward for running away – scared by the threat of Aragon Zaragoza. I should have stayed in Sacandaya and faced the consequences if that was to show him I wasn't ever afraid of his threat."

My grandfather was the most ideal person, the most respected in town, but at that moment, Hiroshi Yamasaki was about to convince me the truth about the real Aragon Zaragoza. He couldn't be lying. I was inclined to believe that when my grandfather was still alive, he committed an enormous sin that no amount of prayer could save him from hell. What my grandfather did to my mother, he also did to his other daughter.

Lots of thoughts whirled in my mind that ended up with a question how did I come to that point? I never expected the dream of finding my father which I already have learned to forget would come back to me that moment as a nightmare. I found my father and he opened to me a skeleton in the closet inside Villa Zaragoza. All the while, I had the feeling there were still lots of things that Hiroshi Yamasaki wanted to reveal.

"Did you tell my mother about this? About what Aragon Zaragoza told you?"

My voice was trembling when I asked. There were tears about to fall from my eyes, but I tried hard not to let him see me cry.

"I didn't have the nerve to tell your mother the kind of person her father was for I thought that might come unbelievable to her. I only told her I was joining the PhilCAG for the remuneration that America promised which could have helped me become a lawyer."

"But why did you not come home from war when you got the chance?"

"I got a letter from your grandfather before we left for the reconnaissance patrol. I didn't have time to read it but kept it because I anticipated there was something quite important in that letter. I survived the ambush. I wrote about the incident to your mother; she never wrote back. I remember reading your grandfather's letter. He wrote that Patricia got married to another man and had given birth to a baby girl. That devastated me. I should not have saved myself from death in Quang Nam if I had nobody anymore to go home for. I thought of ending my life if not because of Minh Le. She was also alone in the world as I was. We needed each other to go on living.

"I was sired by a Japanese soldier, the very reason your grandfather despised me, but my father was murdered before I was born. And so, I grew up without a father. I didn't know any relatives of his for all of them perished after America bombed Hiroshima, my father's hometown. My mother died before I graduated from high school; her relatives disowned me. That left me all alone – had nobody to run to."

Mr. Hiroshi's account of his own life gripped my heart real hard. Tears were streaming in his face while telling me those miseries which he must already have forgotten through the years. I was chilling while listening to Mr. Yamasaki's account of his life. I thought of leaving immediately but to find the truth was the reason why I wanted to talk to him. If he intended to destroy my grandfather's reputation, it was because I brought him to that situation. My heart was bleeding profusely those moments that I wanted to scream to ease out the excruciating pain gripping the whole of me. It never occurred to me that the person who I thought to be my father had gone through a life that was more severely painful than what I had gone through. If I grew up without a father, my very own father grew up without a family.

I didn't want to hear more what he had been through, and I wanted to get out – to get away from there but at the same instance, on realizing it was me who brought him to that situation, to hear more how devastating his life had been, I was nailed where I stood. I had to hear more of what he had been through, had to let myself realize that growing up without a father was better off than living a life without a family.

"I joined the military," Mr. Hiroshi continued his account, "but I had this passion of becoming a lawyer. Your grandfather learned about it. He bribed me with a huge amount to use in pursuing my studies, but with a condition that I must stay away from his daughter for good. If I'd go against his words, he said he'd hire somebody to kill me or he'd make my life extremely miserable that I would wish I rather had died. Knowing how powerful he was in Sacandaya, I joined the PhilCAG for that was the only way open to me, but I never accepted the bribe he offered.

After the ambush in Quang Nam and after reading the letter he sent me, I decided to change my identity – wanting myself to exist as a new person. I assumed the name of Hiroshi Yamasaki, the real name of my father and realizing I didn't have a country to call my own, I claimed Vietnam as my own.

To be a son of a Japanese wasn't of my choice. But Aragon Zaragoza hadn't given me a chance to prove what I was capable of. All he cared about was vanity. He thought of me as a stain to the prestige and honor of his family. I wasn't afraid of his threat but if only to save my future family from a life of misery, I followed his demands in the long run. I sent a letter to Mr. Zaragoza telling him I won't be returning home anymore. His wish was fully granted."

Finally, I found my father, but I learned of his miseries and uncovered the ugly side of my grandfather who was looked up to as the most ideal person our town ever had. Now, I found out that the person I adored most in life was the very same person who caused me profound bitterness. Hiroshi Yamasaki tore my grandfather's reputation to shreds. Could he be lying to spare himself from my resentment?

It was only my mother who could shed light on what really had happened. She could confirm whether Mr. Yamasaki was telling the truth about the real Aragon Zaragoza.

I closed my eyes tightly squeezing out the tears blurring my sight. I thought of those years when I was growing up. How I wished there was a father to watch over me, to protect me from harm, a father who could have given me a hug during my desperate moments.

Mr. Yamasaki was staring at me when I opened my eyes. In his looks, he was pleading for forgiveness, begging for compassion. In the next moment, I saw him forcing himself to stand from his swivel chair. I thought of helping him stand but I never did; never even tried to touch him.

I kept watching him. It was when I found out he was walking with difficulty which I hadn't noticed the first time we met. He was dragging his left foot as he moved towards me, kept his eyes on me - perhaps to give me a father's hug which I yearned for in all my life but was deprived of.

I didn't take off my eyes from him and while he was limping towards me, I was moving back gradually until I sensed I had reached the door. He was at arm's length and when he tried to stretch his arm, when his fingertips almost touched my hand, I turned around as quick as I could and slipped out of the room, leaving the place hurriedly, left without looking back at him - leaving him without saying goodbye.

So, at that moment, that moment when I only had to wait for my father's hug in a matter of seconds, I loathed to have it. I must convince myself I never had met my father in all my life; never had seen him at all.

LXIV

The Final Chapter

I was completely relieved of the burden
I'd been carrying in my whole life through
on knowing what really happened to my father

I believe that my mother had identified the Japanese pianist even on the first time she had seen him in Yuki No Hana and that made her sick instantly that she wanted to return home immediately that evening.

My mother would have already known I had a confrontation with Hiroshi Yamasaki. While driving back home, I thought she would ask me about it, or I expected her to say something about him; she did not.

"You're hiding something from me, Mama," I told her upon reaching home.

"About what?" Mama asked in reply; all the while she avoided looking at me.

"Something about Yoshiko's father. Why don't you tell me what I need to know?"

I waited for her to say something; she did not.

"Now is the time to tell me about him. I'm ready to listen to the whole story. Is he the person you've been waiting for to come home?"

She cast a glance at me. Our eyes met. I could see she was hiding fear behind the paleness in her face, but in her eyes surfaced the same pain that I saw in her when Aunt Merriam banished us from Villa Zaragoza. That same pain flashed in her face when she conveyed to me that my father wasn't among those who were washed ashore in Sacandaya. I saw those miseries she had had in her life. I felt those and I cried them out; I was drawn to empathize with her. I would have done the same if I were in her situation.

"Your father never got any of the letters I sent him while he was in Vietnam."

It seemed I was out of breath when my mother started to talk. Then she stopped.

"I'm listening!"

I must have raised my voice, but I didn't mean to be rude to my mother; I must have unknowingly hurt her. I saw her wiping her eyes with her fingers.

"Those letters that I was sending him were pulled out by the postmaster per my father's instructions. He burned all those as what he did to the letters your father was sending me. I heard my father's confession when he was dying. How I wanted to hate my father, but he earnestly begged for my forgiveness, and I must forgive him; he was dying. He wanted to tell you the same thing, but you ignored his call."

"I refused to talk to him because I was afraid; I was just being afraid."

"Your father had gone to Vietnam when I discovered my pregnancy. Knowing my condition, my mother wanted me to return to the villa, but I was afraid of my father's plan."

"What plan . . .?"

"At one time when he called me to his office, he suggested abortion . . ."

"What do you mean, Mama? Did Grandpa think of getting rid of me?"

"One day, when I was five months pregnant, Santiago came up with a message that my father wanted to see me at the villa. When I got there, nobody was around but Benito who offered me a mug of tea as soon as I came in. That was strange. Benito had never shown that kindness before. I remembered my father's suggestion to abort you to save the prestige and honor he built for his family. I suspected something not nice was going on. My trepidation worsened when I noticed the infamous abortionist in Sacandaya. Out of nervousness, I was about to quaff up the content in the mug in my hand that Benito had given me when Flora suddenly came out of nowhere and bumped at me dashing off the mug from my hold. At that moment, Rafael and Thelma arrived. Benito disappeared and so was the abortionist. Only then I realized that what Benito offered me to drink was a concoction that the abortionist must have prepared. Flora must already had learned about my father's plan, so she kept watching over me whenever I was in Villa Zaragoza."

"You never told me about this until now . . ."

"I didn't want to spoil your good impression on your grandfather. To save the good name of the Zaragozas, I asked Flora to keep the incident a secret. My mother and my younger siblings never knew about it. When your grandfather was dying, he wanted to confess it to you and to ask your forgiveness, but you refused to hear him."

My own grandfather, who was believed to be the most honorable man in all Sacandaya, had wanted his first grandchild dead. It was traumatic to learn it, but I had had enough. Remembering the epitaph in my grandfather's tomb, I realized then how easy could a lie be told and written.

What Mr. Yamasaki told me collaborated with my grandfather's confession to my mother which he kept through the years until that time he was in the verge of death.

"I only want to hear it from you, Mama, because I always believe in you even at times you were telling me lies. Now, I want to know directly from you if Hiroshi Yamasaki was the person, you'd been waiting for to come home."

She looked at me. I perceived she was begging for my understanding.

"When you were there alone with him, did you ask him to come home with us?"

Mama vowed down her head. She started to speak without looking at me.

"We survived those years without him, but to his other family, he's alive and well. It hurts to leave but there's more pain to suffer if you're the one left behind. I don't want that to happen to your father's other family. I know it's the same reason why you gave up Richard to Samantha."?

"Richard has a child with Samantha; my father has me."

"You never had him even for a day whereas half of his lifetime was with his other family. We had become strangers to your father as he is to us. Living with strangers wouldn't be nice and comfy. He's happy where he is. It's enough to know that he's alive. He had told me that it was because he thought I left him for another man that he wanted to end his life, but it was because of Minh Le that he wanted to go on living."

"Now's your chance to tell the truth, Mama. Were you legally married to my father?"

"I lived with your father without the benefit of marriage. I never wanted that situation, but it happened, and I had no way to avoid it. We arranged a date to get married by a priest but suddenly, your father left for the Vietnam War. Everybody in my family must have known about you being born a bastard yet we managed to keep our skeletons in the closet to save the good reputation of the Zaragozas."

It was for the family's prestige and honor that the Zaragozas locked off their dirty linens from the public. Mama made the town believe she was legally married to my father – a false thing told several times had become a false truth.

"Jinee, I'm sorry for messing up your life."

"No, it's not your fault. It's my fate, Mama."

"What's your plan now?"

"I want to go back home to Sacandaya and start my life anew. Villa Zaragoza had always been the house I wanted to call my home."

"I'd been waiting for that time to have you always with me while I'm still alive."

"I feel the same, Mama. Please bring me home."

"But America has been your home . . ."

"I reached the end of my journey when I found out what really happened to my father. This time, I want to return to where I came from and spend my life there serving my own countrymen. Besides, Flora is getting old. This time she needs us and now is my time, my chance to pay her back for saving my life."

"If I may ask, do you have plans to marry Vernon Vergel?"

"Vernon was the first man I ever have loved, but he had become a soldier of God. Honestly, he proposed marriage lately, but I'm afraid it might be unacceptable in the society we're in."

"If you're really meant for each other, the Lord finds a way."

As God wanted it, I realized my dream to come to America and lived in a town where people come and go like the years forgone. I thought Middletown wasn't a good working place for me but an ideal one for the superannuated, the ones who were turning weary of living. In Middletown, the ambience was heavenly. Only the tweets of the tiny birds, the honks of wild geese and the rustles of the trees dancing to the whistles of the wind could stir its celestial serenity.

It was where I met Kitty Brown, the woman who preferred a life of misery to save the child she bore. It was where I met an ugly American named Bandy Boor whose rudeness made me look for another place where to work which paved the way in finding my father. At the Lakeside Assisted Residential Community, I met and got acquainted with Elizabeth Taylor Fuller and her grandson, Richard Joseph Fuller and through him I found the person my mother had been searching for.

My ardent wish when I was a child was to see my father and so was my dream to reach and live in America. It was in my adolescence that both dreams vanished from my thoughts, but my mother carried for me my American dream. Never did I know that in realizing it, I'd find the other dream I left behind. If truth be told, before I came of age, I already had accepted that my father had been dead before I was born; that he would never be coming home anymore.

Postscript

"Sorry, Father James if I got you bored. I wrote the details of what I'd been through. It's a memoir but had become more of a love story."

"I love reading books of love stories; it reminds me of . . ." The priest didn't finish what he wanted to say. He moved nearer to the window and stood there for a moment.

Twilight was coming. In a little while, stars would start popping up in the sky. While watching these stars on some nights in his solitude, the priest must have wondered what could have been him if he had chosen a married life.

Father James looked back at me with a smile that reminded me of Vernon. The priest must have remembered some happy moments he had had.

"If you won't mind my asking, Father James, have you ever been in love?"

"Did you ever think that priests aren't human beings?" The priest reacted with a chuckle. "Yes, I had been in love once; she was my schoolmate in high school. We grew up in the same town."

"What happened then?"

"We broke up after graduation from high school per our parents' demand due to religious differences. We were young then. She was my first love as I was to her. To forget her, I left my hometown and lived in Dublin for college studies. But it was hard for me to forget her; I was hoping for a reconciliation. A few years later, I learned that she got married to another guy. In desperation, I quit my studies in Law and entered the seminary and avoided falling in love again."

"It is said that first love never ever dies. It seems Vernon is irreplaceable."

"It only seems but you can forget Vernon in the long run. You can replace him as time goes by. You only need to adjust your standard."

"Even changing for the worse?"

"Loving someone with lesser attributes isn't changing for the worse. If you love someone, it's because that someone is worthy of your loving."

"You're right, Father James, but until now I haven't found someone worth loving, other than Vernon. Until now, I still wonder if reaching my American dream is worth losing him. Coming to America was my mother's greatest obsession for me."

"Your mother had good reasons for it . . . you know, mother knows best," the priest responded. "Tell me, are you still getting in touch with Vernon?"

"We were communicating with each other lately. In his last letter, he said he still loves me and was ready to quit priesthood if I decide to marry him. I'm afraid about it. I want to know it from you, Father James, if it's possible . . ."

"Priests are free to marry but must undergo first the process of laicization."

"But the Lord owns him now as His builder of faith in the heart of humanity."

"*God understands. If you two are sure of each other, then free yourselves from restraints. You've the right to pursue your own happiness. Pursue your dreams.*"

"*I've been thinking about it. Whatever this comes up to, I will tell you.*"

"*Communicate with me from time to time.*"

"*I surely will. I'm afraid it's time to say goodbye, Father James.*"

Outside, the sky was getting dimmer. I caught sight of a huge raven flying towards the western skies, maybe heading to where its home must be.

I used to believe that America lies beneath the western skies, and it was my fondest dream to reach it as much as I desired to see my biological father. I lost interest in both dreams during the years I was growing up. After finishing high school, my American dream hooked on me again but my dream of finding my father had long been gone.

I studied nursing in college following my mother's wish, finished it, passed the board and eventually, got a nursing job in the country I long have dreamed of calling my own. But then, way beyond my expectations, I found in here the other dream I left behind – I met my father. My mother's search for him consumed almost half of her lifetime. It had been part of the miseries I went through. Finally, our search for him had ended.

It was good to know what really happened to my father while in Vietnam but at the same time it changed my impressions towards the grandfather I adored so much. The truth may hurt but it's much better than to remain believing in what had been false. It relieved me of part of the burden I was carrying on my shoulders through the years. It came to me that if my mother carried my dream of reaching America, the Lord carried for me the dream of finding my father. I realized it now why the Lord willed that I should come to America and reached that sleepy town in the state of North Carolina; God did it for reasons.

I have one life to live, and I will live it to the fullest depending on what the Lord wants from me. As with Vernon, if he proposes marriage again, I'll grab it this time no matter what people say. After all, I'd like to prove it myself how true the saying is that "Love Is Lovelier the Second Time Around".

END

Glossary

Anak sa Buho sa Kawayan — literally means 'conceived inside the bamboo hollow tube' - a local saying that refers to an illegitimate child.

"Barracudas and Ilagas" — the opposing bands of Philippine Muslim terrorists and Christian defenders active during the Muslim-Christian War in Mindanao.

Bihag — a Cebuano term in cockfighting referring to a rooster won over by the opponent.

Camarin — a farmhouse where newly harvested crops are stored.

Curacha — a lively Filipino folk dance in quick steps that tells of courtship.

EDSA — Epifanio de los Santos Avenue, a popular street in Manila

Gook/gunk — term applied to a North Vietnamese soldier or a Viet Cong.

Hermana Mayor — refers to a lady heading the executive committee of the town fiesta.

Hija de puta — an expression of anger; a Spanish translation of 'daughter of a whore'.

HUKBALAHAP — a word coined after 'Hukbo ng bayan laban sa Hapon' which means 'Troop of the nation against the Japanese'.

Kamuning — a white-flowering plant like jasmine.

Kamunggay	– a kind of vegetable commonly called horse radish native to the Philippines
Kinilaw	– a dish of white-meat fish, fresh and raw, thinly sliced and marinated in coconut vinegar, mixed with mashed ginger, thinly-sliced sweet onion and chunked tomato, thoroughly soaked in coco milk and sprinkled with a dash of salt and pepper.
Lechon	– a young pig fermented with onions and lemon grasses roasted golden brown over a bonfire of wood charcoal.
LRRP	– Long Range Reconnaissance Patrol.
NCPP	– New Communist Party of the Philippines.
NPA	– New People's Army.
NVA	– North Vietnamese Army.
PAGASA	– Philippine Atmospheric, Geophysical and Astronomical Services Administration; the Philippine's Weather Bureau.
PhilCAG	– Philippine Civic Action Group.
Pulahans	– a band of the pre-war revolutionaries who got its name by the red bands they wore on their heads when under arms.
Sinigang	– a kind of fish soup, spiced with ginger, tomato, and leafy onions, soured with a green tamarind fruit and flavored with lemon grasses and kamunggay leaves.
Sinofications	– the term applied to the values and beliefs introduced by Chinese traders to the Philippine natives during the pre-Spanish era.

Acknowledgements

I'm thankful to those who'd helped me make this book possible. Foremost of all are my sisters, namely: **Zenaida Arranguez Onggue**, of Perth, Western Australia; **Josefina Arranguez Etulle**, of Ceritos, CA; **Mel Rosell Arranguez** of Cebu City, Philippines; **Judith Arranguez Rago** and **Nancy Arranguez Jaboni**, both of Long Beach, CA.

For their literary wisdom, thanks to **Faye** and **Ekron Chelson Crow III** of Raleigh, NC, to **Sr. Mary Kelly** (St. Joseph Order), chaplain of Wisteria Hospice in Long Beach, CA, and to the late **Sor Maria Begona Divinagracia,** (O.P.), of Corpus Christi, TX.

I shouldn't have known what had happened when Saigon fell into the hands of the communists if not for Binh and Bich van Nguyen of Raleigh, NC. I got in touch with them through their daughter, Linda. More heartbreaking stories of refugees came to my knowledge from the Reverend Father Donald F. Staib of St. Mary Magdalene Parish in Apex, NC. Fr. Staib had been to Bataan, Philippines on a mission when there was the heavy influx of Vietnamese refugees.

Thanks to **Brian Bubach** of Fargo, ND, for the Spanish translations, to **Tony Van Phan** of Holly Springs, NC for the Vietnamese, and to the Japanese man for the Japanese translation, whom I met in the plane on my way to Hongkong. I'm also thankful to **Michael J. Young** of NCSU, Raleigh who helped me create the character of Brendan Cameron; ditto to **Mitchell Bowden** for Helga Schwartz. **Sheila Dionson Arroyo** of Melrose Park, IL, happened to be my very first reader, when this book was still in a short story form under the title 'Beneath the Western Skies'.

Thanks to: **Jean Arocho, Mary Grady, Dot Mclelland, Phyllis Parks, Vivian Rainey, Grace Viglione, Khushman Surti,** and **Erlinda Yatta** for their compliments. Also, thanks to **Susan Sullivan,** my former team leader who loves my style of writing.

I'm grateful to **Kim Sabol**, DPPD's former director, who was forever nice and friendly. The same goes to **Debbie Wall, Diana Salmon,** DPPD's division supervisors, and to my dear friend, **Wilma Hopkins,** who was always there for me during my desperate moments. **Lou Marotta** is a one in a million kind of a friend. Special mention goes to **Jordan W. Li** who helped me realize this book's 3rd edition. I also want to thank **Mira Butler** and **Luna Harrington** of Prime Seven Media for their untiring effort to make a beautiful layout of this book.

In my job promotion as information processing technician at the Central Collections Unit, I met some nice people whose kindness was a factor that encouraged me to finish this book. Unfortunately, it was also in this unit where I had my supervisors treating me very unkindly. Their harassment forced me to quit my job and led me to spend more time on writing, my passion in life.

As forgiving is sublime, I bear no hatred towards those who were unreasonably mean and rude to me, however, I'm giving them my thanks for their unkindness had given me the idea on how to define well the villains in this novel. I may forget their names and faces through the coming years, but their maltreatment towards me may always be remembered.

My dear Jesus, after letting me walk across a 'wide field of sorrow', you're leading me to this 'footpath of joy'. It's the best thing to ever happen in my life.

To My Readers:

Some characters in this story are fictitious; some are real whose names are changed to protect their identity. Some places and events are fictional, but some are factual. The Raleigh Assisted Living Community and the Saint Jude Nursing Care, as well as the Middletown in North Carolina are all as fictitious as the nightclub called Yuki No Hana.

Sacandaya is Daanbantayan, the northernmost town of Cebu Province in the Philippines where I was born and raised. Most of my ancestors lived and died here. Some members from the Rosell clan, who are direct descendants of Vicente Rosell and Victoria Rodrigo, my maternal grandparents, are still residing in this town.

The residents of Daanbantayan are deeply religious, generally friendly and extremely hospitable. They still observe old traditions, practice the same old culture, and generally believe in superstitions as depicted in this book.

Villa Zaragoza in the story is a fictional manor, but the centuries-old church of Santa Rosa de Lima is real and still existing.

I'd like to encourage my readers to visit the historic town of Daanbantayan. Feast your eyes on its breathtaking sceneries that have been attracting tourist foreigners. Breathe its breeze that's soothing and fresh from the southern seas and see the sunset that I used to watch in my youth; it's still as fascinating as it had been.

To all my readers, *"Daghang Salamat".*

- From the Author

---

josearranguez291@gmail.com

About the Author

Jose Rosell Arranguez Jr. comes from the Philippines. He earned the degree of BS in English from the University of the Visayas in the city of Cebu, worked as a media production specialist II of the Department of Agriculture Central Visayas Region and was chief editor of its in-house publications. He had published short stories, poetry, news and feature stories in local and national magazines, wrote scripts related to agriculture and produced documentary films for public consumption.

The tenth in the brood of twelve, "Dodong" or "Jun", to his family and friends, is a native of Daanbantayan, the northernmost town in the province of Cebu. In 1994, he migrated to the USA with his family and settled in the town of Holly Springs, NC.

Jun was working as an Information Processing Technician in NCDOR- Raleigh until October 2014, when he was subjected to harassment and discrimination. He quit his state job and has been into writing fiction since then. He had previously published "The Boy Who Hated Numbers", a book for kids and young adults.

"Reminiscence" is a historical/multicultural fiction inspired by actual events and based on a true story of a Filipina nurse the author met in Raleigh, North Carolina, more than a decade ago. This book is specially dedicated to the author's countrymen working abroad and to all the children in the world growing up without a father.

Title: REMINISCENCE: Memories Are Beyond Forgetting No
          Matter How Bitter They Are
Author: J.R. ARRANGUEZ JR.
Genre: Historical Fiction.

The Moving Words book review (Feb. 7, 2024):

"Reminiscence" by J.R. Arranguez Jr. is a compelling historical and multicultural fiction that delves into the complexities of identity, heritage, and the unbreakable bonds of family. Set against the backdrop of the Vietnam War's aftermath and the Filipino diaspora, the novel offers a poignant exploration of the lives of Filipinos working abroad and the challenges they face in their quest for a better life.

The story centers on a Filipina nurse whose life is shaped by the legacy of a father she never knew, a soldier presumed dead in the Vietnam War before her birth. The narrative unfolds as she embarks on a journey to America, a land of dreams and promises, where she seeks fulfillment and a sense of belonging. Her work in a nursing home in Raleigh, North Carolina, becomes a gateway to unexpected discoveries about her father, love, and the intricate tapestry of human connections.

Arranguez Jr.'s novel is a tribute to the resilience and courage of those who navigate the spaces between cultures and memories. The author skillfully weaves a narrative that is as much about the personal journey of its protagonist as it is about the collective experience of a nation and its people scattered across the globe. The characters are beautifully drawn, with depth and authenticity that make their struggles and triumphs resonate with the reader. One of the novel's strengths is its rich historical context and the detailed portrayal of the Filipino experience. The author's deep understanding of the cultural nuances and the emotional landscape of his characters enriches the narrative, making it not only a story of personal discovery but also a reflection on the themes of loss, identity, and redemption.

The book's dedication to Filipinos working abroad and to children growing up without a father adds a layer of poignancy to the story. It speaks to the universal longing for connection and the search for a place to call home. The inclusion of a Filipina nurse's real-life inspiration for the plot lends authenticity and depth to the narrative, highlighting the real-world implications of the themes explored in the book.

"Reminiscence" is a moving and thought-provoking novel that captures the heartache and hope of the immigrant experience. **Arranguez Jr.'s** eloquent prose and keen insight into the human condition make this book a must-read for anyone interested in stories of cultural identity, familial bonds, and the enduring power of love. It is a testament to the strength of the human spirit and the unending quest for understanding and acceptance.

- The Moving Words Review

www.ingramcontent.com/pod-product-compliance
Lightning Source LLC
Chambersburg PA
CBHW020915140626
46545CB00015B/44